Mountain Climber

# Mountain Climber

*A Memoir*

Bill Katra

Toplight
*Jefferson, North Carolina*

All photographs are by the author or from his collection.

Library of Congress Cataloguing-in-Publication Data

Names: Katra, Bill, 1945– author.
Title: Mountain climber : a memoir / Bill Katra.
Description: Jefferson, North Carolina : Toplight, 2020. |
Includes bibliographical references and index.
Identifiers: LCCN 2019058960 | ISBN 9781476679631 (paperback : acid free paper) ♾
ISBN 9781476637785 (ebook)
Subjects: LCSH: Katra, Bill, 1945– | Mountaineers—United States—Biography.
Classification: LCC GV199.92.K38 A3 2020 | DDC 796.522092 [B]—dc23
LC record available at https://lccn.loc.gov/2019058960

British Library cataloguing data are available

**ISBN (print) 978-1-4766-7963-1**
**ISBN (ebook) 978-1-4766-3778-5**



Front cover: In Peru's Cordillera Blanca a climber snakes his way up the glacier toe (photograph by Bill Katra)

Printed in the United States of America

Toplight is an imprint of McFarland & Company, Inc., Publishers

Toplight

*Box 611, Jefferson, North Carolina 28640*
*www.toplightbooks.com*

As the years pass by and remembrance pales
Of weighty packs and rainy trails,
What shines bright
In memory's light
Are those fine friends who have climbed with me.

—From "Climbing Majesty" by Bill Katra

# Table of Contents

Away from the cities and responsibilities, we lived simply, feeling at peace with ourselves and the world. We thought that climbing made us better people, and perhaps it did. Humbled often by the walls, we had to look deeply into ourselves to find out what made us tick. We learned to confront fear, and years later we all would agree that facing dangers on the cliffs, fighting to maintain equanimity, helped us to get through difficult times.... In short, climbing was good for the soul, a calming influence on our reckless natures.

—Yvon Chouinard in Steve Roper, *Camp 4*

Que lindo haberlo vivido para poderlo contar.

—El Sabalero, Uruguayan folk singer,
in the song "Chiquillada"

Something hidden. Go and find it. Go and look behind the Ranges.
Something lost behind the Ranges. Lost and waiting for you. Go!

—Rudyard Kipling

# Introduction

> I write not about [climbing], but about human beings in [climbing]. I write not the history of a [climb], but the history of feelings. I am a historian of the soul. On the one hand I examine specific human beings, living in a specific time and taking part in specific events, and on the other hand I have to discern the eternally human in them. The tremor of eternity. That which is in human beings at all times.[1]

It's impossible to know whether the gods had ordained that I would be a climber. But my parents told me that at five months old I was agile enough to lift myself out of the crib—and they had to tie on a top so that I would not fall to the floor. Then, at about age three I suffered my first fall when, balancing on the top of a 12-foot-high jungle gym, I fell to the ground. That resulted in ten stitches under my chin. Later, I must have already celebrated my eleventh birthday when, at a Boy Scout Camporee, no one could beat my time up the 10-foot rope climb.

In writing the above I have no intention of suggesting exceptional physical attributes, only inclinations. The strength or climbing ability of the child, "Bad Billy"? Above average, yes. But perhaps most important: determination. This means that the stories that follow are by no means heroic, or that my physical accomplishments as a climber are particularly noteworthy. While I am proud to have pioneered a few new routes (duly mentioned in the text),[2] in no way should they be compared to the accomplishments of climbing superstars such as Royal Robbins, Fred Becky, Galen Rowell, or Gaston Rébuffat. In brief, I have not been a great climber, only a persistent one.

It is appropriate here to provide a personal definition of the term *climbing*, or perhaps better, *climber*. Indeed, outside of the community of technical climbers there is some confusion about this. For me a "climber" is not simply a "hiker" or "trekker" or even one who "follows a trail up to a notable summit." No. A climber for me uses technical equipment and/or special physical prowess in overcoming notable objective obstacles to ascend a rock wall or mountain. Accordingly, any adventurer requiring a rope and protective devices obviously qualifies. But, on the other hand, one who hikes the Appalachian Trail is not a climber in my book. Marginal cases? Those who walk up that shit-pile of volcanic ash called Mt. Shasta or follow the mule trail to the summit of Aconcagua qualify as climbers on account of the problems involving acclimatization and uncommon exertion.

There are, also, borderline cases in addressing more specifically the issue of "physical prowess." Two examples. First, a particular individual with whom I have climbed at Devil's Lake State Park (Wisconsin) is able to get up routes of moderate difficulty while well protected with an upper belay, but moves like a cripple over boulders on the approach. (It would court disaster for this person to partake of any climb in the Tetons.) Or a second and comparable case: a moderately fit youth who visits a climbing gym three times. According to my personal definition, when it comes to the issue of "physical prowess," these two individuals occupy the nebulous, grey area.

The issue also has a "psychological" dimension. Ax Nelson, an American pioneer in the sport, wrote in 1948: "One cannot climb at all unless he has sufficient urge to do so. Danger must be met—indeed, it must be used—to an extent beyond that incurred in normal life."[3] Climbers have to possess "discipline" to enhance their physical strength, but Nelson is less than clear about how they acquire the necessary "self-control" to protect against injury from a fall.

"Confidence"—or "self-control"—is for me an essential attribute of a climber. Not all individuals who participate in roped exercises on a given Saturday at Devil's Lake—or at Las Vegas's Red Rocks or Rochester's climbing gym—possess it. Most of those hanging on sport-climbing ropes, however, would wish to be able to "lead" with confidence (and relative safety) even easy routes in "traditional" climbing areas. An explanation:

In the early days (before the 1950s) only "traditional" (trad) climbing was practiced, given the non-existence of climbing gyms or "sport" climbing areas (where one finds "bolts" permanently inserted in the rock to provide greater climbing safety). That is to say, parties had to invent the techniques of rope belaying in order to decrease the seriousness of injuries in the case of climbing falls. It is easy to understand how a climber who is belayed from above, when slipping off the rock, almost always escapes serious injury. But picture a team of climbers wishing to ascend a typical mountain wall that provides no easy way to hang a belay rope from above. The lead climber, who goes first, with a belayer at ground level feeding out the rope, could suffer significant physical damage in the case of a fall—and even with the proper placement of "protection" (or "pro": pitons, nuts, cams, etc.) As such, the age-old mantra: "The leader must never fall." (One could only wish!)

Understandably, climbers over the past few centuries have sought ways to lessen the injury suffered by the lead climber when falling (or by those practicing "free solos"). First, the lead climber must train in order to gain skill and strength. Second, s/he must have an instinct or a developed sense of choosing the best path up. Third, it helps to have experience in down-climbing to avoid getting stuck in a dangerous cul-de-sac. All of these contribute to number four: lead climbers must not let fear interrupt their concentration once they are committed to an action.

Fear. Here are some intelligent words: "The crucial question is not how to climb without fear—that's impossible—but how to deal with it when it creeps into your nerve endings."[4] More precisely, the lead climber must be able to banish from the mind the *irrational* fear that destabilizes one in attempting a hard move, but respect the fear of the *life-saving* type. I hardly need to write that this is easier said than done. But it is the climber, and not simply the weekend adventurer, who successfully deals with fear in this way.

Interestingly, a random sample of today's most accomplished climbers (I've perused writings by Tommy Caldwell, Lynn Hill, and Alex Honnold), reveals that when writing about their amazing exploits on rock or mountain routes, they rarely discuss the issue of fear except in the context of early learning experiences. Instead you read about climbing's "mystery," its resemblance to a Native American "vision quest," the joy of "testing oneself," or "exploring a sense of movement on the rocks without risking life and limb in the death zone."[5] In psychological terms, these climbers have sublimated the "fear" experienced. That is to say, they have successfully transformed it mentally into a positive experience: their mental processing of fear becomes almost automatic. A personality quirk?

Admittedly, climbers possess other uncommon—and not always socially acceptable—personality traits.[6] First, many harbor a fanciful belief that "bad news" might happen to another, but not to oneself. Second, they—we—possess an uncanny ability to "forget" or repress memories of the close calls and dangers of past climbs (after a fatal accident, one climber recounts: "We immortal ones shrugged off [a friend's] death").[7] Third—and very much related—we possess a "morbid" sense of humor about the bad luck befalling other climbers. And fourth, we display a somewhat cavalier attitude about using safety devices advocated by "pedestrians" such as seat belts and bicycle helmets, and we disdain some safety procedures taught in conservative climbing schools.

I admit to sharing to a certain degree the youthful attitudes of the individuals, only a decade before my entrance into the climbing world, who were in the process of becoming the climbing greats of Yosemite Valley (as described by that group's generational historian, Steve Roper[8]): "the dedication (sometimes to a masochistic extreme) for superb physical conditioning; rebelliousness in the dislike of authority, committees, or rules; the acceptance of body stink and ragged clothing as a badge of honor; a fervent commitment to the sport; the recognition that, at most, climbing constitutes a stimulating experience which awakens our minds and spirits to a lust for life and a keener awareness of beauty."

Other personality traits of the lead climber might be highly valued in dangerous or extreme situations. Here I'll write in the first person, since I am drawing upon my own experiences during 50 years of accident-free climbing. First, I possess a deep sense of confidence in my own rope leadership and route-finding skills. (During a technical rock climb I am able to "read" with—almost—unfailing accuracy the technical difficulty and needed protection for the next 40 or so feet above me.) Related is my skepticism or distrust if a rope partner offers alternative evaluations. And third—also related—I possess a hard-headedness about my own responsibility for the welfare of myself and others in a climbing adventure.

I understand that many employers, weighing the importance of all the above character traits, might not wish to offer me a job. I forgive them, I've been there before. But you have to understand that out there someone will value what types like me have to offer. I venture to suggest that this is true for even the most dirt bag of dirt bag climbers. (Well, maybe not. An anecdote: Seven years ago, when I arrived for a week of climbing at Potrero Chico in Northern Mexico, a local there did not believe I was a climber. "Why not?" I asked him. "Because you don't have that glazed expression of being high on something." Hmmm. I exclude that type of climber from my former generalizations.) As I have jokingly remarked to intimate friends: in a former incarnation I would have excelled as leader of a wagon train crossing the untamed American wilderness. So—admittedly—climbers might not make great, obedient employees. But thank goodness our society offers plentiful options for those like me to found our own companies and become our own bosses.

I'm nearing my sixth decade as a dedicated climber, my body still intact and strong, and I yearn for more. This means that over those years I've made good—or lucky—decisions in serious situations. Or: I have never pissed off the Mountain Gods and they, in turn, have favored me. The fact that I'm a survivor means something, perhaps a lot. Maybe there's wisdom in my words and appraisals. Perhaps my grandchildren will treasure my retelling of yet another interesting anecdote about now long-past adventures.

Another take on the idea of "retelling": a combination narrative about experiences a half-century ago enriched with musings nurtured from the wisdom of the present. The duality is also temporal, meaning that I am in a unique position to compare the past status of a particular glacier or the ice on a specific route, with its condition today after decades of global warming. Or, in several instances I contrast climbing technology and procedures: how we did it then and how they do it today.

An additional note about *memory*. The idea of Jorge Luis Borges merits exploration that, given the "unstable world" of the mind, memory does away with useless details.[9] Obviously, the two words "memory" and "memorable" are related, meaning that the former produces images which, for a myriad of reasons, have "survived" or, in other words, are worthy of being retold.[10] My own lesson from this: "Trust my remembrances. As insignificant or irrelevant a detail might seem, its remembrance is certification of its worthiness for being preserved in print." Why not? There is a certain logic to all this. An example: I have a vivid memory of "butterflies in the stomach" when, in August 1973, I critically appraised our proposed ascent line up the north buttress of Alaska's Gurney Peak. Here, in the chapters that follow, the recounting of *that and similar sensations* merits equal textual importance to traditional climbing data (i.e., the physical obstacles and how we overcame them during the actual climb).

I present here a series of essays. For my part, the retelling of such wonderful climbing experiences has been an invitation to immerse myself, once again, in the joys of life and living. For the remaining Augusts that the serendipitous gods may permit, you will know where to find me. Berg Heil![11]

## Chapter 1

# Climbing Snippets

### *1961—Olympic National Park*

At the age of sixteen I participated in my first trek, lasting about 14 days, with a dozen other Boy Scouts. Our packs were heavy. Our food was basic and bulky—freeze-drying had not yet been invented. Jangling from each pack was a #10 tin can, with bent wire handles, that we used for cooking. At that time, there was no use for purification tablets—giardia was, as of yet, unknown.

A week into the trip, a sense of drudgery was setting in. Three hours of hiking in the direct sun had taken its toll: we wearily stopped to rest sore shoulders from the uncomfortable straps of our wood-framed canvas packs (Kelty's divine waist straps had yet to make their appearance), and remove boots to dry out socks and stick moleskin onto bothersome hot spots. Only after the sweat had dried did the cool shade become pleasant. Fatigue and pine fragrance invited a lackadaisical afternoon. All along the trail we had passed a proliferation of ripe huckleberries; now they invited idle hands and appetites anxious to escape from our humdrum trail menu. With two people assigned to each cooking tin, we spent several hours picking berries. That night, we used a considerable portion of our sugar supply to brew up a delicious berry slurp, enough to provide each one of us with two full cups to sip while warming our hands and spirits before the campfire.

### *1962—Mt. Rainier National Park*

The ranger's booted foot had tested the long shaft of each ice axe—his poor excuse for a required "equipment inspection." After a long hike up, we pitched our tent on the ice, about 50 yards from the Quonset hut at Camp Muir—at about 10,000 feet. (At four in the morning we would rope up to begin the four-hour glacier traverse to the summit crater.) We had spent a leisurely afternoon practicing self-arrests on a moderately steep snow field and then simulated rope rescues, with prussic knots, in a nearby crevasse. Now, pretending to ignore the encroaching chill, we were sitting on our packs melting water with a white-gas stove, pretending it was a cheery campfire. Just as the sun was setting, we enjoyed a magnificent view to the south: just to the right of the "tiny" blips representing Mt. Hood (in northern Oregon) and Mount Adams (in southern Washington), we had a perfect view of the conical-shaped Mount St. Helens. Never again would that peak appear so majestic: its eruption in 1980 transformed a gigantic section of its upper slopes into volcanic dust that the winds distributed over a five-state area.

## *1963—Mt. Rainier National Park*

It had been the worst day imaginable: loaded with overnight and summit gear, we had had to ascend the first 4,000 feet in hot sunshine, up to the mountaineers' hut at Camp Schurman that was located on the rocky apex where the Emmons and Winthrop glaciers join. Now, crammed inside the climbing hut, and with throats parched by thirst, the six of us had only my feeble Bleuet stove to melt the gallons of water that we would need: first for cooking our dinner; second, for satiating a night-long water debt; and third, for filling the 12 empty plastic water bottles needed for our ascent on the morrow. For several afternoon hours we had been in the cold shadow of the mountain. Now, nobody wanted to linger outside after dusk, with little visibility and growing discomfort in the increasingly frigid temperature. Inside it was only slightly better: most of us had slipped into sleeping bags to avoid the inevitable shivers. Yet someone had to remain attentive to tend the stove. And since I was the person who had brought it along, that task was largely mine. So there I sat, hour after hour, until tedium, cold, and fatigue finally sent me to bed with the task unfinished. In the morning, our leader admitted to leg cramps, a result of his reluctance to drink the water needed by others. This, when added to the sight of six empty water bottles, justified our abandonment of plans to attempt the numbing plod to the summit.

## *1964—Mt. Olympus*

Never—whether before or after—was a mile ever "psychologically" longer than the space separating each of the 18 markers on the Hoh River approach to the Blue Glacier. I'd "conned" a few of my high-school friends to suffer the tedium of heavy packs and soggy boots, as we proceeded up the muddy rain-forest trail. Our interest was sparked only by the sight of the tallest alder, cedar, and fir trees on record. In the frigid evenings my spirit would rise with every turn to sit near the fire in our bridge-hand rotation agreement.

On the third morning we urged ourselves on with the anticipation of reaching Olympus' 7,954-foot summit. Before noon we emerged from the thick woods and—finally—were able to view the alpine meadows and glacier ahead. Roped up, we wove a path through crevasses and ascended its extreme eastern edge. Two hours later we again were walking over *terra firma*, along an easy ridge that led to the summit block. Triumph was just minutes away!

What? The guidebook said nothing about the 50-foot rock "climb" we would have to accomplish to stand on the actual top! Mouths agape, we just stood there looking at the steep gully shooting upward. (My "mature" self today laughs at the same-named novice of that afternoon: ascending that gulley today would be an easy scramble without the slightest need for protection.) None of us had rock-climbing experience. We knew that we were a "green" party—only days before three of our number had, for the first time, put on hiking boots and overnight packs. What to do? I grumbled. "It doesn't seem dangerous, the scamper up"—yet I suspected that a few of my companions, when contemplating that scramble, were inwardly trembling. I had confidence in my own athletic ability. But Roger? A whiz at math and bridge, but sure to be unsteady going up the rock gulley. Could he be convinced to wait a half-hour for the rest of us to nerve our way up and down? That wouldn't be totally fair, he coming all this way. I, being the second-in-charge and having induced Roger to make this trip, had to make the decision. "I don't like to say it, but I think we'll have to be satisfied with getting up to here. Prudence rules: no further is my vote." That decided it. We took a few (almost-summit) pictures, then turned around.

And forever after, I have regretted our timidity. To turn back 50 feet from a summit: that hurts. Especially since it might have been an easy 50 feet. Hmmm. Perhaps there was one meek consolation: that disappointment proved to be a good motivation for learning the ups and downs of technical rock climbing.

## *1964—Big Rock, Riverside County, California*[1]

At the beginning of my freshman year in college I had met Peter, who would get me started in roped climbing. With his assistance I purchased a pair of Austrian-made klettershoes (as of yet there were no such manufacturers in the U.S.), my first 150' white nylon rope, and a CMI rock hammer. I still depended on Peter's rack of chromoly pitons[2]—not wanting yet to splurge to buy my own set.

My new passion? For seventeen years I had been athletically inclined, but had excelled in no specific sport. In high school I had played on the frosh basketball team, but then left that sport behind—or perhaps it's more correct to say that it left me behind—because while the jump shot of my other basketball buddies developed, mine didn't. And it wasn't for want of trying. Then, every springtime I was out there at the track. What event? Almost by process of elimination I was placed with the pole vault crew. In four years of training, practicing, and dual meets, all I had to show for it all were two third-place medals. In other words, mediocrity. But—at the very least—I had demonstrated to myself and to others a stick-to-itiveness. Persistency. I would not quit. It was like going back home when you have no other place to go.

It must be stated at the outset that neither Peter nor I were "superstar" climbers—as one might currently understand the concept. That is to say, I have the impression that new climbers, today, are self-selected. To explain: a young person decides to give climbing a try and, after speeding up an easy 5.1 route, will decide to attempt one of mid-difficulty: 5.7 for example. And, with natural talent, s/he might even top-rope or follow up a 5.9! So, if experiencing success on these, s/he will probably want to return the next weekend. In contrast, the novice who experiences difficulty (or fear) getting up the 5.1 will probably decide to pass on the invitation to climb the next weekend, preferring to go to the beach or stay at home texting. This is what I mean by a "process of self-selection," meaning that perhaps the majority of young climbing enthusiasts today are going to belong to that small minority of the super talented.

But Peter and I, back then? The idea of being able to go up a 5.4 or 5.6

route on our first time out? Forget it. Because there were no sport areas with pre-established routes of known and varied difficulties. Because there were no climbing gyms where an athletic novice could rope into an upper belay, stumble about, and discover whether climbing was possibly his or her "thing."

No. In the 1960s the only option presenting itself to Peter and me was to go out with our rope, swinging leads up a trad route. One of the two of us, both novices, had to lead. That was not fun—even on easy 5.0 routes—because the vertical exposure sent willies down our spines. The risk of falling meant that fear became a constant companion (the trad leader always incurs risk upon advancing 10 or 20 feet beyond the last piece of protection—whether a driven piton or a sling around a bush). But we had no choice: it was either he or I going first. Week after week we "pushed ourselves," meaning that we tempted danger in order to improve our technique and accustom our nerves to fear. Even with the excitement, sense of adventure, and wonders of the natural world, it was scary. We had to choose easy routes to build up our experience base. Repetition and determination: that was our dual agenda. We had to make routine, in order to gain confidence, each simple act of placing a toe on a dainty crystal or trusting arm strength to lay back up a crack.

To hone the point even further: during our whole first two years of climbing together, we struggled to build up our trad leading skills, our fitness and—most important—our confidence. We continually wondered, and would enquire one to the other: would we ever be able to climb confidently at 5.7? Our goal was a route called the Jam Crack—which we, trembling, attempted a few times, but always backed down with a case of the jitters. In brief, we spent our entire first two years struggling to master climbing skills sufficient to feel enough confidence on a 5.7 route!

Our routine: after five days of studies, we would take off in Peter's rickety VW bug bound for Big Rock (about a two-hour drive) or Tahquitz Rock (four hours away). During two winters we made two trips to the super-abrasive rock of Joshua Tree (six hours away), a new "national monument" with a single primitive campground. During the week we had begun a rigorous schedule of workouts.

Then, there were few climbers at Big Rock—a modest 200-foot-wide granite pinnacle. Parking our car within 20 feet of the main rock, we joked about being able to "belay from its bumper." With shoes and rope ready, we would do our best to get up, at least partially, a few of the 20 or so

**April 1969. Here I stand alongside my newly purchased VW bug as we took a break on the road leading to the Sierra Nevada's Sawtooth Ridge (CA). Visible are the "mountaineering skis" that we carried on the top of the car. Our skis featured home-made bindings that held down the toes of our leather climbing boots while allowing us to lift our heels to "walk-glide" up the snow path. These skis with "skins" attached to the bottom were far preferable to snow shoes for walking up a snowy incline.**

existing routes. Come evening, if we were staying the night, we would scrape around to find enough wood to make a campfire, cook our meals over a camp stove, and lay out our plastic ground cloths, foam pads, and sleeping bags to pass the night. The only interference came from an occasional car venturing near with a young couple disappointed at us occupying that isolated spot usually reserved for erotic recreation.

My first day there I had experienced the magical power of positive thinking. We were standing on the ground, examining what the rock offered about hip high for a delicate left-foot friction placement. There would be only balance holds for the hands. It would require leg strength to perform the lifting move: at all costs I had to avoid a lower-foot thrust that might cause the left to slip off its delicate perch. In the first moment I doubted whether my left foot would stay on in order to make the move. And, sure enough, that instance of doubt proved to be a self-fulfilling prophecy: while gently lifting myself off the ground, the foot slipped off.

Then, two minutes later, I was ready to try again. Re-examining the sloping friction surface, did I see a sand-sized crystal that hadn't been there before? It gave me confidence. Now I was not doubting. I carefully placed my left foot—just as before. But this time I did not doubt. I lifted my body up—slowly—*and the left foot stayed glued.* Then I was able to straighten the leg. Next, I moved my right foot up to a secure foothold. I was on my way. I had made the move.

Subsequently, I have experienced relatively the same phenomenon a hundred-thousand times: before a dubious move, my positive attitude—that is, my ability to exile doubt from the mind—has been a key factor. Call it the psychological dimension of climbing. It's real and it's powerful.

Then it was my turn to lead, with Peter sitting on the ground belaying. With that brand of face climbing, each new foot placement involved finding either a slight depression or an especially large crystal jutting out from the surface. Then, grasping fingers around a pebble-sized crystal a bit higher up, I used the strength of my arms to assist the leg muscles in slowly shifting my weight up onto the raised foot and maintaining my balance the whole way. I had proceeded about 10 feet up fairly easy stuff and had pounded in a somewhat decent pin in the crack to the left. Then I had to leave the relative security it offered and venture out again onto the unprotected face. Delicate. Not much there. Ouch, that crystal cuts into my finger. Slowly, slowly I shift my weight. Another few feet gained, diagonaling up.

I was now about 12 feet out and above my last piece of protection—meaning that a slip there would result in me falling all the way to the ground. Not a pleasant thought. Straining to lift my head to glance up, I saw that the same distance separated me from a comfortable ledge with a thank-god bolt. The next move was going to be difficult—there was nothing significant for either a foot or a hand to assist. For a few seconds

I studied the foot-placement alternatives. Hmm. It was not going to be easy. A few more seconds … *ouch*, my bottom-foot toes, cramped inside the shoe that was delicately perched on top of a tiny crystal, were beginning to hurt. (Suppress panic.) Hmm. Is there a crystal up there for two left-hand fingers—after I step up with my right foot? … I'm taking too long … I'm violating the first rule of lead climbing: do not delay, it will only tire you out. I've got to make the move. It'll be tense. I could slip off … and down I go. Not a nice thought. Yes. Now I'll make the move … in a second. What's that? My right foot beginning to tremble? No! *Damn foot*, you'll make me slide me off the stance! Sewing machine shakes. *Stop!* I cry out silently, as if that foot belonged to someone else. *Goddammit, stop.* I'm using up energy. I can't delay anymore: I'm frozen on this move and I've let fear dominate my thoughts. I silently yell at that leg that is not mine: *Stop shaking*. I force myself to begin the move. With way too much weight upon my hands I lift my body up and stand crouched on my right foot. It holds! *Thank God.* Quickly I place my left foot on a decent protrusion and gain instant security. Whew. I'm sweating like a cow. I un-tense my shoulders and drop my aching arms to the sides. Two deep breaths. *Whew.* A moment of respite. That was nasty. Or was it "much ado about nothing"? Did I make an easy move hard? Well, it's history now. A thirty-second rest has restored my calm—I have already almost forgotten about the fear I was feeling only a minute before. I glance on up. The next nine feet look clear. Easy going. I move up with smooth control like a cat, and reach the sloping ledge to clip into the bolt. Nerves: relax now. *Whew.*

## *1965—Tahquitz Rock*

After grunting 20 minutes up the eroding trail, we reached Lunch Rock. "Let's leave our stuff here," Peter instructed. "We have to follow the base of the rock around to the right." So we continued, Peter carrying the leader sling from which bounced the pins that would be needed for the climb. Rounding the corner, we ogle-gazed at Royal Robbins' 5.9[3] Open Book route which—I was as convinced then as I am still today—was way beyond my capabilities. After another five minutes of scampering along the base, our route came into view just above us. There they were, beginning about 40 feet up: the two more or less parallel cracks shooting diagonally skyward to the left. “Bill, I led the last pitch on White Maiden, so you get to go first.”

I felt only mild trepidation, being that our route, Ski Tracks, was rated only 5.4. We uncoiled the rope, with Peter setting up an anchor and belay. I roped in and slung the trash sling over my shoulder. *“On belay?”* “Belay on.” *“Climbing.”* “Climb.”

Looking up and seeing the steepness of the wall ahead of me, I automatically pushed my fear-repression button while, at the same time, obeyed the unwritten climbing rule of never verbalizing—either to oneself or to one’s partner, even minimally—whatever suggestion of displeasure, discomfort, or trepidation. “The weather looks OK. No wind, and good temperature for climbing,” I murmured to Peter, without mentioning the flutter of butterflies in my stomach. Up 15 feet: I placed a good piton. After another 25 feet, I was able to place another piece of pro at the start of the diagonal crack.

Then I began the psychological game: the cracks lent themselves to layback moves, but it was too scary lifting myself out of the mama crack and trusting the strength of my hands and arms. That would have been good technique. But fear was whispering in my ear. I felt much more secure, even though it demanded much more force and energy, keeping my body wedged inside the lower crack and squirming on up.

Fifteen feet higher, and I was able to place another piece of pro. Then, at the end of the left diagonal, I pounded in yet another piton just after changing direction and grasping, somewhat frantically, whatever I could in or on the corner of the—now—right-veering cracks. Wiggling up—with energy-consuming friction against my body—was still my choice of movement. I simply lacked the confidence to climb it in “proper” style, that is, using the lower crack for feet placements and lay backing it on up. Unspoken (and unspeakable) fear was in control, it—and not I—was deciding my chosen technique.

But after placing a fifth piece of pro, another factor entered into the equation: rope drag. With every squirm onward I had to battle against this new enemy by tugging on the rope as it passed through the 90-degree angle resulting from the route’s change of direction.

Pulling on the rope was not an easy task. One hand/arm had to be jammed into the upper crack to simply hold my body on the wall. Rope tugging had to be accomplished with only the free hand and—at times—my teeth. It wasn’t fun. Soon, I was sweating profusely, with one thing unclear: was I perspiring more on account of the ever-increasing drag on the rope, or was it because of my mounting frustration—and *fear*?

I had to keep squirming. The remedy for fear was pounding in one more piton. Yet every time I clipped in anew, the drag increased on the rope. At first, continuing was merely difficult. Then, add the adjective "exhausting." And I have to repeat that hated word, "fear." Yet I continued. I had to. There really was no alternative.

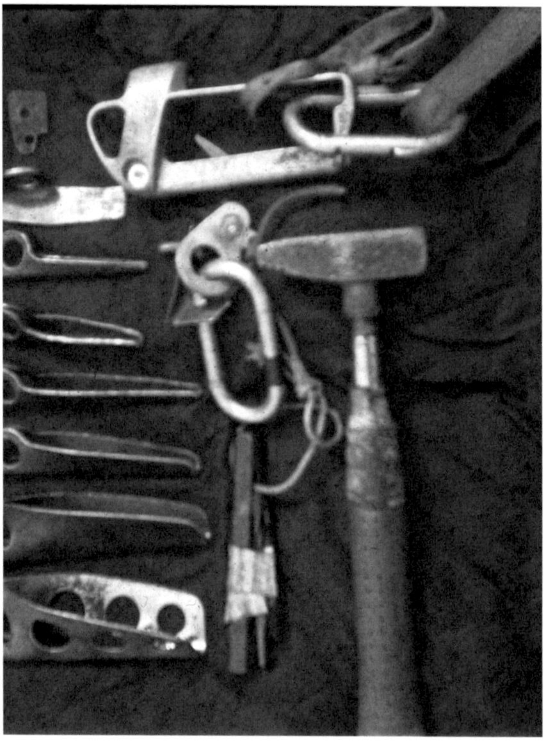

**"The age of pitons" lasted until about 1975. When "pro" was necessary, we would choose the most appropriate one—depending on the width of the crack—and then hammer it in. Only a few times did I use the bolt kit (in the middle) to protect a crackless stretch. At the top is a jumar that we used for aid climbing on big walls.**

Well, it's time to bring this painful narrative to a close. Yes, I made it to the top of the pitch, and then with deadened arms I belayed Peter on up. Yes, we finished the route and came back down. Blah, blah, blah. And forever after I have engraved in my memory the association of Ski Tracks and fear. Yes, that route has been catalogued, in the vaults of my personal memories, as one of the most "difficult" that I have ever climbed.

## *March 1969—West Buttress, El Capitan, Yosemite*

Little time to plan, less to prepare. But the Nixon Administration's invasion and bombing of Cambodia triggered a near universal wave of

**About halfway up El Cap's Salathé Wall (Yosemite, California), I point the camera straight down to capture Don, jumaring up and about to reach my small belay ledge.**

indignation. We had little to do with the politics of the situation. But when irate students closed the Berkeley campus down, Mike Caldwell and Don Fredrickson jumped at the chance of getting on a major route with at least a week free of classes. Mike was the prime instigator: weeks earlier he had stumbled across Steve Roper alongside his camper-library at Camp 4 and obtained a copy of the route's topo—that is, a graphic representation of its features and difficulties. Why the West Buttress? Who knows. Even the most accomplished of big-wall climbers avoided it, due undoubtedly to its endless A4[4] and A5 moves. At best, the route would be slow and tedious.

It's an understatement to say that I was not too excited about the route. But … days, possibly weeks, of cancelled classes? The situation caught me unprepared: I hadn't even dreamed of an alternative way to spend my time. And I was flattered by their invitation to join them, even though my assigned task would be not to do any of the actual climbing but to merely haul the bags. They and I knew that I had absolutely no experience in—nor desire to learn about—the placement of insecure rurps to get up that humongous granite wall. Having nothing better to do, and never eager to turn down yet another adventure, I agreed to join the team.

So we made midnight preparations. All of us were green on big walls, which led to the bad decisions we made in packing the haul sack—which in turn led, three days later and six pitches up, to our having to abandon the climb. I need not go into the particulars. Suffice it to say that the protruding corners of eight-to-ten one-gallon containers, when packed into the army-surplus-duffle-bag-converted-into-hauling-sack, wore so heavily against the wall that after three pitches we had bled so much water that to continue would have been suicidal.

Nevertheless, the three-day attempt was, for me, memorable. First, my raw, rigor-mortis hands, pulling upward or downward on the rope leading to the haul bag that was braked by a tied-off jumar. Second, the sheer immensity of the wall above us. Third, the manner in which belly butterflies calmed and became routine.

Picture the situation: Caldwell on lead on pitch four—for example—with Fredrickson standing in stirrups belaying him from a bolt at the top of pitch three, and me, sitting on top of the hanging haul sack 150 feet down, at the top of pitch two. Since the nailing was painfully slow, a typical pitch would take three to four hours. I can't remember whether boredom was an issue; somehow, when on a wall—any wall—I've dealt far better with dead time than in any other situation. Had I been down at sea level, sitting with minimum movement for four hours, the monotony would have been infernal. But, in my belay seat hanging from a vertical wall, slow time is pardonable.

(On the Salathé Wall some four years later the prolonged look across the valley proved spectacular—in contrast to our shortened stay here: the daily gain in verticality became an experience in itself. Day One on the Salathé: belaying with my back to the wall, the tops of the Cathedral Peaks a kilometer away hovered way above, and in the late afternoon their long shadows covered half of the valley floor before me. Day Three: glancing down, their summits were now below us. Day Five: peering almost straight down, they appeared as mere humps hardly protruding from the ground.)

Back to my perch on top of the haul sack. Luckily the weather, for the middle of March, was decent. With absolutely nothing to do, the sun warmed me and induced drowsiness. I had long since tired of repeating every bit of data I had taken the time and trouble to commit to memory over years past: the periodic table (horizontal and several vertical columns), "Sam Magee," "Gunga Din," the multiple verses of "Mountain Dew."

Then—something on the wall to my left, just at eye level, caught my eye. A spider? Way up here? It didn't fly. Perhaps the wind blew it or its ancestor into the crack. Hmmm. Also enjoying the sun rays? Small, about 1½ inches from (rounded, black) toe to toe. It must have come out of the shallow crack a foot away… Possible but not probable… Not moving, just poised there… Eight jointed, thread-like legs supporting the reddish round body, a half-inch above the rock… Small movement.

O h m y G o d, it's doing push-ups… D o w n … and … u p. A g a i n. A n d a g a i n…

And again… A g a i n… A g …

A shout from above interrupted this stupendous scene: "Bill, get ready. Caldwell's finally on belay."

## *1973—Salathé Wall, El Capitan, Yosemite*

*What am I doing here? It's Don's and my second morning on this gigantic face that, only since yesterday, offers that exhilarating feeling of looking straight down 1,000 feet to see the ground. Looking up, 3,000 vertical feet to go—with the last third actually overhanging. The entire route is rated 5.9 A3—a bit over my head.*[5] *Up until now I've led only the even-numbered pitches, all 5.8 at max so I'm doing OK. Knock on granite. Up ahead, on pitch 14, there's some 5.9—it could be real hard for me. But—not that I'd like to—I can always call on Don to lead it.*

Over the past four years our climbs together had become increasingly more difficult, with a few weekends—and then entire May weeks—spent at Lovers' Leap (west of Sacramento) and in the Sierra Nevada, but primarily at Yosemite. Perhaps we were subconsciously preparing to get on this route but—today when I'm writing this paragraph—I can't remember us having nurtured a deliberate plan. How much can I trust the brief notes that, years past, I jotted down in my 1971 edition of the Roper Climbing Guide?[6]: That in the Spring of 1970—when students shut down UC-B in angry reaction to the U.S. invasion of Cambodia—we (joined by Mike Caldwell) bailed out after three days on the West Buttress of El Cap (and in doing so learned valuable lessons about how not to pack water for a five-day climb). And then, between 1972 and 1973, we got up—among several lesser accomplishments—the regular routes of both the Lower and Higher Cathedral Spires and spent three glorious days on the NW Face of

After the previous day's exhausting climb up Fairview Dome (Tuolumne Meadows, Yosemite, California), Don—at 10,000 feet—doesn't want to stir until he's warmed by the early-morning sun.

Half-Dome. Then, in the early months of 1974 we ascended the left side of Koko Ledge (and its continuation), the East Buttress of Middle Cathedral Rock, and the NE Buttress of Higher Cathedral. All these were the prelude to our presence now on the Salathé.

There, at the route's start, Don and I were pathetically alone. Other parties attempting whatever route on El Cap had a "support team" or—at the very least—a faithful girlfriend or roommate. This type of assistance was handy for ferrying heavy loads (mainly a minimum supply of water) on up the 200 yards of steep incline to the base of the route. Most important, however, would be their role in communications if and when a problem would arise. Think of the logistics. A typical party back in those days would take 5½ days to make the ascent. (That, as it turned out, was our approximate duration too.) People might have possessed walkie-talkies but, because of their bulk and expense, I remember no valley climber remotely considering packing them on even the most demanding of climbs. More importantly, there did not yet exist the—today ubiquitous—cellphone that makes it possible for any climber to have leisurely evening chats with an intimate friend down below or even as far away as New York City. The truth of the matter is that, back then, once any party got a single day up—say, 800–1000 vertical feet—verbal communication through shouting was totally impossible. Warren Harding and Dean Caldwell, months earlier, on their (outrageously publicized) first ascent of the Wall of the Early Morning Light (now known more simply as Dawn Wall) resorted to writing messages on pieces of paper crammed into either an empty bean can or film canister and dropping the assemblage down to an awaiting messenger.

During our multi-day ascent, Don and I suffered neither accident nor rain, so we ended up not suffering majorly from our total lack of communication possibilities. But this issue did assume the status of a distasteful bother at the end: our deliberated plan had been to spring-start the climb by fixing ropes up the first four pitches—an easy first day for the climb. This would eliminate the burdensome task of bag hauling for the whole first day. With these ropes fixed, we were able to descend to sleep our last night on *terra firma*, at the base of the face, then—bright and early on the second day—we jumared up to recommence our climbing labors. Once we ascended to the top of our fixed ropes at the beginning of the second day, our plan involved dropping to the ground the first two ropes (the third and fourth would be needed for climbing and equipment). We had no one to call upon to retrieve those abandoned ropes, or even to report to someone back in Camp IV about our desire to be able to reclaim them—somehow. We nurtured the illusion of finding them there after our eventual descent five days later, still waiting for us lying on the ground where we had dropped them. We knew at the time that this was a foolish hope. More probable: they would fly away, into the pack of some lucky tourist poking around at the El Cap base. But—we silently reasoned—would not their loss be a small price to pay for the satisfaction of climbing the route? It was no real surprise to see, at our finish, that the ropes had indeed disappeared. One mini consolation: being that Don had already retired them from active climbing service, he hardly shed a tear. But—over the years—I have felt guilty for not having offered at least a measly $50 to my buddy as my share of his small loss.

*Only having to fix four pitches made the first an easy day. Ditto for the second: seven more straightforward pitches got us to our bivouac spot on Heart Ledges, which we made by mid-afternoon. Don had taken the first lead—it had been my choice—meaning that he would go first for all the odd-numbered pitches. I had been climbing strongly, feeling my oats and gaining confidence.*

Perhaps many readers don't understand this, our modus operandi, on big-wall climbs. In actual fact, one climbs only about half the pitches and jumars[7] the rest; the other half are led by one's partner. This saves time and energy. So, did I really "climb" the Salathé Wall? You, dear reader, will have to assume the position as final judge.

A few notes on our preparations. First: equipment. The guide suggested "60–65 pins, from rurps to a 4" bong." (We were not yet in the age of chocks, nuts, or cams). Unlike every other route up the mighty El Cap, we would need no hammocks, being that every ten or so pitches—a reasonable climbing day—we would find a ledge large enough for two sleeping bodies.

Second: water. The rule of thumb for Yosemite during the hot months is a half-gallon of water per person per day. For the two of us that totaled up to a minimum of five gallons in the haul sack, which translates into a weight of 42 pounds. *Ouch!* From our earlier botched attempt on El Cap, we had learned of the importance of packing that life-preserving water so that no protruding corner would be the cause of a hole worn through both canvas and plastic when the dangling sack was being hauled up the near vertical wall.

A third memorable note: Don had prepared and wrapped ten fat sandwiches, each with a 5⁄16" slab of irresistible ham, for each dinner. It's funny: I remember distinctly that precise thickness because we laughed at the fact that those ham slices were only a tad narrower than our 7⁄16"-diameter rope. Majestic choice.

Yet a fourth preparation, with a not so fortuitous result: my camera. On most climbs, but especially on extended trips, I always brought along a camera, and almost always preferred taking slides, and I valued the colors of Kodachrome over those of Ektachrome. But, how to climb with a camera? Only with difficulty. I finally had developed a method of securing it in front of my chest. That had its advantages over the tedious and sometimes impossible task of taking off the climbing pack and withdrawing it from an outside pocket—for every desired photo. But the major disadvantage: when nervously gripping a corner with sweat-slippery hands while standing on a nebulous foothold, or when desperately hand-frisking inside a squeeze chimney to jam my fingers into a ¾-inch groove, the camera would suffer inevitable blows and thumps. After all, what was more important, my life or the machine? As a result, climbing cameras had a short life span. I had already relegated my trusty ol' (but really too large) single-lens-reflex Nikon to the junk heap, as I had to do just weeks before with a smaller and more automatic Olympus. So, imagine my consternation with only a week of anticipation between Don and I and the climb of our lives! I had no functional camera and was already economizing to pay my rent. Idea! I approached a friendly department at UC Berkeley, leveraging my status as an illustrious alumnus, to request that they lend me one of their student Instamatics. They obliged. There I was, outfitted with the cheapest, most inadequate camera commercially available. With that Instamatic toy, I would document, for all time, in the form of slides, the greatest climbing adventure that I would ever attempt in my life!

During our historic 5½ days, that Instamatic fulfilled all those negative expectations. Did I mention the amateurish 1"-square slides it produced?—as opposed to the ⅞" × 1⅜" ones taken from any decent camera? Much worse: having neither adjustable nor automatic aperture, the images came out OK only if snapped in intense sunlight. As a result, I ended up with worthy pics for at most half the climb. No decent slide emerged for any of our bivy-night ledges. Nor did I end up with preserved visual memories for nearly half the 35 total pitches, which we had climbed in insufficient light, either early in the mornings or late in the afternoons.

Perhaps there is a positive side to all this: had one of those intense days been overcast, I would have ended up with even less than I did.

*Third day: early start. The first three pitches offered no great challenge, with a bit of easy aid and even a long stretch of 4th class. Hmm. Pitch 14, just ahead, would be my lead. According to the 1964 Roper guide, I will have to "pendulum into a striking jam crack which leads to Hollow Flake Ledge." "Striking"? Hmmm…? The later—1971—edition leaves out that adjective and indicates no special difficulty for the climber to get up the "120 foot lie back/jam."*[8] *Hmm. The most recent description gives no indication of special difficulty. If there were, I could always yield the lead to Don—as we have done in the past. It's my decision. So—not knowing any better—I say nothing. And Don—even if he knows stuff I ignore about the Hollow Flake—remains his silent self.*

I've explained about the camera. Now a note about using it. El Cap is huge, more than huge. It's as high as three Empire State Buildings stacked one on top of the other. Have you ever stood at the very base of a similar building? Well, it's unimpressive. It might as well have eight stories as 800: right next to its base, you can't tell the difference. Similarly, you only begin to appreciate the immensity of El Cap when you stroll a half-mile out into the Meadows and squint, trying to convince yourself that those two small dots are, in fact, a pair of climbers high on the wall.

No one should expect to see impressive photos of the giant taken from its base. Ditto for climbing shots either looking up or down: they simply don't cut it. Over the years, constantly practicing climbing photography, I've learned of the difficulties and disappointments and I don't take photos either looking up or looking down. That is to say, still photography does not and cannot capture the verve you feel, the fear, the tremendous excitement: all these are impossible to capture when aiming the camera in the only two directions available—up or down. In short, the only decent climbing photos are those looking horizontal. And, unfortunately, the climb up El Cap provided very few instances offering that type of view.

*I'm on lead, pitch 14. Leaving almost the whole rack and most of the contents of the pack, I prepare for the super-long pendulum. I make my way past Don, who is on belay. Fifty feet up and to the left I find the fixed pin with a ring. Secured, I thread the rope through, then start lowering myself down. About 80 feet. Sufficient? I walk laterally and instantly see that I'll have to go at least another 30 feet down. Oh my gosh, now I'm well below Don's level. Here's the pendulum—I've never done one so long—I'll have to*

**The last third of El Cap's Salathé Wall overhangs. In the 1970s, we and other climbers used lots of aid on this section. Today's climbers will climb free over most of it. In negotiating a roof, one of my pitons came out, and I was left dangling.**

*push, to hustle. With the first real try I realize that simply running to the left while hanging is not enough: my destination is the vertical-sloping flake, way off to the left, which hangs there suspended, perhaps a foot separating it from the steep wall. In my first two attempts I only got within ten feet of it. I hang there resting; a few deep breaths. This will require major effort. I have to adjust the length of my rope one more time so that the swing will land me exactly at the flake's lower point.*

*Now, another attempt. This time I strain to get as high to tension-traverse to the right as high as I can. Slowly I push with the legs to power myself as high as possible. Now I need to get the fastest running start possible. It'll take everything I can give it. I begin my second—crazy—hanging run to the left. I face sideways, body vertical to the rock face. And I run… Go! Go! … gone. But I did touch the flake. Almost!*

*One more time. I begin—again—the tension-traverse to the right. Three's a charm, they say. Then I burst into my hanging run-swing to the left. Straining, at my maximum. I am able to grab onto—barely—the flake's rounded corner. Then I desperately squirm a few feet up in order to lessen—just one little bit—the tension of the rope. I swing my body to jam it a bit further into the wide crack, with my back now against the underside of the flake, while my right hand—in a panic—passes over the smooth wall surface seeking a ridge or crystal to grasp. Whew. I'm stable—at least for now. Will I slip out? Horrible thought. Goddamn, the flake is so flared. And smooth. No cracks to sink a hand into. At least it's not overhanging!*

*I made it here—wedged in. It's like a squeeze chimney: my dangling feet have nothing to push against, and my knees sustain me, bruising themselves against the face. No time to relax. I have to exert force simply to stay put. But how to move up? After a half-minute I'm sweating. Somewhat frantically, I look around: no possible protection for the next 120 feet. That means I'll end up 20–30 feet above Don's level—and 50 feet across—before I get to the flake's top and an easy ledge. Ouch! A slip-out fall right now would mean a nasty long swing. Can't even let myself imagine it. But if and when I squiggle myself up the flake, then a fall from there? Also too frightening to even contemplate. God, why didn't I give Don this lead? I'm way over my head. And there's no going back.*

*Got to suppress panic. Butterflies, get your ass out of my gut! Oh. A cramp in the right arm? I've got to move. How? Hard to squeeze on up, it's too narrow. Lie back? That's what the Roper guide says. This means I have to maneuver my body out of the mother crack and, while grasping the rounded edge with my sweaty hands, move my legs out and up. Shit, the corner is smooth, it has nothing—and now it too is slippery with my sweat. Nerves: Get lost, there's no other way.*

*I'm making some progress, but this is scary. Hooray, one sharp-corner section for a decent lie back hand. After that, everything rounded, again. My shirt wet under the arms. God. Sweating hands. This is disastrous: I could slip off. Calm, Bill. If I panic it's all over. Reach up again. Delicately. Got to keep going, even if it remains hard. Have to avoid hands cramping. Mouth dry now, can I induce salivation? Sun now directly on me. This is a nightmare. So far not so good. But I'm still here—barely. Hands, stay put. I rub the right one against shirt, but it's still clammy. Now I can't see too well above: the sun is making sweat to drip into bleary eyes.*

*Slowly, painfully, I move on up, trying not to think. For, as Hamlet didn't say: "to think perchance to fear." I have to suppress fear.*

*That is near impossible—but necessary. The realization again flashes across my consciousness that slipping off here would be worse than horrible. Yet—the temptation is there: my over-tired arms could simply relax. No. Can't oblige. Falling is not an option.*

*Suddenly an epiphany—which I remember vividly to this day. This—this existential situation—is akin to the mind's confused meanderings at the moment of death. At what point does one simply decide to stop resisting? To relax, to slide off, to go sailing into the Netherland?*

*Not me! Angry with myself, I rebuke that voice of softness, I clench my teeth yet one more time, and silently repeat to myself: falling is not an option.*

*I continue struggling ... the slope eases off ... I'm beginning to find real footholds. But my body is almost at the point of going no further. I have to drag myself up the final—easy—forty feet to the ledge and clip myself in to a bombproof fixed pin. Opening the pack, I take out my day's allotment of water, and instantly begin to chug. Thirst will remain.*

*It's only 9:30 a.m. and I have a whole climbing day ahead of me. I've gone through most of my day's ration of water—it'll be a long day. I'm wasted. Don will have to take the rest of my leads today.*

## *1978—The A, B, Cs: Accidents, Bears, Peter Craig/Canada*

Four times a buddy tied into the other extreme of my rope has ended up in the hospital—and three of those accidents involved my lifelong friend Peter, an unfortunate Jonah mountaineer.

Most climbers have a few experiences of peeling off the rock while leading over particularly difficult or demanding route sections. But most know how to minimize any possible injury through their anticipation of potential problems. First, they make sure they are high enough from the ground or a ledge so that the fall ends with them hanging in midair from the belay rope, and suffering at most a light hand or arm abrasion, a sore waist (from the harness or—in the 1970s—a swami belt), and possibly a bruised ego. Second, they are careful to place a piece of pro as high as possible—and possibly a second piece for moral support. Third, they know exactly where a slip is most likely. And fourth, they are mentally prepared to take the airy tumble. A typical reaction: the fall pisses them off so much that, after a minute of arm rest, they climb back up to attempt the difficult move one more time.

Unfortunately, Peter's falls were not of that type. In two of the three instances he came crashing down against the ground. Ergo, a broken leg (fall number one) and a dislocated shoulder (fall number three). On fall number two, he was high enough, but out of panic he attempted to jam his hand into a horizontal crack. As a result, he later had to relearn classical guitar strums with only three intact right-hand fingers.

I hurriedly pass over these gory details in order to get to my chosen emphasis: Peter's psychological disposition vis-a-vis climbing. Obviously, his climbing abilities were far below those of the Yosemite elite. Interestingly—according to one account—no "super climber" of Yosemite fame seems to have suffered comparable injuries to those of Peter. Yes, there were deaths from rappel accidents. Yes, there were long falls after which climber after climber was able to "shrug" off the fright and climb back up to resume ascending.[9] So what is at issue here?

I must return to the topic of "climbing mentality" that I touched upon briefly in the introduction to this book. Peter and I were very aware that we were not gifted climbers in either the physical or mental domains. For that reason, we spent years pushing ourselves to master basic climbing techniques and to acquire an ever greater "confidence" for lead climbing. I would venture to say that the great majority of climbing novices share similar motivations. A typical climber's ambition: "I was able to get up a 5.7 route last weekend, so this coming Saturday I'll attempt a 5.8." We push ourselves with the hope of improving—in both technique and lead-climber confidence.

Physical skill and confidence are inevitably intertwined: one feeds off the other. And obviously, Peter's desire for improvement exceeded his abilities. Unfortunately, this is not an uncommon mindset; in fact, it alone might account for the majority of accidents and injuries in the whole history of alpinism and climbing.

Yet in spite of his limitations, Peter's desire was extreme. Since childhood he had sported a passion for the mountains. When he looked in the mirror, he must have seen, or have wished to see, little other than a climber. Even after all that self-mutilation he continued "breathing" mountains and dreaming of rock faces. (A few years later, when he would choose a location to establish his neurology practice, he chose Lander, Wyoming—the gateway city for the most remote wilderness areas of the contiguous forty-eight states: the Wind River Range.) Vivid in my mind are the multiple—and frustrated—attempts made by Peter over perhaps two decades to become, once again, an effective lead climber. Such was his love of the experience.

**California has its advantages. I always spent spring vacations doing mixed climbing in the High Sierras. In the early morning sunshine at our campsite before a frozen lake, I took off my dark goggles and squinted as a buddy snapped this photo.**

The year 1978 would see yet one more attempt. Peter was eager to see if by following my roped leads he could once again improve his level of confidence. He was now married to Eva—studying neurology at Seattle's University of Washington—and the two still resided in the Pacific Northwest. I, married to Sara and sporting my child of ten months, Dani, was visiting old friends and parents in the same city. "*Can we climb together?*" "You bet—let's decide on an easy peak somewhere near Banff. The weather will be passable, if not superb. We can take the wives. Sara might begin liking the campground experience—B.C. has no rival for mountain beauty. We've already been camping a few times with little Dani, so she ought to be okay. And Eva will not have to feel committed to remain with Sara at the campground; she'll love going out hiking to look for wildflowers."

We were off to Mt. Sir Donald—one of the "50 classics"[10]—somewhat near the U.S.-Canadian border. Peter and I did not yet share with our wives that it would be a longer climb, over somewhat sharp rock that required a bivouac. This means that we would leave our wives for a whole night to fend for themselves in the two tents we would pitch next to the car in the campground. "Not to worry, delinquents and criminals don't thrive that far north, and we won't even take off for the route if there is threatening weather." But Peter and I had not anticipated the bears. Or perhaps I should say, *the* bear.

Here, a rather long digression. One has to understand that there are bears and *bears*. First, the kind that is furry, bothersome, but essentially harmless for humankind. By that time I must have had a score of experiences with Yosemite's brown bears. One Camp 4 climbing rat described them as "fat, tourist-fed, insolent, and monstrously facile at stealing food, contemptuously impervious to indignation, rage, terrified screams, outraged threats, or supplication."[11] I could rattle on for paragraphs over how the camp service at the Valley (shorthand for the Yosemite Valley), changed each decade the design of garbage containers or Camp 4 procedures for protecting climbers' food, but I remember no specific incident involving an unfortunate human encounter.

Three "bear" memories. On one occasion I had taken off by myself for some long days of hiking in the contiguous Sequoia National Forest, and returned late and very much fatigued to an open camping spot in the Valley. In the darkness I carelessly chose a spot to throw down my plastic ground cloth, pad, and sleeping bag that was precisely (if you draw a straight line) between two garbage cans. There I was, slumbering—perhaps barely entering the REM stage—and dreaming of a circus (!) where I was lying on the ground, super frightened by an approaching elephant coming directly my way. With a lurch I then awoke sufficiently to jump out of my unzipped sleeping bag, yank it two yards to the side, and watch a huge darkened mass tread exactly over where my body had been positioned two seconds before. It was an adult bear making a beeline for the garbage can only thirty feet away. *Whew!* The power of the unconscious saved my butt!

A second anecdote. In the summer of 1972 Fredrickson and I had parked my new VW Bug (brown, or "color de caca," as my office mate had described it) at the tourist lodge near the Bugaboos (located in the Interior Ranges of British Columbia) and—in the heaviest pack I've ever carried!—lugged half of our food up the very long hill to the Magic Ground-Squirrel Campsite (who could have taught those small critters to climb a two-meter boulder and drop onto the top of a hanging pack?) A week later, when hunger motivated us to return back down to my parked car for the rest of our food, we found the whole back-side window ripped out—metal frame and all—and claw scratches marking a few of the windows. I had been under the naive impression that only a diamond ring could leave such marks on windshield glass! Lodge personnel informed us that only a "baby bear" would target a car, because they—unlike adult bears—were not able to satiate their appetite for human grub remains by climbing into the dumpster.

My car: even worse off. We saw that after the baby bear's window destruction, the smaller forest creatures had been able to enter, gorging themselves for at least a week on Jell-O and Wyler's sugar drink mix, cocoa packs, etc., and had left sticky paw prints over every imaginable interior surface. We had to spend three hours washing and scrubbing everything except the interior roof. For the drive back to Seattle, we patched the glassless window with cardboard and tape. Thankfully, the personnel at my car insurance company did not cast too much doubt on what might have seemed a tall tale of baby-bear destruction.

Yet a third "bear" experience. There we were—it must have been around 2012—several of us were sitting around a wooden picnic table in Camp 4 as night was approaching. Along came a young female ranger, cute and friendly (this is the truth: not all rangers are male, ugly, and mean!), urging us to comply promptly with campground regulations and move any type of consumables, plates, or pans, to the assigned steel storage box a few feet away. She informed us that within the last hour the radio-tracking technology in her small office had indicated that two of the Valley's well-known bears were just minutes away, awaiting the onset of darkness to come visiting. *"The mother bear is down near El Cap—she probably won't get over here tonight—but you never know. The little bear, however, is over there, somewhere up the hill and behind the large climbing boulder. We've had a few near incidents with him over the last month. One more and we'll have to send him to the farm." "Really? You have a farm for the most bothersome of the critters?" "No, that's just a polite way to say that we'd have to put him to sleep. About ten years ago the practice was to capture them, fly them by helicopter to a remote area of the Sierras, and then release them. But all that proved to be ineffective. Because once a bear tastes human food, it will settle for nothing else. On several occasions, the released bears ended up finding their way back to campgrounds and causing problems again. You've read the sign we have posted at our office: 'A fed bear is a dead bear.' You campers and climbers will be kind to them if you leave absolutely nothing on your campsite tables."*

Now some notes about *bears*. Near the end of Chapter 7 I write about a near encounter in the Tetons with a mother brown bear that, because she was with her cub, might have proven to be dangerous. But here the subject is grizzlies, with which—fortunately—I have had no personal experiences. My assumption is that these primarily reside in the lowlands where stream-bred salmon are plentiful. In contrast, us climbers, if in the wilderness, hurry through the low elevations in order to arrive as promptly as possible at the beginning of our intended climbing route at a higher elevation.

Perhaps, decades ago, a grizzly or two would have made its appearance in Yellowstone National Park—before that place became a car-bearing tourist Mecca. Or, one occasionally hears a scary story about a bear surprising a lonely hiker in Alaska or British Columbia. A half-decade ago, when I first arrived at Glacier National Park, I—just like almost all the tourist hikers—dutifully carried a canister of "bear spray" strapped across my chest and ready to frisk out at a second's notice. After a few days I left it behind in the car when I realized the diligence of the rangers in completely closing off a whole section of the park and advising all visitors when a grizzly was sighted. But they are still wary about one surprisingly appearing. At every trailhead in that park there are signs posted to prohibit hikers from proceeding unless they are accompanied by at least four companions. So much for grizzles. End of this digression about bears in general.

There we were, having decided to climb Mt. Sir Donald and leave on the morrow. It was Monday, about lunchtime. Eva had ventured out to stretch her legs and Peter and I were warming up on the nearby rocks. Returning to the campground, we found a terrified Sara clutching little Danielito in her arms. She had been laboring to open a small can of chicken meat when a medium-sized bear approached her totally undetected. Screaming, she had grabbed the baby, dropped the partially opened can on the ground, and enclosed herself safely inside the car.

Next morning, Peter and I were barely successful in persuading her and Eva that they would be OK. The two of us left, climbed all day, and then prepared for our less-than-comfortable night in a rocky cave.

Unfortunately, at about that same time, but down below in the campground, the two women were struck by bear terror. Later they told us: at about eleven o'clock, both—accompanying Danielito in one tent—were awakened upon hearing a disturbance some thirty feet away at the site of the picnic table. They had "forgotten" to clear it of any and all dishes and—sure enough—the bear had come back. The two women spent ten frightful minutes screaming and banging whatever in the hopes of scaring it away. They survived—of course. But Peter and I ended up taking the brunt of their anger when they blamed us for their bearly fright.

Moral of the story? Bears are going to be there whether you like it or not.

Oh! And Peter? Although spending his adult life in or near the Wind River mountains, he never was successful in regaining that *je ne sais quoi* that one needs to be a successful lead climber.

## *1992—Liberty Ridge on Mt. Rainier*

*A stubby candle positioned in a small cavity about three feet above the nylon floor tarp—it alone illuminates the whole interior space. Its pale light reaches everywhere. There are almost no shadows. It's as if the snow walls were glowing. Funny, it must be totally dark outside and the temperature must have dropped to four degrees. Yet I need to take off the down jacket, what with my sweating body and the interior heat. Scott just made the last trip outside, before cutting a few last hard-snow blocks off from his side of the cave in order to seal the door. Snow caves are so comfy!*

**Snow caves are—you have to believe me!—warm and comfortable. The secret is to choose a near vertical face in order to facilitate the number-one problem, which is snow removal.**

How does memory

work? My curiosity about this—could it be a sign of the waning years? (Please gods, grant me at least twenty more—as long as they're good ones.) I'm prone on the bed, on my back. In the darkness I close my eyes and "invite" the inner eye to take over. Does it project or does it record—like a mental video camera? Sometimes what happens is by association: I "picture" the living room's dinner candle and a memory "pops up": I'm now "seeing" the snow-cave candle stub.

*The cave measures about eight by eight feet—big enough so that no part of either sleeping bag will touch either a wall or the ceiling. We had anticipated an extra space for the stove for the inevitable melting/cooking rituals.*

For the second consecutive year we had driven across the state to go up Liberty Ridge, on the north side of Mt. Rainier. Entering the park, it was eerie to pass through a roof-less tunnel, with a snow-covered road underneath and five-foot white walls on either side. After parking the car at the lonely road end, we secured ice axes, crampons, and snow shovels to our packs, and then fastened skins to the bottom of our skis. After inserting gaiter-covered boots into the ski bindings, we threaded our mitt-hands through the pole loops. Then, up with the Kelty packs, fasten belt straps, and off we went.

After a few miles on skis, we confronted what turned out to be the most difficult part of the whole climb. Crossing the small stream in the summer takes simply a prance, but with the winter snow accumulation, you have to cross, somehow, an impressive eight-foot-deep chasm measuring three feet across at its narrowest point. The running stream, apparently, never freezes. Since we couldn't fly over or jump across, we resorted to bridging the gap with two horizontally positioned skis. Would the snow-ice underneath them hold? Thankfully it did. But the difficult maneuvers involved took an hour of our time.

Then, a bit further, the steep incline forced us to take off the skis and stick them vertically in the snow—in a place where we would not fail to find them on the return. Then we put on crampons to begin the real ascent. It's funny: winter here has its advantages over summer for a climb like this. First, there's no hot sun to dehydrate your body. Second, if enveloped in a cloud you don't have to wear dark glasses or yuck your neck and face—including ears and lips—with sunscreen. Third, this route—believe me!—is more dangerous in August, with hidden crevasses, rock missiles, and crumby hand holds (on the whole mountain there's not a trace of decent rock to be found.) And fourth: if the snow has an ideal consistency—like today—it's a breeze kicking in with boot and crampons and not having to worry about unconsolidated fluff, slippery ice, or loose volcanic sand/dirt. The only danger—it happened once about noon—is kicking my front points into either the gaiter or the laces of the other boot. Tripping up there would have been … better not to even think about it.

Truth be told, it was so easy going that we didn't even consider roping up. But not because it wasn't dangerous. On the contrary. Protecting ourselves with a rope would have meant losing precious time putting in anchors and belaying. On a long climb like this you've got to move fast—you don't want to be caught on the face in darkness. A second discarded option was simul climbing, but that is also time-consuming and none of us owned even one picket—probably the only type of pro that would stay put in the consolidated snow. What's more, why use any rope at all? Because if one person slips then two people fall. Better no rope at all.

Most of the day we were enveloped in the clouds. Fortunately, there was enough visibility to not mistake the ridge outcroppings that define the route. But only a few times was I able to see the impressive Willis Wall a kilometer off to the left (gads, this mountain is huge!) On a water break I spent a whole minute tracing a possible route up its broken ledges and steep gullies. Would a rational person even want to get near it? But some suicidal climber just might choose to attempt it in winter, when there would be fewer loose rocks ricocheting on down. Did I write that I "saw" the Willis Wall? Better stated: "I heard it."

The four of us just cramponed up, keeping to our side of the ridge. On the steeper parts we would hold the ice axe in the self-arrest position; on easier parts my buddies liked to use it as a walking stick, but I usually preferred to free up my arms by jamming it in between my back and the pack—where it would stay put. I made sure to never position myself immediately below a buddy, because I realized that his slip would end it all for me too. But each of us felt confident: for years we had trained ourselves to not make even the slightest mistake. Yes, the route was "dangerous"—because of the exposure—but it was not hard. We just kept stepping on up, as if each were alone in the world. Concentration meant silence. Step by step, as if in a trance.

Passing alongside of, and then around, a 20-feet-high gendarme: impressive, intimidating, exhilarating. A different stretch of the route resembled … a Disney movie? Everything was coated with sparkling ice crystals—like Tinkerbell's pixie dust! Only much better, because you're breathing in the fresh glacial air.

It's hard to put into words the strange species of joy that I was feeling.

An hour before darkness we identified an appropriately steep slope for our cave. After taking off my pack, I delicately cut a path with the shovel to arrive at my chosen spot. It takes only two minutes to cut out a platform. Then, the fun part: on my knees facing in, I imagine an 18" square on the new vertical wall, and give three shovel thrusts straight in and out to cut three of the sides. Then, a thrust into the square's bottom, followed by a push downward, and a snow chunk breaks free and I let it slide down the slope. Next order of business: to cut out a low horizontal passage—the future door. By then I'm down to my T-shirt for the most strenuous part: aiming my four thrusts upward to hollow out the ceiling. As soon as space allows, I move inside and sit. Now snow removal is a piece of cake: I can use my feet to push each new snow block out and away. Within an hour I'm all done.

By the time I spread out the plastic floor tarp and pads, carry equipment inside, and remove crampons, I'm dripping with sweat and panting—an effect of my exertion and the altitude. We'll leave the door open until after the last pee. Inside, it's cramped—and definitely snug. There's only room to stoop. It's more comfortable sitting down with my back against the wall. Or I can lie down with the legs stretched out—to keep them from cramping—while propped up on an elbow. It might be dark outside, but the light from the candle stub that we have positioned in a wall hole is multiplied several times over by the reflecting walls. Another double plus: no wind and flapping noise; and the white walls provide more insulation from the cold than four inches of house insulation.

Yet another advantage of our snow cave: we can run the stove for 90 minutes of water melting and cooking and not have to worry about damage to tent nylon or asphyxiation from fumes (they instantly disappear into the porous walls). Also pleasant: with the stove's heat, I can comfortably violate the skinny climber's number-one rule for winter outings: that "either you're moving or inside the bag." But there is also a minor downside: after a half-hour we have to smooth out the shovel cuts in the ceiling so that condensation does not drip down upon us.

We sip cup after cup of warmed brew, pretending it's wine to toast to our unforgettable day. We engage in pleasant conversation—but no communication is possible with our other buddies, even though they're only twenty feet away in their own cave. I'm positioned to look straight at the candle flame. It has a hypnotizing effect. My thigh muscles tingle pleasantly with fatigue as drowsiness sets in. Eyelids grow heavy…

## *1996—The Needles, Black Hills, South Dakota*

"Dad, do you think I could get to the top of Devil's Tower?" What? Does my daughter even know where it is? Oh yes, I remember now: on a family outing years back we must have spent a night in the campground at its base. But now? In her 17 years she's never done serious roped climbing. I remember eight years back when I protected her and Dani—little kids then—with a short top rope to scramble up truck-sized rocks in Icicle Canyon.[12] Hallelujah, the bug must have bitten!

There we were, Esti, her high-school and cross-country friend Gina, and I, camped out at certainly the most beautiful spot in the USA, Horsethief Lake, just a few turns beyond Mt. Rushmore. I had taken the two girls into the woods to locate ideal cliffs to practice rappels—first easy ones, then hard ones, then raps that, to get started, would scare your booty. And, of course, rope work: my leading with one of them belaying, they in turn following to my small belay stance in the middle of a cliff, then going through all the necessary moves for a second roped pitch. They had to have it down, because on the real thing they would be alone and would have to make the right decisions. And climb safely. Which means, climb, belay, tie a figure-eight, clip in, yell out the standard signals, unclip and collect anchor gear, then climb up with confidence. Doing all that I forged a new, not-so-difficult, route up the backside of Horsethief pinnacle. Were the girls ready? Almost. We needed to do one more shake-out route. Hmm. The Third Cathedral Spire, about twenty miles away, in the northwest corner of Carson State Park. A good route: not hard, has a spectacular summit, and offers a chance for the girls to confront and deal with vertigo. And, after that, the half-day's drive west into Wyoming and to Devil's Tower.

I led the first pitch up the obvious chimney, squeezed through the chockstone hole, and sat down on the wide belay ledge where the girls, on their separate ropes, soon joined me. The second pitch took me up a chimney and into a shallow gully to an exposed, sloping, mini summit—just 15 vertical feet below and this side of the actual summit—where I

Devil's Tower, in the northeast corner of Wyoming, was featured in the movie *Close Encounters of the Third Kind*. Almost every crack separating the weird hexagonal columns constitutes a route, but the easiest is the Durrance, on the right-hand skyline.

placed a solid nut that offered good protection for establishing my belay. Then, I brought the girls up. Each, in turn, clipped in and sat down. Then, they watched me step across the airy, scary, gap, and scamper up to put on another, short, belay. On that real summit we spent an obligatory few minutes to snap some pics, while watching a cavalcade of ants scurrying around as we opened up the canister and signed the summit register. Then, back down the tender 15 feet to the security of our protected spot, where we sat, pulled out sandwiches and sipped some water. Esti was enjoying herself, sitting in the comfortable sun, being able to peer straight down on three sides to the ground way below.

Then my eyes shifted to Gina. Hmm. What was going on in her head? I noticed that one of her hands was firmly grasping the sling leading from her harness to our anchor. And her feet were positioned to withstand an earthquake. She smiled, making small conversation. (Too deliberately?) "How you do'n, Gina?" *"F-fine."* "Like the view?" (my camouflaged attempt to have her reveal what she was feeling). *"It's wonderful up here. I really like the verticality."* (Hmm. Her tone? Was she merely stating what she knew I wanted/needed to hear?) Then I shifted my gaze from her (feigned) calm face to her free hand. It was slightly trembling.

How could I say what I had to say without hurting her feelings? "Gina, I'm really sorry to say that tomorrow, when we drive up to Devil's Tower, I'm not going to be able to take you up the route. You'll have to join the tourists. From down below you'll be able to follow Esti's and my progress."

## *2002—Devil's Lake State Park, Wisconsin*

My aleph-like memory captures in simultaneity various past moments:

*"Sue, hopefully there's a younger climber among us who, in a future outing, will remember how to find this trail." "Don't worry, Bill. Olle made sure to include the GPS coordinates in the new edition of the Guide."*[13] *The "veteran" group—which I always lined up with on Saturdays or Sundays to climb with the CMC (Chicago Mountaineering Club)—always selected the most remote of the park's 170 (or so) climbing areas. In this we always deferred to Olle, who eschewed the gawking stares of tourists—which leads one to question a popularly held misconception that people like me climb out of a certain "desire for glory."*[14]

*Was the 5.8 rating for Laughing Sioux too low? After the four most endowed members of our group struggled on up it, the inevitable pow wow: Ben: "It's super strenuous: for me, 5.8+"; Brad: "That finger hold is a doozy: 5.9–"; Pete: "I was straining on the inside corner: 5.9–. If majority rules, we should up it to 5.9." Then the deciding word from Olle (heavily accented): "We won't change that rating. 5.8." End of discussion.*

*Thirty feet away and ten minutes later, I recruit a belayer and start up White Wasp, knowing I'd not get past the scary 5.9 overhang halfway up. "Bill, the route doesn't go over there; it keeps to the corner." "Sue, for us trad climbers the only important thing is getting to the top."*

There's so much to be said of my association and experiences with the CMC that had begun about six years earlier. Over the past thirty or so years since our family had moved to Wisconsin, I had never considered it worth my time to climb in the state's best park, Devil's Lake—located in about the center of the state and less than a two-hour drive from my home. But beginning in 2002 that changed.

Why had this not occurred earlier? The simple reason is that I was—by fact of my climbing past and committed consciousness—a trad climber. Or, a West Coast climber—in my mind they were one and the same. This explains my yearly junkets out West. In contrast, Devil's Lake dogmatically and almost exclusively offered top-roped climbing. Its reddish rock, quartzite, was as hard as granite and featured great cracks and a high variety of climbing obstacles. But the hundreds of vertical "outcroppings" in the park rarely exceeded 50 feet in height. So top-roping was the standard practice. Why not? Similar to sport-climbing areas that now proliferate, these offer the advantage of super safe climbing: a fixed rope from the top nearly eliminates the number-one danger of trad climbing—and the major cause of injuries or accidents—which are the long leader falls. This factor, among others, accounts for how "climbing" has become dramatically safer and, therefore, widely practiced. Climbing gyms share with outdoors "sport" (and top-roping) areas this basic characteristic of offering safe climbing—unlike my preference for areas featuring "trad" climbing.

So being a trad climber ("to the marrow of my bones"), I had (somewhat haughtily, some might say) disdained Devil's Lake. And I was rather uninterested in other, "lesser" types of climbing experiences, as long as I could make my annual trip to some worldly Mecca of trad climbing out West. Or—another way of expressing the same—I had little need or desire to partake of such "practice-climbing" areas as long as my palate continued to be satiated with "the real thing."

But come 2002 or so, my adolescent children were making fewer demands on my time, work was becoming boring, and each year's spring revival was awakening memories of past climbing adventures that I now wished to relive—if possible. My age: 50 plus and counting. Could a trad climber be reborn? I felt good physically and the desire was there. Was the bod capable of attaining—once again—the high state of physical conditioning necessary for demanding mountain experiences? Over the previous two decades I had maintained a respectable degree of fitness in my activities as a soccer referee. Hmm. Could I now regain strength in the arms and upper torso? The least I could do was try. I installed a pull-up bar in the basement and—lo and behold—my repetitions increased, in the short period of three months, from about seven (in a ten-minute duration) to 24. This surprised me in the most favorable way imaginable, because while all the literature says that after about the age of 20 or 25 the body loses muscle mass, here I had demonstrated to myself that I was capable of gaining strength, at the ripe age of 50, through a consistent workout schedule!

**A new generation of climbers prefers warm and accessible sites with short routes. Notice the "pro" (cams or "friends") hanging from my friend's waist.**

After my recent two summer visits to the Tetons, I was a bit more sanguine: I remember distinctly having to tolerate the Alpine Club's Camp, what with its hard bunks, claustrophobic wooden cabins, and especially its total ban on evening campfires. But the crown of my trepidations revolved around my realization that while the bod was still capable of putting in a very long day for my evolving practice of "scamper climbing," I needed to spend the entire next day in immobilized physical recovery. (A definition needed? Scamper climbing means that I'd carry a super-light pack with no technical equipment except an emergency "spaghetti rope" for a possible rappel. I'd leave the trailhead at the break of day; and—moving constantly to avoid chills—I'd reach a summit and return back to the car by nightfall.) This was not like forty years before, when I could go day after day without experiencing the now day-after *rigor mortis* of the legs. Hmm. I began to realize and then accept that this was the type of aging that, for at least this over-the-hill climber, was unavoidable.

Then there was the issue of my previous ability to lead climb. To all appearances it was still there, relatively intact, but in a rusty state. Back in about 1995 I had successfully introduced my daughter, then my son, to serious roped climbing in experiences culminating in my leading them up the Durrance Route of Devil's Tower. This had involved purchasing new climbing shoes and a set of cams—that continue to amaze me with their holding power. At the beginning—upon resuming my lead-climbing activities—I continually lost time in misjudging the cam size needed for a given crack. But I was convinced that this minor problem would disappear as I accumulated more experience with their placement.

So initially I was attracted to the idea of climbing with the CMC at Devil's Lake. What worked for me was preparing the Friday or Saturday night before, and if—at 6:30 a.m. on the morrow—the weather looked favorable, I'd leave home by 7, stop at a Kwik Trip for coffee and breakfast muffins, and arrive at the CMC campground (adjacent to the park) before 9 a.m. The assembly of climbers would then go out to a selected location to fix from eight to ten double ropes. I personally made it a point to climb multiple variations of the easier climbs, but I usually exhausted myself on the 5.8s and 5.9s. I have to admit: when climbing with a top rope, it was pleasant not having to suffer the fear of a leader fall.

Within that group I was noticeably different—due largely to my long personal history as a trad lead climber. First—and curiously—I was the only one who consistently down-climbed (instead of being passively lowered) after reaching the top on the easier routes. I had my reasons: in addition to enhancing my physical condition, I was—and remain—convinced that down-climbing practice enhances my ability as a "scamper" climber.

A second difference: in contrast to other CMC participants, I have an

**At the top of a 60-foot cliff (Devil's Lake, Wisconsin), our "rope leader" inspects each of the three anchors (for each climbing rope) that are tied with webbing to trees or climbing nuts wedged into rock cracks. When he gives the "thumbs up," we descend to the bottom to begin our day of climbing and belaying.**

inability, when attempting a very hard move, to push myself to the point of falling—even though slipping off would result only in dangling safely at the end of the rope. Why? Because as a trad leader I have trained myself not to fall. In 50 years I have not taken a significant leader fall (here I'm not including those calculated slips right next to a solid pro placement) because my unconscious dominates: it will not allow for a "conscious" decision to push myself until I peel off the rock. That type of mental conditioning—which has saved my butt countless times in trad ascents—proves to be out of sync with a generally accepted CMC practice.

There's a third difference, which requires a few introductory paragraphs. I was coming to realize that in spite of my increased frequency in joining CMC friends for top-roped climbing at Devil's Lake, I was feeling less and less confident in leading trad in divine places like the Tetons or Yosemite. Ditto with regard to my emerging passion for scamper climbing:

I was fearing more and therefore attempting less. In other words, I was beginning to feel "over the hill" as a climber.

I remain convinced that although the top-roping experiences at Devil's Lake are far superior to anything you could do in (smelly) indoor climbing gyms (and far better than just staying home in everyday La Crosse), they are still far inferior to the adrenaline rush and joy of vertical nature that I crave to experience in the "real" mountains. It is also true that the top-roping experiences at Devil's Lake—for instance, on the park's strenuous 5.8 and 5.9 lay-backs—do enhance my technical ability and physical strength. That, and my pull-up routines at home.

But the added arm and shoulder strength is only one aspect, and perhaps the less important part, of trad leading. Even more important is the confidence/fear factor. Throughout the 1960s and 1970s—with Peter, with Fredrickson—we were training ourselves, most of all, to deal with fear. That is to say, we were struggling to gain climbing control so that fear would not jeopardize effective lead climbing.

What was my solution? I began to spend considerable time at CMC outings moving along a wall, ascending unroped up to about 20 feet, down climbing, then moving some five or ten feet to the right or left to repeat the same maneuvers. My motivation for doing this? I'm training my mind, I'm accustoming (or re-accustoming) my subconscious by simulating the psychological situation of the trad leader when he gets some 20 or 30 feet beyond his last piece of pro.

No other CMC participant does the same, and I have been singularly unsuccessful in convincing any of the others to join me. Some have told me that they consider this type of activity to be "unsafe," that a possible fall would cast bad light on the reputation of the club—as it possibly could. On one occasion I answered that my name was not Alex Honnold, but that surely he—and other super-skilled climbers on the American scene today—trained in somewhat the same fashion.

All of the above points to my own special situation: that even though I participate in "sport" (or top-roping) situations, I remain, psychologically speaking, a trad climber.

## *2005—Camp Omache, Monroe, Washington*

What took me back to Omache was news that the Seattle Boy Scout Council was planning to reopen that summer camp. Forty years had passed since a downturn in membership forced them to close it down. The gods were speaking to me! Was it possible? Could I—possibly—wrangle a position on the camp staff and then perform the improbable: two times in one lifetime, could I take the axe in hand to build, construct, and carve out of the woods my dream laden Camp Omache? So I applied. They must have been desperate for warm bodies to fill all the summer-camp positions because they accepted me. Then I was able to convince them to name Ari, my young Mexican wife, to a position, any position.

At our home in Wisconsin, we packed up and then drove our big blue truck across the country, arriving at camp a week early. Most of the construction had already been completed: rebuilt roads, a water system, a wholly new dining hall, program buildings, and 30+ all-weather cabins. But still not ready for operation was the climbing tower. Volunteers were working 12-hour days nailing the ¾"-thick treated plywood sheets to the 40'-high walls, anchored at the corners by vertical cedar logs. When I mentioned my experience with cement, they put Ari and me to work immediately on the side of the tower with metal stucco mesh that now awaited a preliminary layer of mortar. A two-person crew was permanently assigned to assist us by mixing and ascending—via pulley-assisted corner ropes—the heavy buckets and scaffold pieces. We began at the bottom, constructing our platform as we progressed upward (40 frickin' feet!) Then, we had to disassemble the jointed scaffold and lower or drop each piece to the ground. Then, the next application, starting again at the bottom: "gluing" with mortar the artificial rock pieces (each with a flattened surface from 8–12" across). Again: hanging on ropes doing acrobatics to build up and then take down perhaps the (96 in number?) scaffolding pieces. And then, yet a third time up and down (scaffolding and all) to squeeze mortar from "caulking" tubes, and then smooth it over with a spatula in order to fill all the holes and gaps.

And meanwhile the rest of the staff had arrived. They were going through their in-service training, they were getting to know one another. They were sitting on their duffs, warm, well-fed, and happy. But Ari and I were hanging from ropes out there, our hands cracking from the constant contact with cement. Our arms ached from the rope and scaffold work—like they had on the Salathé Wall some forty years before. Each morning hauling ourselves out, with stiff fingers, deadened arms and all. We were beyond any desire for cleanliness, as we put on mortar-covered pants and overshirts to start yet another day. We were way past any pre-

The 40-foot climbing tower at Camp Omache is under construction. When finished, we will belay at the bottom with a double rope dropped from the top. Only a few strong-fingered climbers will make it up the side with masonry rock.

occupation with belays or double-checking knots when we clipped in. All day, hanging from above, jumaring up and down with yet another bucket of mortar, attaching or disassembling yet another countless piece of scaffolding. And then, each night falling asleep from exhaustion.

For normal human beings these tasks might have taken weeks to complete. But Ari and I finally finished, after five horrendously long days! Funny how memory works: today I consider it all as constituting one of my most glorious experiences as a climber! In a masochistic way, we loved it. From start to finish we were "high" from being "on high." That tower was ours: we had made it.

But meanwhile what was not happening in the social realm was that we were not "bonding" with the rest of the staff. I have to admit it: from start to finish we were kind of an appendage to the group: the two of us were different. We were merely tolerated. So what's new? That's a description for how each of us separately, and then together, had always lived. Ouch! Am I describing how a "climber" fits into normal society?

Then, a week later, when the campers arrived, I was assigned to direct all the climbing activity at "our tower." Also, the honor fell on me to establish six climbing routes on two of the tower's four sides. Wanting them to be well done, I carefully positioned dozens of climbing holds for each of the routes. We rated one at 5.1, a second at 5.3, and a third at 5.4—all three routes ended up being highly appropriate for younger scouts who were beginners at climbing. I made an even more challenging route on the tower's third side: using the available handholds, I was able to construct a decent lay-back move—for normal-sized people. In short, the tower was my baby. It was "my baby."

Even more impressive for real climbers was the rock side that Ari and I had constructed during the training week. It was a mini work of art: any professional mason would have been proud. Also, it offered a bona fide challenge to any advanced climber: in the course of the summer only two individuals were able to withstand the terrible fatigue it demanded of the fingers in ascending from bottom to top. One of those two persons was yours truly. Yes, that tower—with its rock wall—it was "mine." Through it, the gods had spoken to me.

But then came that fateful week, about four sessions into the summer. It was in the middle of a hot afternoon when I was supervising all the climbing activity—my normal role. It must have been a rascally god who pushed me into deciding to take a turn on belay. I sat down, with grigri fastened to my waist, and leaning against the eight-foot linked fence that—following anal-retentive Boy Scout regulations—had been tightly constructed around the tower's perimeter. A scout roped in. Then he started to climb. When he got about halfway up, I had to suffer a crick in the neck to twist my head back in order to see him. And, when he slowed down in his ascent, I stopped trying to watch him. And meanwhile, I became engaged in a conversation with one of my assistants.

Have you ever texted while driving? Imagine that at some point your texting becomes more interesting than the driving. That is more or less what happened: I kept conversing, now earnestly, with the buddy standing on the ground behind me. Honestly, I must have forgotten that I was on belay! It must have happened that the scout, who had been making slow progress upward, had chosen to take a very long rest, standing on solid footholds, about two-thirds the way up. For at least two minutes he had not moved. This meant that, for me sitting on the ground directly below, there was no rope to pull in. The belayer, who (coincidentally) bears the same name as I, must have forgotten about him.

I got to my feet, took the belay rope from the grigri, dropped it on the ground, and took three steps forward. Luckily, my assistant immediately jumped onto the rope and quickly put the scout back on belay. But—for my reputation anyway—the deed had been done. There were several witnesses, a few from the scout's own troop. Within ten minutes his scoutmaster found out about what had happened, and only another five minutes had to pass before my misdeed was reported to the camp director.

The next day I found myself removed from the Climbing Tower directorship and demoted to supervisor of the Scoutcraft area, where nothing interesting really happens—ever. There, they don't even teach the three or four knots most basic to climbing. There, for the next two weeks and until the end of the scout camping season, I spent my time, never to return to the climbing-tower grounds. Exiled. Exiled forever.

So there! Finally, I've come clean. I've released myself from the agony of silence all this time. I feel like a character from Edgar Allan Poe[15]: "You knew. All this time you were making a mockery of me. Villains! Dissemble no more. I admit the deed."

A few weeks later, camp ended. Then the sad drive home. I drove in silence, passing, one by one, those settings of past climbing glory: Index Town Wall, Peshaskin Pinnacles, Tiny's—with its incomparable Applets and Cotlets—Castle Rock looming above the highway, the Icicle Canyon approach to Snow Creek Wall (and its unforgettable, trembling—almost unprotected—step-across on Outer Space). Memories, emblazoned in my consciousness, which the mighty mountains themselves will long outlive.

## *2004—Turned Back in Yosemite National Park*

Hmm. Unique in the corpus of climbing literature is this short section dedicated to the climbs I attempted but had to abandon—a topic quite anti-heroic but nevertheless interesting and perhaps entertaining. Of the scores of routes falling into this category, I have selected four.

Memorable was one of my earliest weekends in Yosemite Valley—it could have been in about 1971—when a pick-up buddy and I convinced

**At the beginning of the 1970s, you still couldn't buy climbing "nuts." So we had to sneak into a UC Berkeley workshop to cut and drill our own pieces of airplane aluminum.**

ourselves that we could and would get up the Lost Arrow Chimney. Ha! Well, according to the guidebook it was only rated V, 5.8 A3.[16] "Only 5.8? It'll probably be hard. But let's go for it. In our sleep we can get up the A3!" In theory we could do it! But we didn't ask around—*Big Error.*

We were decided. In the early morning we made our way up the belabored approach to Sunnyside Bench. Just before roping up my buddy drew out of his pack nothing less than a sparkling new white shirt, cardboard under the collar, straight pins, and all. Ceremoniously, he put it on. A good luck ritual? I don't know. But he was fit for a wedding and he only lacked the tux. I'll always remember that elegant gesture: a new white shirt for what could be a stupendous climb! Correction: "what—only very remotely—could have been."

In retrospect, the most memorable part of the climb is what I have just described in the previous paragraph. Because within an hour we were back at Camp 4. Minutes after my buddy had buttoned the last shirt button, we passed into the cave to rope up. After that, there's very little to tell: we couldn't even get up the first 20 feet! Gads, that stem chimney was so hard that we would have needed giant legs to bridge across it! And looking straight up, there was no place to put in any piton in order to aid up the difficult beginning. More so, the wide chimney above us looked definitely scary. Definitely impressive, The Mountain Gods certainly had done a creative number there. And the first ascenter, John Salathé? Before he had been for me a mere climbing legend. But now he appeared in my imagination as a superhuman being. Who—or what—else could have gotten up that horrific chimney? "You're a better man than I am, Gunga Din." Hats off to John Salathé.

Now, the second instance of backing off a route; this also occurred in the Valley, maybe two years later. Fredrickson and I were feeling our oats. I suppose our hubris at the time was due to us having bested in recent months the NW Face of Half Dome. Now—as usual—it was Don calling the shots. He must have had more faith in my technical ability than I had myself. Or perhaps this was an instance of the "steamboat" phenomenon: he would decide where, he would (if I couldn't) lead, and at the very least I would do my part in belaying him going first, and later jumaring up the route.

We were on Sentinel's vertical Psychedelic Wall, a 2½-day climb with a lot of (sometimes difficult) nailing. Well, the *two* days were easy to account for: on Saturday and Sunday we students had no classes. But the other ½ day? Hmmm. More difficult. What to do? We had to squeeze the last ½ day out of a Friday.

But it wasn't so easy getting an early Friday start for the drive to the Valley. We arrived there about 2 or 3 o'clock, and then it took much longer than we had anticipated to trudge up the steep ledges, weighted down with our heavy hauling sack, to the beginning of the route. In fact, we were so late that daylight was ending as we finally put on our swamis, and me getting on belay for Don to begin the climb. For him, the nailing was slow—rated A4. This means that even the best of nailers was not going to race on up. But I, seated on belay within 15 feet of the start, was not uncomfortable. A half-hour passed, and daylight faded. Don continued climbing, but now with headlight turned on—it was fastened to the front of his helmet. I, meanwhile, was bathed in darkness. He was easily 40 feet up. The nailing was very slow.

"Here's a fixed pin. It has a sling attached"—he shouted on down in the now total darkness. "I'm clipped in." Just sitting there on the hard flat ground, my butt began to pain slightly. I had already slid into a bored daze. I lazily thought, "Hmm. Nylon sling … how many years has it been exposed to sunlight? Not to worry: Don's super-careful about such things." And, in the next two minutes I fed out about six more feet of rope, figuring that he had gotten to the top of his stirrups and was now tenuously pulling his body as high as possible while deciding on another pin placement.

Then: "*R I I I P.*" I heard it. The sound could only be … *the nylon sling*!!!! Then I heard a faint, quick jingling of iron. I instinctively pulled in whatever rope slack, leaned back bracing myself, and clenched my hands on either side of the rope. It all happened so fast. *Whuuup.*

*Oh My God.* In the near darkness I saw Don bounce against the ground just three feet in front of me. For a few seconds no movement. No voice. No sound. Images were racing through my mind. Then the realization: *Oh my God.* I'm … going … to have … to carry Don's grey matter down in his brain bucket (dirt bag climbers' term for helmet). I … was … stunned.

Then—*shock*—I barely make out Don in a kneeling position, slowly getting to his feet—*or was it his ghost*? Now he was standing, bending forward. Now he was turning around to face me. I saw his hands slide-slap across his buttocks, as if brushing off dirt. He spoke: "The goddamn sling just tore off. I must have zippered out three of my pins. But the last one held. It must have caught me just as I was approaching the ground.… I guess … that's enough climbing for today."

Definitely the understatement of the year. We gathered up our stuff and began carefully treading on down. We found an appropriate place to throw the hauling sack into the darkness, calculating (correctly, it turned out) where we would find it a thousand feet below. Using the faint glow of our headlamps, and trying not to tumble, we butt-braked down the gravel-covered ledges. About midway down Don admitted to me a bit of soreness all over. I, in turn, would have to weather for the next few weeks a raw rope burn across my whole back waist.

Oops. Any other misadventure after that last one is bound to be anticlimactic. But I've sworn to eschew the heroic. Here's the third yarn … that I swear really, actually, happened.

Same place: the Valley. But a different time. Ouch! Another chimney story! (What do they have against me?) Hadn't I learned anything from my fiasco inside and under the Lost Arrow? No.

Here a digression. I'm convinced that successful climbers have to be endowed with a superb capacity to forget. Because if you're planning for your next challenging climb, you cannot let memories of a recent bad experience immobilize your expectations. Or, if you lead, you cannot be saddled with fear—you simply have to learn how to prohibit it from clouding your thought process as you are struggling up the next hard move.

Somewhat similar: the good climber has to be a dogmatic optimist:

**If the little pine tree could "hold on" to a Yosemite wall, then we figured that we'd be able to do so too.**

"Accidents happen to others, not to me." Or: "By mid-afternoon we'll be over the worst part of the wall, so we won't suffer if the thunderstorm hits." End of digression.

So one can readily understand if that young climber, coincidentally borrowing my name way back then, had all but forgotten his relative incompetence in getting up hard chimneys.

But there I was a few years later—it could have been around the year 2004—again slumming away in Camp 4, again trying to snag a rope partner for the morrow. I wandered into another campsite and found a likely prospect. Half self-convinced, I described to that individual my climbing ability as just one level below "super-climber." After all, over the years I had been able to get up a few great routes.

At this distance—here Bill the writer is speaking—it's somewhat amusing to imagine Bill the younger climber strutting around, realizing that he'd been able to climb respectable routes on almost all the Valley's great walls—except for the Sentinel. (My near fiasco with Fredrickson on the Dihedral Wall obviously didn't count as "an ascent.") And that he had convinced himself—he had fantasized—that the Sentinel now awaited his reverent hands. Yes! "I can climb it"—why not the famed Steck-Salathé? With that illusion (had it been induced by a liquid substance consumed at the campfire the night before?) he convinced another eager climber from another campsite that this was what they should attempt on the morrow. The other would take his rope and trash sling, and Bill would bring along his spaghetti rope to facilitate all the rappels. Both climbers would take light bivy stuff and a minimum of water. OK. They were all set, and early in the morning they set off.

(Switch back to first person.) Here I'll have to abbreviate, because I really don't want to prolong any more than necessary my memories of the resultant shame. We started huffing up those medium-width chimneys, swinging leads. But *oh*, they weren't easy. I began to realize *big time*—and I remember to this day—that I might be a champ at face climbing, but my technique for chimneys was deficient. That's not to say I couldn't do the first three pitches, but that in getting up them I was expending far too much energy! Uff! uph! Scraped knees, two fingernails torn from jamming into rope slits. *Uff!*

To make the painful story much shorter, by the end of three pitches I was exhausted. My arms felt like lead and were resisting a lift above my head one more time. Looking up, I realized that another 14 mother pitches still awaited. *Fourteen more of the same?*

What embarrassment when I turned to my buddy to admit that I couldn't go on. We'd have to rap back down. And the unspoken message that I'd deceived him about my own abilities. (Heavens, I had deceived myself first!)

We tied the two ropes together and set up the first rap. Gads, hadn't I ever used my spaghetti rope for this before? Was it the static electricity? The thinner rope stuck to the fatter one, and in places was winding around it. Hard—no, impossible—to keep them separate! It was my disastrous rope, and I was the one turning back, so I went down first. My nearly impossible responsibility was to separate the two lines with the index finger on my brake hand. But they wouldn't separate—only by force. Every ten feet I had to stop, loop the duo of rap ropes over my shoulder to free up my hands (remember, dear reader, that I was hanging in midair), then coil, pull, tug the two lines apart.

Gads, I spent three tedious raps doing all that. In fact, it got real scary, because while hanging vertical, with nothing to support the feet, on several occasions I almost had to undo my rappel.

Finally, the bottom. *Solid ground.* But there was no celebration, because I then had to suffer the horrible hike back to Camp 4: me ashamed to speak, and he probably pissed off—royally—at an incompetent partner who had wasted his whole day.

## *2013—Snake Dike, Half Dome, Yosemite*

Marvelous to the third power. First, Yosemite; second, Half Dome; and third, Snake Dike.[17] Any more superlatives needed? I thank the gods that they have allowed me, on so many occasions, to experience any of these wonders. My cup runneth over upon realizing that in the early summer of 2013 I was able to savor all three, at the same time, in the course of a spectacular day.

First of all, we are not talking about the Half Dome that is seen from most areas of the park. No. You only see *this* Half Dome from the area around Mirror Lake (hmm, more appropriately called "mud-flat" lake in the recent dry-spell years). That is to say, you have to be able to view head-on the huge, flat, vertical face of the Gorgeous Monster, so that its right side appears to you as the perfect quarter-circle arching from the summit and down to its perpendicular intersection with the flat plateau upon which the massive rock is positioned. For the unschooled in the topography of this issue: Once you get up upon that flat plateau—to the west of Half Dome—you'll find the start of Snake Dike about 50 yards in from that abrupt, curved edge. The nature of the route? Picture a bent pole-vault pole: climbers start out on a near vertical wall that loses about 10 degrees with each new pitch. This means that by the end of four serious rope lengths the rock angle has significantly lessened. In fact, when the slope reduces to a mere 40-degree angle, most that climb this route choose to unrope and scamper up the remaining distance. Which is not inconsiderable. (It felt a mile long, but Roper—1971: 180—states that it's only "1,000 feet." My interpretation: climbers, moving a very considerable distance, gain only 1,000 vertical feet.) "You've got to do it to believe it."

Perhaps all readers might not understand what a dike is. I don't have a geological history of the Yosemite on hand, but I'll wing it. Imagine a first geological "moment," several million-million years in the past (and

**The white dike is at our feet as we celebrate the completion of a most amazing route up Half Dome in Yosemite National Park (California). Imagine the route's beginning, where the slope progressively steepens until it's vertical, about 2,000 feet down to the left.**

itself lasting millions of years), when molten substances miles beneath the earth's surface cooled to become hard granite fracturing slightly to produce crack systems upon cooling. Then, imagine a second geological "moment"—a millennium or two later—when extreme pressures shoot a new molten substance into the existing cracks of this granite mass, still miles underground. In time this new substance solidifies and now appears as salmon-colored streaks crisscrossing Half Dome's surface. Then, imagine a third geological "moment"—after another few millennia—when tectonic ("*yosemetonic*"?) pressures lift this granite mass to the surface. Give us yet another few millennia for glaciers to shear away one side of this massive granite dome. Then, after yet another few millennia the ravages of surface weather wear down the hard surface granite a few inches, leaving the even more resistant dike material as ⅛-inch, and sometimes ¼-inch, protrusions. Surprisingly—in light of the difficulty of every other climbing route up Half Dome (I exclude the cable tourist route up its back side)—these freakish protrusions make for relatively "easy" friction climbing. Well, "easy" but breathy, due to the fact that a few of the pitches require the leader to "run-out"—that is, pass over long climbing stretches between points of protection.

To summarize the above paragraph: the Snake Dike Route is yet one more testimony to the fact that the mountain gods must have really, really, delighted in making for us this marvelous Valley. Your heaven, in almost every way, comes out far less glamorous when compared to the Yosemite!

I've checked and rechecked the notes I usually make after each climbing season in the back pages of each relevant climbing guide in order to remember better the routes climbed, with which rope partners, and the approximate dates. Unfortunately, after lead climbing up that glorious Snake Dike route, sometime during the summer of 2013, I made no notation. At this moment I have no explanation for why. I project that the glitter I felt and saw for months after that glorious day must have blinded me from performing normal, mundane tasks. Anyway, here's to you glorious—now unremembered—climbing mates! We did it together and in grand style.

A few notes about that climb: Before daybreak we were able to find a parking spot in the Happy Isles lot, and then started passing by the parade of tourists determined to sweat up the long trail and ascend hand-by-hand the fixed cable route at the back of Half Dome. In the emerging light I recognized the bridge under which Fredrickson and I—back in 1972—had hidden to strip down and wash off the dust and sweat after 2½ days on Half Dome's NW Face. But now, my two buddies and I carried little water, knowing that we could add purification tablets to what we'd find after ascending 2,000 vertical feet on the trail paralleling the small stream at the top of Vernal Falls.

Walking on up on that long approach, it was impossible to stop memories from flowing. I remembered passing those same marvelous falls on my first Valley visit in 1965; then: the same trail on at least a dozen rest-day excursions between 1968 and 1978 when I was a regular May climber in the Valley. Then, the same hike to access route starts in 1974, 1977, and 2004.

One of my buddies had, in the previous week, made it to the beginning of the route, then had backed off—he had realized that his partner was not "up to it." Fortunate for us, because he immediately saw the very small cairn that marked the faint trail branching off from the soft-sand

***Opposite:* Don is balancing on Thank-god Ledge (NW Face of Half Dome, Yosemite National Park).**

highway-trail, that led to the base of the Snake Dike. I must have been the most experienced climber, because it fell to me to lead the first and third pitches. There I was, easily a generation older than either buddy, and silently battling to regain the leader confidence that had bubbled forth two and three decades before.

But I shut up. I remembered clearly the maxim of climbing partnerships: when a doubt springs forth, the best treatment is silence, because doubt is not only contagious; worse, it can become a self-fulfilling prophecy. One has to shut up. And also enforce the mental operation of repressing mental doubt. Immediately. This is the climbing way, at least the way I have always practiced it.

It fell to me to lead that hard first pitch. Climbing, in this regard, is so macho. There I was somewhat trembling inside, but keeping my mouth shut. I repeat: a good climber cannot let himself think or mention doubt. Because to imagine that you're going to fall is akin to causing you to fall. So, I had to masquerade, to present myself to my two companions with the guise of "assured," confident, competent for what awaited us.

The lead is mine. I sling the thin rack over my shoulder and, when the belay is ready, I start out. Delicate. Oh so delicate, traversing across a smooth face (this pitch would even be unappealing for the two who follow, because any slip will result in a nasty swing out). Whew. I reach the undercling and clip into the historical fixed pin. Safe for now. Then I continue frictioning across the face. Difficult. Looks scary, but feet are not slipping. Slow, careful foot placement, balancing. I continue going across and somewhat down, using leg muscles to slowly lower my weight onto the forward foot that I place flat over the surface. Absolutely nothing for the hands. Long live friction climbing: it can look horrendous, but the shoe soles stay put. That is, if I don't do something stupid. Or if I cease moving like a cat. And only if I don't begin to fear.

I have no scientific explanation, but this was but one more instance of me banishing doubt in order that with each new tenuous foot placement I would not slip off and go sailing downward. The skeptic might call this a mental illusion, and who am I to disagree? I project that every successful climber gets to know the powers of positive mental energy.

I round the corner and step up onto the first nubbins of the dike. *I'm safe.* They really protrude. Some, a whole ½-inch high, offer bombproof foot placements and—sometimes—decent finger grabs. I keep ascending, now with confidence growing. Thirty feet up: a bolt. Thank God.

**Tuolumne Meadows, in Yosemite National Park, features several domes, whose glacier-polished surfaces provide for many spectacular climbing routes. Many a tourist has scampered up one of the Water Cracks—the deep grooves in the center of the photograph—without realizing that it's much more dangerous, and scary, getting back down.**

Just above that bolt, the surface—for long stretches—appears almost bald. I have to keep calm. Luckily, the sun warms and there is no wind. A strong puff would really be a bother. The angle has dropped off somewhat. But here, no huge nubbins. Only small ones. Again, I have to perform friction climbing at its most delicate, but now it's a breeze given what I had to pass over five minutes before. Better not to even think, to just keep moving forward and upward. It's difficult, but not overly so. Best to move steadily, not stopping.

Suddenly a memory streaks into consciousness of a previous friction climb on Glacier Point Apron. It was harder, it was nasty. This, in comparison, is a piece of cake. A light tremor then jolts memory back thirty years to yet another climb: the scary friction traverse at the top of Royal Arches. Funny, the memory has a reassuring effect. "Been there, done that." Yes, I've done far harder before. Thinking stops. I continue moving, slowly, daintily. These dike nubbins are magnificent. It's airy here—I'm thirty, now forty, feet past the last bolt. I'd feel fear if I'd let myself. But I've been here before: *No fear allowed.* Just got to continue. Keep on jugging. It'll end soon enough.

*What?* The yell from my buddy breaks my numbed concentration. He shouts to inform me that the rope is almost out. *Ouch*, I've still got 30 feet to go and it doesn't ease off. It's not comfortable standing on small nubbins and having to turn around to shout back. *"Free up rope. Take off belay"* (knowing that he's clipped in to the other end of my rope). *"Start climbing if you have to. I need 30 more feet."* The lead climber should never have to make this dangerous request. But there's no other option. I realize that we're lucky being three of us roped all together. The last buddy is a fast thinker: with no hesitation he puts himself on belay to protect now the two of us. (A note to future climbers: be sure to use a longer-than-usual rope.)

With that extra length I reach the belay stance. Hooray, it has two bomb-proof bolts. Peace. Turn off adrenaline. Relax into ritual, quickly clipping the rope into the biners going to both bolts. I then begin to belay my first buddy on up. Twenty minutes later—with the three of us together at the airy stance, we are ready for the next pitch. The rest of the climb is anti- (or better, post-) climactic.

Indeed, the climb got no harder. Getting over that first, run-out pitch had been the crux. And, with each new pitch, the angle kept easing off.

The three of us proceed and, in less than an hour, the angle has eased off so much that there's no need to keep belaying. We coil up the ropes, sling them over our heads and shoulders, and begin walking. We don't want to slip, but we hardly feel danger, given what we had had to climb over the first four pitches. Now, we just have to keep on walking. And walking. The angle keeps easing off. There! A quarter mile away: that must be the summit, with scads of tourists. It's like the top of an anthill.

We emerge onto the summit plateau, like landing on the moon. We've accomplished something magnificent. Nobody there gives us applause. Thank goodness!—they wouldn't be able to imagine the grandiose sensations we had felt every step up that marvelous route. Now: the top of Half Dome. The Top of the World. Climbing doesn't get any better than this. It couldn't. What a privilege: to stand on top, on the very top of this incredible hunk of granite. All glory to the Mountain Gods.

An hour later, after a generous rest with food and water, we angle over to the top of the cables leading 400 feet downward. Heck, can you believe it? Descending those cables gave me more pangs of trepidation than ascending that first pitch on Snake Dike. Such is life.

## 2014—Palisade Glacier, Sierra Nevada Mountains, California

What did I remember after 49 years? There I was, huffing and puffing up the hot, dry, park-service trail leaving from the Glacier Lodge parking lot, then going past the three Pine Lakes. At that point, I turned west on a well-marked mountaineering trail and began a fast elevation gain.[18] I was not feeling so chipper, with my pack carrying only a minimum of overnight stuff and a day's allotment of food. Was it the heat—and a stingy intake of water? Definitely two factors. In addition, I knew that at this early point in the season, I was not yet in the prime of physical conditioning.

Looking at the map, in this moment of writing, I (the writer) have a sudden realization: of course—back then—I hadn't been feeling my oats! Early in the morning upon leaving the car I was at about 2,400 feet of altitude. Then, upon meeting with a three-person climbing party, I was already at about 6,400 feet. (The threesome was making ready to leave the trail heading east to climb one of the spectacular arêtes on Temple Crag, all reputed to be "long, exposed, and incredibly fun."[19]) Four thousand feet of elevation gain! In anybody's book that's a day's quota in itself. But the additional factor: above 6,000 feet one begins to feel the effects of altitude. Of course I'd feel it—under any circumstances.

But truth be told, at the time I ascribed my sensed weakness to the accumulation of years. Sixty-eight years old! Some friends my age were stumbling around with walkers; others had declared defeat before an expanding waist line; and 99 percent of them had left in the past the former goal of physical fitness. But not me. I had attempted to maintain myself fit: running up a two-mile-long hill a few times a week—when the weather was decent—and then ending with repetitions of pull-ups and weight lifting.[20] So, returning to the narrative about being on that trail, I was disappointed with myself when I began to feel beat—about the time when I encountered (and envied) the well-equipped climbers.

Near the three new friends I spread out my foam pad and passed the night. In the early morning they started toward their climbing objective, and were out of sight when I continued my slog on up the main trail. Soon I branched onto a faint mountaineering trail, which disappeared after an hour, leaving me to jump across the boulders that formed the Palisade Glacier's frontal moraine. I kept going up and up, and I felt progressively weaker. A sad truism in the mountains: your (mental) eagerness to continue onward erodes in proportion to your degree of fatigue. So, as I approached the elevation of the glacier toe—at about 12,000 feet—I was already contemplating a "pull of the plug" to my former plans. With that low energy level, there was no way that I would want to continue onto the glacier, ascending the U Notch, and scrambling up the easy back-side route to the top of the North Pal. An added disincentive: the morning sun was now hidden behind a midday haze. Add to that the unwelcome chilly breeze that probably blew from the nearby glacier.

With no possible trail I continued skirting up, down, around, and on top of ever larger rocks. Soon, I gained a promontory—could it have been the glacier's frontal moraine in years past? There, I took off my pack and sat down in order to take advantage of the clear view, looking downward, of the glacier ahead. *Downward? What? Had most of the glacier simply disappeared?*

There, seated on a flat rock at about 12,400 feet, I gazed out onto the glacier before me. Its toe was still a mile, or a half-hour, away. Then I lifted my eyes to mentally follow a desired path to the top of U Notch, then further up and right to the summit, still off in the distance and way above me.

**In the last thirty years—the age of "climate change"—glaciers such as this one are rapidly disappearing.**

No, given my fatigue and obvious *soroche* (high-altitude symptoms), I was far from enthused about the former plan of continuing on.

Furthermore, I was confused. During the previous months of anticipating this trip, I had continually conjured up the engraved memory of a gently sloping glacier transitioning into a steep white pillowy rise to the notch. Forty-five years ago we had ascended that path safely, without using either crampons or ice axes—and certainly without a rope—without needing to place protection or to belay. Then, we had simply kicked easy steps into ideal-consistency snow. That pleasant memory of the past climb is what had fueled my anticipations a few days earlier.

But now I saw, there before me, a wholly different setting. There—*yes*, as anticipated—was the rather smooth glacier rise. But now the passage leading up to the notch was scary steep and at a considerable distance. And—even worse—the fluffy snow of before had been replaced by glistening—read: dangerous—ice. To make things perfectly clear: any possible ascent to the top of the U Notch would now be a perilous, dangerous undertaking.

How to explain this disconnect between rosy memory-induced expectations and harsh, stark—current—reality? Answer: glacier melt. Another two words: climate change. Yet another pair: global warming. Indeed, in the intervening half-century the Pal Glacier had lost perhaps 500 vertical feet of ice! Maybe less, but still a huge amount. And that melt had transformed completely the former, somewhat "agreeable," approach into a tenuous, difficult, and dangerous ascent.

A sense of foreboding filled me.

Adding to my sadness was another realization at that moment: that the Bill Katra of a half-century past was an energetic, ambitious, gutsy guy. And that if the graying Bill Katra of the present could ever perform a climbing exploit even remotely as bold as those of his same-named predecessor, then this would merit the applause of the Mountain Gods.

## Chapter 2

# Aconcagua

In case you, dear reader, are a non-climber seeing for the first time the name "Aconcagua," here is some basic information. This mountain, situated in Argentina's north and only kilometers from the country's western border with Chile, has the highest summit in the world outside of the Himalayas: 6,962 meters (or about 22,975 feet). Compare this to Mount Everest, at nearly 9,000 meters, or Mount Whitney (the highest in the lower U.S.) at about 4,400 meters.

I had not planned to return to Aconcagua, but perhaps the Mountain Gods had decreed otherwise. Way back in 1970, I had followed the mule trail up to its summit on the north side; now, 46 years later, I would spend a week in Mendoza, eager to talk about any and all aspects of the mountain, but without sufficient enthusiasm to venture even to the entrance of the national park (established 20–30 years ago) some 40 kilometers away.

Why my lack of enthusiasm? Years of climbing on hundreds of majestic mountains have confirmed what I strongly had felt during the three weeks spent on Aconcagua many years ago: that, with the exception of its colossal South Wall, it is hardly a pretty or interesting mountain. According to one sober writer: "All of Aconcagua is either loose dirt or loose rock … its high Andean desert … free of trees [and] plants [makes it] a bit depressing."[1] The same author continues, in reference to the misery he suffered—mainly on account of the altitude: "Oh, how we laughed on Kilimanjaro. It is a pretty party cake walk. Imagine making out, let's say to second base, on a summer night in the back seat of a fine car. Let's say this is happening with some hot person on whom you have a crush. Feel those glorious titties? That's Kilimanjaro. Now imagine being punched in the face, then tied up and dragged down a dirt road behind your worst enemy's shitty pickup truck on a day so hot even your shoes are sweating. That's how I was feeling [from start to finish] about Aconcagua."[2] That writer and I are in agreement: even though I never felt his depth of suffering, climbing *joy* was not part of my experience.

So why did I return? There I was in Buenos Aires's municipal airport on December 26, 2016. I had left our humble house in Uruguay some seven hours earlier: plenty of time to make the two-hour bus ride to Colonia (Uruguay's westernmost port), traverse the estuary in a rapid ferry to Buenos Aires, and navigate via city buses to arrive here at the municipal airport. I had made no advanced reservations—a mistake!—and was weighed down by a backpack crammed with gear for a sport-climbing adventure. I wanted to snag a stray seat on an airplane bound for Bariloche, a touristy area in the north–Patagonian Andean foothills (and where, after descending from Aconcagua in 1970, I had spent a delightful week getting up a half dozen trad routes on the area's remarkable towers). This was not to be. I quickly rejected my only option of waiting a week for the next available seat.

Where to go for an alternative adventure? I found an open seat on a flight to Mendoza, an area which—I figured—must have a few good sport-climbing areas. Hmmm. When there, I could get up-to-date information about Aconcagua and take advantage of the city's libraries and archives. (Mendoza was of interest to the historian in me: it was where General San Martín had outfitted his army to cross the Andes and win Latin America's independence in the early 1800s.) Mendoza … why not?

Thank you globalization: they accepted my USA–issued plastic card to pay for the last available seat to Mendoza. Whew! I passed by the crowd-constipated area for baggage check-in, mentally celebrating that I would probably be able to weather minor hassles carrying my bulging pack aboard with me. Then (ugh) the security check. Hooray, no shoe inspection! I looked for my boarding gate. (Hmmm.) It was an hour before the designated boarding time and the flight was still not listed on the digital wall display. (Irritation, double hmmm.) I walked the length of the gated corridor, inquiring if other individuals were waiting for the same flight. No one? (Control anger.) Half hour before scheduled flight. What was going on? Nobody to ask. (Suppress panic. Gads, were they filming me in some *Twilight Zone* episode?) At the prescribed boarding time I, with six other stupefied people, heard the PA announcement that our flight had been cancelled and that we could obtain a seat on the next available Mendoza flight at such-and-such an office. (Pissed off, but resigned.) We stomped back to the check-in area and joined one of the interminable lines that were advancing at the speed of ten-persons-per-hour.

Well, a flight finally did get me to Mendoza—but at 2:00 in the frickin' morning! It was totally dark outside, and all we passengers were in a sleep-deprived stupor. When I learned that the city center was a distant half-hour away, I briefly contemplated slinking away from the terminal building about a hundred yards to some bushes where, unobserved, I could pull out my ground cloth and sleeping bag and pass the rest of the night unperturbed (a memory flashed through my mind of doing the same at the Spokane airport back in about 1982). (For the uninitiated reader, we old-school "dirt bag" climbers tend to think of crazy ideas like this.) But I hastily rejected that idea when I was able to bum a ride with some friendly people willing to scrunch me into their family-filled car. Forty minutes later they dropped me off at a youth hostel somewhere in that now unfamiliar city.

Over the next two days I asked, without result, in every sports equipment store and tourist agency, about sport-climbing areas. I did see a guidebook for sale, but its $30 price was unacceptable. I finally got one lead: some people told me about a place off the highway leading to Uspallata—that is, about half the distance to (what is now) the Aconcagua National Park. So I concocted a plan to board the bus, travel the two or so hours to that small city, find my way to a camping area at its outskirts, and then make contact with potential rock climbers. Sitting on my pack in the bus terminal, I spent a pleasant hour talking with a well-equipped Swiss climber who was headed for the Big A.

In the bus, the Serendipity Gods must have smiled at me: I was seated across the aisle from four scrubbily dressed young men. Overhearing their conversation, I correctly surmised that they could be nothing but rock climbers and I butted my way into their conversation. I can't remember if they actually invited me, but when they scurried to get off the bus in the middle of nowhere, I impulsively gathered up my own stuff and followed them out. It turned out that I and my equipment were welcome additions to their party—soon to be joined by two others accompanied by girlfriends—since my rope and biners doubled their (our) climbing possibilities. All of us had shoes and harnesses. At that stage I could only guess about their climbing prowess. That is to say, I know by experience that the majority of younger athletes everywhere, who train rigorously in climbing gyms, have attained a level of climbing technique that far exceeds my own. Indeed, by the morrow I was able to see the high athletic potential of all of them—a fact that left me feeling as if I were 70+ years old.

The area, called Agua de las Abejas (Bee Waters or Spring) was the combination of a discontinued limestone quarry (with its 60–80 vertical feet and two dozen bolted lines), and a wide—and beautiful—natural gully leading up and up (with perhaps twice the number of routes). They honored me with the first lead that featured a shaky 5.8 move at the very top. Given the heat, we avoided climbing in the direct sunshine. None of them had brought along sufficient water—their excuse was that their friends, arriving later, would be bringing enough beer to satisfy the $H_2O$ deficit of all of us. Meanwhile, we had to take our chances with a natural spring (no bees visible) whose water, luckily—over the next few hours—caused no diarrhea or vomiting in any of us. That night they and their friends, and minus any beer (at least for me), prepared a generous meat barbecue over the coals of our campfire. Time was plentiful. With quaky voice, and *sans* guitar, I impressed them with a few of the classic Argentine folklore songs stored—and still in mint condition—in my memory vaults. Given the vastly insufficient quantity of beer, we were all sober when we finally laid out our sleeping stuff to pass a memorable night.

The next morning we got in a few more routes before scurrying down the hill, only to wait three hours for the delayed bus that took us all back to Mendoza. From there, it was only a six-block walk back to my hostel. The next day, via internet, the lead climber from that group generously invited me to join his extended family (easily 40 people in attendance) two nights later at a delightful wine-enriched New Year's Eve party.

With almost everything closed over the holiday weekend, I spent most of my hours at the hostel. Luckily, I was now accompanied by Ravi, an expedition guide from (surprise!) Malaysia. Parts of eight of his fingers had been amputated due to Himalayan frostbite. (I kid you not!) Days before he had dragged a client to the summit of the Big A and now had to wait a week for the arrival of a new one. Most memorable was his comment to me one morning: "Bill, our dinner out last night was remarkable: there we were, three generations—you, 71 years old, me 46, and our German friend Hans 22—all three of us have been able to make it to the top."

On Sunday I eagerly listened as Ravi gave advice to an ambitious, but somewhat naïve (a better word in Spanish: *despistado*), software engineer from Hong Kong who bombarded us with questions in anticipation of the frustrations he would experience when offices and stores would open on the morrow. He needed to complete all of the complicated preparations to join the line of trekkers slogging up toward the summit. At least he knew that this would not be a Ya-Ya-land jaunt: perhaps 40 percent of the 2,000 people each season fail in their struggle to gain the summit due to the inevitable problems associated with high altitude, cold, and winds. We had ample time to discuss issues related to money, equipment, acclimatization, and park rules.[3] (Listening to all of this, I mentally celebrated the fact that some 47 years earlier things had been much less complicated and touri$ty.)

First, the average cost, per person, is now about $6,000: $900 buys your permit to enter the park (the price goes down considerably during the off months when the weather is less stable) for a maximum of 20 days. Most people contract with mule drivers to carry some equipment and food about 15 kilometers in and some 5,000 feet up to Plaza de Mulas—the north side's base camp, which is a small tent city (outfitted with a hamburger restaurant, no less) at 4,270 meters (14,000 feet). Most people also pay for a guide, because you have to carry far less weight if you pay to stay in agency tents and eat their hot, prepared food. In addition, when a trekker pays for any of these s/he automatically qualifies to use free of charge the simple chest-high kybos along the route. Otherwise, you'd better carry spare change in your pocket to cover the cost of every kybo visit.

Time needed for making the painful ascent? It's best not to hurry because all bodies have to acclimatize: all trekkers must plan for high-altitude stays of about 12 days (doing what—for god's sake—in that visually sterile environment?) before the body has sufficiently adapted in order to push for the summit. Some trekkers have to wait additional days—bored to death—at a high camp if they are out of sync with the weather: high winds at high altitudes can be devastating. (Forty-seven years ago we had no way of obtaining accurate meteorological reports—and I have to conclude today that back then we had lucked out not having suffered cold, high winds.)

One new safety feature: at two different points in the park's lower elevations authorities require a reading of each trekker's "oxygen saturation" and pulse levels in order to assess whether s/he has acclimatized sufficiently. Most of the trekkers toe the line with regard to the recommended ascent timetable and, therefore, are allowed to proceed. In the case of trekkers whose bodies show signs of insufficient acclimatization, the health officials often prescribe Diamox (i.e., acetazolamide), delay trekkers' stay at lower altitudes before being retested, and are even empowered to order people with health risks to descend and exit the park. Even with these "medical" checks, the altitude remains a formidable obstacle for all trekkers: the same "spicy" account quoted earlier goes on to explain how three of the author's party of five elected (or were sternly persuaded) to head back down after they themselves assessed the misery they would suffer from high winds if they were to continue plodding up the trail for the last 500 vertical feet.[4]

This same book provides amusing anecdotes about how trekkers use the kybos at the different established camps— which I won't repeat here. But worthy of mention are the helicopters making daily flights from the mountain, dangling from ropes the containers of human waste from as many as 400 tourist-trekkers on the mountain at any one time. This would be at the peak of the climbing season. Also interesting are the official instructions given to all participants about the need to consume five liters of water per day for maximum acclimatization, and about the messy process of peeing every four hours during the night into personalized plastic containers.

Equipment? Best to fly into Mendoza with almost everything you'll eventually need on the mountain. This especially applies to double boots: Ravi told us the engaging account of how his recent client had decided beforehand to rent a pair from a local agency. And—because they were not sufficiently broken in—he suffered painful foot sores. Even worse, the client's feet swelled slightly as he gained altitude, which contributed to a nearly disastrous experience with frostbite.

The book, and Ravi's anecdotes, touched on other important equipment issues. Trekkers not subscribing to a guide service must carry in and stay in a tent that can resist high winds. Second, the park service provides bags for poop and garbage and then inspects those bags before allowing trekkers to exit the park. Third, most aspirants carry ice axes and crampons that are sometimes needed for the mountain's final stretch.

Forty-some years ago I was fortunate in my trip to the summit of Aconcagua, with less park bureaucracy and rules, vastly fewer fellow adventurers, and far fewer monetary expenses. Here, I'll share some anecdotes drawn from the vaults of memory.

Rewind back to the latter days of December 1969. My Yosemite climbing buddies, Don Fredrickson and Mike Caldwell (the biological father and trainer of the now-famous Tommy Caldwell!) shared the ambition of becoming the first North Americans—and the sixth party overall—to climb Aconcagua's formidable South Wall. Imagine their hubris! A successful ascent of El Capitan had put into their heads the idea that they could ascend, on a single push, the route on which most of the first-ascent French climbers, a decade earlier, had suffered frostbitten toes. At the last moment they had induced me to accompany one of their financial sponsors, Vance Koerner (aerospace engineer and marathon runner from Sacramento), on the mule-trail route up the easy north side. (Over the past twenty or so years I have had to suppress a chuckle every time I have recalled my naïveté at that time, when I sincerely believed that his 43 years made him almost "over-the-hill.")

The flight down was memorable. Our search for the cheapest fare landed us on the last commercial propeller jet I would ever fly. Because we flew at a relatively low altitude in nearly cloudless skies, I was able to peer out the window to follow the Central American coastline almost the whole distance. Changing planes in Quito, we waited in the airport wearing double boots and our fluffy down parkas, with ice axes in hand and the ends of our climbing ropes bulging out of the carry-on luggage. A dark-skinned shoeshine boy ingenuously asked us if we were the American astronauts who had landed on the moon only months before!

From Santiago, Chile, it took us a half day to cross by bus into Argentina via the high mountain pass. Upon arriving at Puente del Inca, the small military outpost that marked the beginning of our trail (where they trained teams of huskies for mountain rescues), it was late in the afternoon of December 24—Christmas Eve. Of course we had made no previous contact! (The internet was still decades into the future.) We were promptly informed that the post commander, whose written permission was required, had departed hours earlier to pass the holidays with his family in Mendoza. I, being the only Spanish speaker of our group, recruited Vance to accompany me. Standing on the side of the highway, we waved our thumbs and, six hours later, we were knocking on his door in a neighborhood of Mendoza. He enthusiastically signed a statement giving us the needed permission and, before noon of the next day, Vance and I were back with our buddies, the huskies, and the soldiers at Puente del Inca.

In the meanwhile, Vance and I had missed the show of shows. Our two companions, after wheezing through the physical test of running 100 meters uphill—at Puente del Inca's elevation of 8,900 feet!—were required to view a slide show featuring military squads loading onto mules the 29 frozen bodies that they, over the previous 20 years, had hauled off the mountain. Even the two of us who had not been present clearly got the message.

The next day belonged to the heroic mules that carried us all the way to Plaza Francia (at 13,451 feet) and the base of the mighty South Wall. To this day I have an enduring admiration for those hardy animals: their strength and sure-footedness minimized the trepidations I felt at the trail's many precipices and while crossing scary silt-stained torrents on the way up.

Turning a corner, still on muleback, I caught the first view of that magnificent wall, with the rest of the mule-mounted party ahead of me. (I still display an enlargement of that photo in my La Crosse home.) There was one of the most challenging climbs in the world, and its mere sight made me tremble. Later, Don imparted a piece of advice that would serve me well six years later at the start of our climb together up El Cap's Salathé Wall in Yosemite Valley: "Bill, you'll freak out if you attempt to anticipate the whole climb at once. It's much better to consider the difficulties one pitch [rope length] at a time. This way you will feel confidence, because you will know that, move by move, you've done far harder stuff before."

Our plan was for Vance and me to accompany our buddies to Plaza Francia, spend five or so days helping them ferry loads up the first third of the South Wall, then the two of us would descend and walk two days around to the mountain's north side. From there, over four or five days we would slowly gain altitude by following the famous mule trail to arrive at Aconcagua's summit. The four of us had naïvely speculated thus: being that circumnavigating and then ascending the mule trail would take more or less the same number of days as Don's and Mike's technical ascent of the South Wall, Vance and I could meet them on the summit and help them navigate down the easy descent trail. It's hard to believe today that back then we might have believed that this plan was at least remotely possible.

Vance, totally intimidated by the vertical topography of the South Wall, was content to twiddle his thumbs in and around Camp Francia. Meanwhile I advanced with Don and Mike up the beginning of the South Wall's French Route, reaching about 15,000 feet (to the base of the Great Towers). Three vivid memories. First, the scads of equipment, and even hardware, abandoned by two previously successful Japanese parties. Sec-

**Don, Vance, and Mike ride ahead of me as we approach the base of Aconcagua's fear-inspiring South Wall. Ten days later Vance and I would reach the 23,000-foot summit via the mule trail on the mountain's other side.**

ond: nervously jumaring up the thin (and weathered) fixed-ropes on a hard fifth-class segment that had been abandoned at least two years before. Third—and even more memorable—finding out that I truly enjoyed (unlike my two Yosemite buddies) ascending on shit rock. I experienced a whole new dimension of adrenaline thrill in anticipating the almost inevitable disintegration of one of the four hand/foot placements at any given stance. (This would prove to be good mental and physical preparation for future ascents at Huascarán, Mississippi river bluffs, and Glacier National Park.)

A few days later Vince and I finally left our buddies and began our hike around the mountain. The downhill part went fast: by late afternoon of the first day we reached Confluencia (literally, "where two streams meet"). There, we located a place to cache a rope, along with unneeded technical equipment and food. However, we wisely decided to continue carrying the ice axes and crampons that we knew would be needed to proceed safely up the north side's mule trail to the summit. (Stupid us: two days later at Plaza de Mulas we trustingly informed the pair of military mule drivers about our stashed equipment, which we would never see again.)

There, at Confluencia in the early afternoon, we puzzled over how we would cross the glacier-melt stream which, given the heat, had become a raging torrent. I stripped down, with only outer boots on my feet, to brave the near waist-high water. As a precaution, I grasped my short ice axe in the downstream hand, positioning its point between the slippery rocks. In the other hand I clutched a loop from the thin rope I had anchored to a rock some thirty feet up-stream. Ankle-deep, I could feel the thrust of the moving water. Knee deep, I realized that crossing it was not going to be easy. At thigh depth the danger became apparent. Suddenly, I slipped and went tumbling downstream. The thin protective line was yanked from my hand. If I had not taken the precaution of threading my hand through its strap, I would have lost the ice axe. I nearly drowned as I clawed my way toward the shore. Choking, and thoroughly weakened by the struggle, I did succeed in extracting myself from the raging torrent—barely. (For the next half-century I would tell interested listeners that this event constituted the closest I had ever come to my own demise in a mountain-related incident; a reader of desperate mountain dramas might interpret this as a sign of my lucky star.)

With no other option, Vance and I were forced to call it a day, and we spent the night 20 meters above the stream. In the early morning we gingerly danced across rocks protruding from the much-diminished flow.

What stands out—via the prism of memory—about the next four or five days is the sensory-deprived setting of our walking ascent up Aconcagua's north side. Not a trace of plant life! Forget any fauna eking out a living in that barren, moon-like landscape. No variation in rock color or formations. Nobody would call Aconcagua a pretty mountain!

Hiking on, what I remember most is the tedium. We experienced no undue suffering (at least until the last, summit, day—which I will get to presently). Of potential interest to future Aconcagua trekkers: in our packs we were carrying all the equipment, including a tent, that we would use over the next week, as well as all the food we would consume. (Almost all trekkers today would hire mules to carry some of this at least to Plaza de Mulas.) But Vance and I, placing one foot ahead of the other, continued on … and on … silently tolerating the pack straps pressing against aching shoulders, following the unmistakable mule trail. Trundling on and up. We just kept doing what we had come there to do.

We must have felt the increasing burden on our breathing as the altitude steadily increased. But we were mentally ready to suffer the "grit" of the climb. The mounting fatigue due to altitude gain was well within our expectations. The intervening years have blotted out any particular memories.

I must confess here that, at the time of our ascent, we knew beans about altitude sickness or the need for taking prescribed steps to achieve a necessary level of acclimatization (gads! few people knew about any of this at that time).[5] The terms "cerebral edema" or "pulmonary edema" were hardly known among members of the climbing community. (I can personally attest to the fact that written information about these issues had only begun to circulate after the successful American ascent of Everest a few years earlier.) After all, we were (primarily) "California rock climbers" for whom acclimatization had never been an issue. Although unschooled, we still didn't fall for the local folklore, imparted to us by our military hosts at Puente del Inca, about the medical advantages of biting into and chewing on a raw onion. In all our ignorance, we were just going to "go for it." Long live youthful folly.

The photos I had taken during the trek are perfectly preserved in my basement as if I had taken them yesterday. Paul Simon, you sang it: "Kodachrome …"—those slides will probably last for hundreds of years with their "living" colors suffering no significant fading.

The word *mounters* is often used in reference to those thousands of trekkers who attempt to reach Aconcagua's summit from the north side's mule trail. I agree with the word choice, because absolutely no technical climbing skill is involved. You simply need determination and stamina.

**Even the mule-trail ascent of Argentina's Aconcagua is difficult because of the altitude (23,000 feet). In the 1970s "cabins" such as the one I'm standing next to here offered refuge from the bitter-cold winds, but only if they weren't filled with ice.**

You simply have to commit yourself to start out, then to "keep on walking" up the blessed mule trail. Today, while snaking your way up in single file, you will pass by the same camps that we passed a half-century before: Alaska, Refugio Antártida, Berlin, and Independencia (back then this last camp was called Juan Perón).

Today I imagine that during the busy season each of these becomes a tent city alongside a park-serviced kybo. My own photos reveal that back then there were humble structures in at least two of these camps: I remember 8' × 8' plywood walls and roofs with guy wires anchored firmly to the ground to protect against the high winds. Each had to have a tightly closing door. The exception was at Juan Perón, where we found only a 2-meter-square, 1.5-meter-high wooden A-frame structure. I am amazed that the most current guidebook includes a photo of that same structure, with the same boards missing from one side of its roof—exactly as one of my photos showed the shoulders and head of Vance sticking up through it some 45 years ago. Also memorable in my bin of memories was one of the structures at Berlin that was chock full of wind-packed ice: a careless climber in the previous weeks must have failed to secure the door from the strong winds that blast snow crystals into every possible crevice. We had to chop ice for a half hour inside the A-structure at the mountain's highest camp in order to pitch my hearty two-man REI oxford-cloth tent inside—that was our best option for protecting ourselves from the incessant winds.

Un-erasable memories flood my consciousness now of the problems that resulted from three separate decisions I had made weeks before Vince's and my painful—but successful—trek up to the summit. These involved the selection of equipment and food. First the stove. I'm from Seattle, home of both Jim Whittaker and REI equipment; both had made it to the summit of Everest only months before. And in dozens of celebratory photos I and a whole generation of young climbers saw that they had carried the Bluet stove. However, REI sales propaganda did not explain that the fuel cartridges they carried on Everest contained a mixture of butane *and methane*, and that the cartridges later available at REI contained only butane. On Aconcagua we learned that the latter vaporizes only if warm, and even then—at best—it provides a minimum of heat and only if insulated from the ground by a patch cut from a foam sleeping pad. On Aconcagua, we quickly (and painfully) learned that our stove could only produce a bare minimum of heat if, during the day, we carried the cartridges inside our shirts and, at night, slept with them positioned next to our skin. Even doing that, the afternoon before summiting, the cold was so extreme that, even covering the bare cartridge with woolen gloves, it took six tedious hours to melt an insufficient amount of snow for our interminable thirst. Moral: future adventurers on this mountain should take along only a stove fueled by hot-burning white or camping gas, and certainly not butane.

This leads to my second grand mistake: the choice of soup for every cooked meal. (Experienced winter climbers know that this is hardly a marginal issue.) I had anticipated the near impossibility of boiling a prepared mix due to the high altitude, so I had ruled out most dried soups containing noodles. This didn't leave too many alternatives. Split-pea soup? Not the most savory, but nutritive and no need to boil; it could be drunk half-warm. Bingo! Split-pea soup would be the constant of all our high-altitude meals! At sea level this sounds like a reasonable line of reasoning. But it fails to take into account the food-induced nausea that almost all mounters or climbers experience at high altitudes, and especially Vince and I on Aconcagua.

To this very day the mere thought of split-pea soup still revolts me. There we were, summit eve, jammed into the sagging REI tent that imperfectly lined the inside of the broken A-frame shelter at Juan Perón, shivering in spite of our fluffy down jackets and thick sleeping bags. In addition, we were miserable with headaches, fatigue, and thirst. Light the Bluet stove. Barely any output. Picture the gymnastics feat of lying prone and simultaneously warming up the cartridge with two cold hands. After 25 painful minutes, melted snow became warm water. Tear open the envelope and dump the split-pea powder into the pot. Hunger tormenting the stomach. Barely heated, I attempt to pour the "soup" into the two awaiting cups, but in the act much of it freezes to the sides of the pot. Nausea only from its smell—and double nausea with its taste. My spoon mashes against the icy chunks. Ugh. Up to the mouth. Will it go down?

Got to melt more water. Lots. Minutes turn to hours. Push open the A-frame door and stretch forward slipping out of the sleeping bag—brrrr—to bang the ice pick against hard snow. Pull myself back in to both the tent and the sleeping bag. Stuff the ice-crystal/snow into the pot. Stove sputters, butane barely vaporizes. Slow, slow. Elbow hurts, no room to roll over. Cup eternally lined with frozen split-pea soup. Pot also. Any new water that we produce has that horrid flavor. Misery has the odor of split-pea soup.

We needed, and did not have, clean water to moisten any food that we might want to ingest. This was the issue of my third grand mistake. The contemporary reader has to remember that this Spartan climber, back then, could not buy (the not yet commercially available) freeze-dried dinners or granola bars—and I must have considered it "unmanly" to consume things as simple as energy-potent candy bars. During my infamous visit to the Seattle REI I had also come across what seemed to be the perfect solution for our anticipated high-altitude food needs: foil-wrapped, Austrian-made (no less!), thick-book sized packets of energy food, each of which (according to the instructions) would supply the necessary calories for a two-person meal. In the warm store at sea-level Seattle, my reaction was: "Fabulous! But somewhat expensive, so I won't waste money opening one ahead of time to sample its taste." I ended up buying four and, weeks later, packed them for the flight down to Chile on the way to Argentina and the Big A.

There we were, jammed inside the A-frame at Juan Perón Camp, with our frozen fingers attempting to peel the foil cover off our first super-calorie meal. Hmmm. Inside were four smaller foil-wrapped cubes. The first contained about ten wafers of crumbly sucrose. In the second we found greenish crackers that, by taste, resembled dog biscuits. The third contained virtually the same, but this time with a weak strawberry scent and color. And in the fourth, virtually the same but with a light chocolate color (*¿color de caca?*). "Come on, Vance, try to get it down." No luck. What with the split-pea flavored water, he was having a very hard time (at that stage a split-pee flavor might have even been preferable). I ended up giving him the sucrose tablets from all the mountain-lunch packs. That left me with the task of overriding my own nausea to choke down five or six of the "cookies"—the different colors or flavors didn't really matter, because they all tasted very much the same: appalling. I did succeed in choking down four. They would have to constitute my "dinner." The same for my summit-day "breakfast," and ditto for the "lunch" on our day of *triumph*. But poor, starving, water-craving Vance: on that M day (reader has to choose from the following: miserable, memorable, but not majestic) he had only two dozen big tablets of sucrose to power his suffering body up the trail and then down. (His troubles were just beginning.)

Frozen in memory are scenes from that day. I did write "*frozen*." It was hard to pull on those stiff over-boots, and even harder lacing them up (with mittens, difficult; without mittens, good-bye fingers). Finally, I crawled out of the A-frame structure and then had to wait an interminable time for Vance. I took a picture of his upper torso sticking out of the hole in the roof. We finally started walking.

Well, we simulated walking. It was as if we had to move against the 2.4 G's of the planet Jupiter. One step, two breaths; another step, two breaths. After twenty such paces, the need to count to 20 to "catch our breath." The whole way, the whole half-day.

I already wrote that we knew next to nothing about altitude sickness. Perhaps that was a good thing, because had we been more knowledgeable we would have recognized dangerous symptoms in Vance and would have turned around and abandoned any summit ambitions. I myself was suffering no severe headache, and my will was unimpaired. But that was not

**Vance, on summit morning, Aconcagua (Argentina). Taking two breaths after every step, we would spend four miserable hours hiking up to the cloud-shrouded summit at around 23,000 feet.**

the case with Vance. Being a marathon runner, he knew how to deny the warning signs of pain and proceed through sheer force of will. In retrospect, that was probably a bad thing.

It was after about 20 minutes—and only a hundred painful yards—when Vance stops and mumbles, "I // for // got // my // wa // ter // bottle." And I answer, gesticulating forcefully with my arm and mitt, "Go // back // Vance. Go // back. // Go." And I sit down for an interminable wait. Finally, he re-joins me, but I am trembling with cold due to what seems like a half-hour of inactivity. We continue on. And on. Huffing, striding, huffing.

"Thank goodness"—I must have been thinking—"we have to ascend only 70 vertical meters and we have all day to do it." The trail seemed endless.

I finally reached the summit in a near white-out—ten meters of visibility. Standing two meters from the waist-high cross honoring the still-exiled ex-president, Juan Perón, I just stood there, with my back to the wind, waiting for Vince—who was delayed another 20 minutes. But he made it.

Up there, no visibility whatsoever. Forget our (insane) anticipation of gazing out from the summit ridge to view the Pacific Ocean. Or even more futile: the idea of rendezvousing with our two companions lifting themselves over the South Wall and onto the summit ridge. Mentally befuddled by altitude and cold, we hardly needed to mumble agreement over our shared intention of hurriedly performing summit rituals and getting our butts on the trail downward as quickly as possible. So among the dozen pieces of summit paraphernalia left by previous parties, we selected two small colorful banners, spread them out over the snow-rock ground, and snapped a few photos. Then Vance—barely recognizable with his sheik-covered face—posed for yet another shot holding a small metal cross he had also found. I snapped what resulted in a picture with my blurred thumb clearly visible. (As it later turned out, this sad photo was—for a critical third person—our one indisputable piece of evidence that we had truly made it to the top.) Then we turned our backs to the summit shrine and began walk-sliding on down. It might have been a "cake walk" were it not for the stabbing hunger pains and our parched throats.

Then, halfway down to Plaza de Mulas, the first of two pleasant surprises: a mule team had just unloaded supplies for a pair of Argentine climbers who, to facilitate acclimatization, had decided to spend two weeks at one of the high camps. (Two whole weeks? What would they do to pass the time and keep their warm blood flowing in that wintery desert? Gads. Just the thought of all this gives me the creeps. Perhaps it's best that the end to my lifelong climbing career is now approaching.) Their offer to carry us on down on the mules: readily accepted.

The other surprise: Within a few hours we reached Plaza de Mulas and, much to our surprise, we saw piled up inside the shelter perhaps a half-dozen gunny sacks full of oranges, spaghetti-sauce cans, bread loaves, and baked rotisserie chickens. Our first reaction: *Hallelujah*—a God-sent salvation for our hunger and thirst. But two hours later, I personally experienced a second, and opposite reaction: the extreme discomfort from *empache*—that is, stomach pains due to overeating. And from gases. Interminable, disgusting gases—for the rest of the day each expulsion would briefly elevate me from the mule saddle.

What was the origin of that food bonanza? It was hard for Vance and me to believe it: during the four days that it had taken us to get to the summit, a huge party (from Austria?—serves them right for those foil-wrapped dog-biscuit lunches!) had ridden in, had suffered from their overly hurried gain of altitude, had panicked, and then had fled. In doing so, they had gifted all their food to the military wranglers.

It seems to me—only now, at the moment of writing all this—that the leaders of that Austrian group must have been much more learned than Vance and I. Recognizing the initial symptoms of altitude sickness, they knew well enough about the need to descend as soon as possible in order to avoid what might have resulted in a medical emergency.

By afternoon, Vance and I, resting our weary shoulders and legs while mounted on the trusty mules, made it back out to the military barracks and the national highway. On the way, we had insisted on halting at Confluencia to recoup our stored equipment. Not a trace of it remained. Our military "friends" concocted the tale that the area was frequently visited by "unknown" individuals, or by the "regional delinquency," and most assuredly they had stumbled across our equipment cache and had absconded with all they found. Bye-bye to an expensive rope and other valuable stuff. Hello to pathetically unreal stories about a proliferation of civilian thieves.

There was other news: Our California buddies, advancing up the South Wall for a whole day after we had left them (probably to the top of the middle glacier), had experienced such severe symptoms of altitude sickness that they decided to abandon their attempt. (This, according to the retelling by the military people at Puente del Inca.) Turning around, they had hiked out, caught transportation back to Santiago, and rescheduled flights to hurry back to classes at UC Berkeley. Don—as it turned out—was so irate over Mike's panicking that he decided to never climb with him again. Good thing for me, because within weeks Don eagerly sought me out as a climbing partner. That was just the beginning: for the whole next decade he and I would go on to accomplish a long string of glorious climbing exploits. Thank you, Mike, for pissing Don off so totally.

Mike's story: Go on to attempt El Cap a few more times; move out to Golden, Colorado, to become a body-building competitor and male model; get married and have a child whom you will train to do fingertip push-ups even before he gets out of the crib; when your own body becomes arthritic, wallow in the glories of Tommy C; remember forever the nausea and headaches, legendary in your own life story, that you experienced on Aconcagua in the first week of the year 1970.

## Chapter 3

# North to Alaska

*Excited, I descend the basement stairs to retrieve one of the two 7" × 18" metal boxes holding my treasure trove of slides. Let's see … here's the one with light pencil marks on the top: "Yosemite-Sierra Nevada; Alaska [Eureka!]/Lovers' Leap, Shucksan, Rainier, Bugaboos, Aconcagua." I carry it back upstairs to examine the contents while sitting in my daylight window.*

*Bonanza! Over a hundred Kodachrome pics from our Alaska summer, and all in mint condition! This will be delicious!*

*But it wasn't. There was a disconnect. I was looking for slides showing "human beings in climbing" and found very few. Hmm. An "anthropological" question: what does this physical evidence reveal about the state of mind of Bill-the-young-climber?*

*I, the gristly veteran, can offer only two speculations: First, the total absence of "selfies," or pictures of the photographer himself, suggests that "ego" might not have been an important motivation.*

*And two: easily 85 percent of the photos are of mountain scenery, meaning that they exclude human presence. Added to that, of the remaining 15 percent that show (mainly from the back) views of climbing partner Don, not one is a close-up that might reveal aspects of his character or the psychological aspects of his struggle up a crux move. Another speculative conclusion: the "human factor" was hardly of interest to the young climber-photographer named Bill.*

Alaska and Don Fredrickson: my memories of both are inexorably intertwined. If you've read the accompanying essay on Aconcagua, you'll know how he and I became climbing partners.

What did we have in common? At the beginning—in 1969—we were fellow students at Berkeley; we traveled together to Aconcagua; we were both from the state of Washington (he: Tacoma; me: Seattle), and for a decade we prioritized devoting weekends and vacations to climbing. Our partnership benefited from the near coincidence of our "availability" and respective dream lists of future climbing routes. A near-perfect couple.

I chuckle at having chosen this last expression: I use it with absolutely no sexual connotation, because the two of us were "ascetic" individuals when together. I can categorically affirm, at least in my case, that our intense commitment to the climbing task at hand supplanted or ruled out any suggestion of sexuality. I wonder today—in an epoch of public "sexual" scandals—whether I (always with unquestioned heterosexual orientation) was blessed with a (perhaps relatively) low libido. (Did others—including my parents—ever wonder about my own sexual orientation when I would explain how Don and I, on multiple-day routes would, come nighttime, slip together into a single bivy sack and pass the night shivering with our two bodies pressed together to preserve heat?) In short, I must conclude that the intensity of the climbing experience simply ruled out any aspect of "sexuality" or "desire." Had I (unconsciously) perfected the practice of sublimation? I do remember mentioning to my wife, during a moment of reflective conversation, that even during a month-long climbing trip (to the Alps, to Peru) I had almost never suffered from, or been plagued by, sexual desire. I repeat: the climbing urge, year after year, was so intense that it must have overruled any rival desire for female corporality. Not even mental imagery. Again, I speak only for myself. I have no idea what might have been running through Don's mind in those days and weeks climbing together (or earlier with Peter). Indeed, this was a topic that we never would even touch upon in our many conversations.

Don and I—I repeat—formed a near perfect climbing team. I totally welcomed his slightly higher technical ability. Our rule of thumb in selecting the food, equipment, or hardware to be carried in our backpacks: "If in doubt, we leave it." To this day, I thump my chest in telling friends and aspiring climbers: "Of the ten essentials listed by the Seattle Mountaineers,[1] we carried only one—an extra pair of dry socks."

A related factor about Don: he was the epitome of toughness (without it—back in the 1970s—I would not be writing these words today). Before a difficult pitch, my infrequent trepidation would always disappear before his quiet resolve. Both of us implicitly knew—as must all successful trad leaders—about the self-fulfilling prophecy that if you permit your self to harbor the most minimal doubt that your shoe will stay on that minuscule crystal, then—lo and behold!—your foot will slip off! Expand that awareness to any type of negative thinking: the mere suggestion of a possible afternoon storm, or about the difficulty of getting over that flared jam crack on the third pitch above, could prove to be contagious. So, we shared in the unspoken pact of our preferred silence. Yet, that was not absolute. On several occasions, upon contemplating a particularly hard or scary lead, I would reluctantly turn to him and request, "Can you take it, Don?" His response never varied: he would silently oblige, without even a minimum glance of "disappointment" (in me) or put down.

Yet I myself was hardly a "climbing slouch." On the contrary, a few of my special skills contributed to the success of our team. Heading this list are my route-finding skills. Time after time, with both of us standing at the bottom peering upward toward a route or pitch, I was able to distinguish physical characteristics—a granite nubbin, a barely visible handhold—that he, burdened with glasses and defective long-range vision, could not see. Also important was my (for my different partners over the years) uncanny ability to assess the climbing difficulty and possible protection needs of a given route. In trip after trip, Don came to trust this type of assessment that I, assisted by good vision, was able to make about the technical difficulties we would confront.

Yet a last ingredient to our success: our shared steadiness and successful planning—when added to our good luck (with weather and other external contingencies)—account for the fact that, in our ten years of climbing together, only few times were we forced to abandon an attempt and not once did either of us suffer a bad injury. We amassed a remarkable record of completing the vast majority of climbs we set out to accomplish.

I must share a few anecdotes about Don before commencing my reflections about our trip to Alaska. One early morning we found ourselves in Tuolumne Meadows (upper Yosemite National Park) putting on our climbing shoes and getting ready to go unroped up the classic Water Marks. I commented on his gnarled toenails. He explained that if, in a given season, he didn't lose three or four of them, then either he had erred in purchasing shoes that were overly large, or he wasn't trying hard enough. Hmmm.

We moseyed up to the start of the route, a low-sloping, rather smooth-sided gully. But as you proceed on up, the angle steepens. Fifty yards up it ends as a rounded crack on a 60-degree wall. Initially we were just walking; soon we were cat-crawling using all fours. Then we were carefully identifying and using solid feet placements. A bit further we needed easy hand grabs over obvious bumps. Within minutes we were carefully placing both toes and fingernails on selected crystals. Finally, we reached a point where the route somewhat leveled out, just before a steep near-vertical rise. It was the obvious place to turn around and go back down. However, looking back at our path, we realized that this was going to be harder, and perhaps more treacherous, than coming up! And we had foolishly decided not to bring even a spaghetti cord to do a simple shoulder rappel! Carefully, very carefully—and with butterflies in the gut—I started down, facing outward using my spread-out hands to avoid a slide, and using my butt as a brake. The first forty feet were dicey, but the rest was a piece of cake. Reaching the bottom I looked up to see that Don was just beginning his descent—*in only his underpants.* "Why'd you take off your pants?" I asked him two minutes later. His reply: "It would cost money to repair a hole in my knickers. But if I lose a bit of skin, it'll just grow back, not costing me anything." Reader, do take note: The Gods did not use a normal cookie cutter in their crafting of Don Fredrickson.

One fine August morning in 1973 Don pulled into the driveway of my parents' Seattle home, at the wheel of an ancient faded green Volvo. Previously, we had decided that flying gravel on the 1,400-mile Alas-Can highway would do irreparable damage to either my rather new VW bug or his (very inappropriate) TR. I agreed to match his $200 and he would buy the used car of his choice to make the trip. He knew that his forebears would approve of what he had purchased.

"Gads, Don. Do you think it'll make it there and back? Its tranny [transmission] doesn't sound terrific."

"I figure that if we just drive straight there, we'll not have to do too much shifting. It was made by Swedes, it'll make it."

"Hope so."

We spent the day buying provisions for a month, piling all onto the backseat. Then, we chicken-wired the headlights to make them ready for the legendary flying rocks on that endless unpaved highway. And we were off.

But we didn't get too far. A hundred miles this side of Spokane the car just stopped. An hour of Don's tinkering (in this and other mechanical matters he was really smart), and nothing succeeded in making the motor show new signs of life. Resigned and desperate, we half-heartedly took the spare gas can—that in a near serendipitous decision we had brought along—and poured a gallon of gasoline into the car's tank. It started! What was going on? Lying on our backs and peering up, we identified the gas tank. Shocked out of our willies, we realized that it held only 6.4 gallons and that, after a mere 150 miles, we had run out of gas! I had never even imagined that a car, of any make, would have a tank that small.

That newly discovered reality decided a key feature to our trip: we would have to stop every eighty or so miles to fill the frickin' tank.

Later that afternoon when we got to the border to cross into Canada Don looked around for a "duty-free" store. "We don't drink. Why stop here?" I asked.

"I want to buy a cheap bottle of whisky for my ol' man for when we come back."

"What? Cross three more borders with contraband whisky? You're out of your mind."

"Crossing by car into Sweden as a kid we did it all the time. My parents hid whiskey bottles under every kid in diapers. They never looked."

"Well, we have no kids in diapers here."

"Don't worry. At the borders I'll be sitting in front of the wheel with the bottle under my belt and hidden by my shirt. If they're suspicious they'll say nothing; they'll be too embarrassed, thinking I've got a h.o."

"It's your bottle, Don."

We headed for the Bugaboos. It would be our third trip there in four years. Driving on that 40-mile dirt road, the car started slipping out of fourth gear every few minutes.

We had such glorious ambitions there, after having accomplished at least two difficult grade V routes (with bivies) on the Hawser Spires the year before. This time we were not so lucky. After carrying monstrous packs up the five-mile trail from the ski lodge's parking lot, it started to rain. And it rained all the next day. On day three we exchanged books, Don's Tolstoy for my Dostoevsky. There was one consolation: we were comfortably seated, and very dry, inside the small Quonset hut—and our food was totally protected from the voracious ground squirrels. On day four there was a lull in the rain and we, totally bored, attempted to get on a wet route, but a near slip of Don's motivated us to return back to the hut.

Day five, drizzle again, but at about 9 a.m. we heard the unmistakable sound of a helicopter landing just outside the door. *Whaaaat?* A few somewhat elderly, portly women, with backpacks, got off, as the chopper made ready to fly back down to ferry more people—and, a half-hour later, lumber. The two schoolteacher-faced women came into the

Quonset hut and solemnly invited us to scrunch ourselves into the corner. They told us that the hut was to become the kitchen for the work crew that, over the next few weeks, was going to construct a new climber's refuge. A half-hour later, the two women changed their tune: they made it absolutely clear that their "kitchen" space would require the entire hut. Not so delicately, they made it known that Don and I had to move ourselves and our equipment out. Beaten down by boredom and with absolutely no desire to continue our sitting ritual in a soggy tent, the two of us sullenly decided that it was time to shoulder our packs and hike back on down to the car.

Bye-bye Bugaboos. I've never visited you again, but your exciting routes and breathless verticality are forever etched in my bank of memories.

Driving back on the long dirt road, and then on the highway, the tranny just got worse. Were we cruising in third or fourth? Couldn't tell. Good thing Calgary was just ahead. We'd stop in the Volvo shop and seek advice. Or even the installation of a rebuilt tranny? Ouch! The cost of that might jeopardize our Alaska plans if it cut too deeply into the funds we had reserved for the two fly-in trips we had planned.

Turned out that whatever the Volvo people might do would have to wait a week, because on the morrow they would close shop for several days during the city's local summer celebration, Stampede Days. So Don and I optimistically reckoned, "Perhaps the tranny problems have bottomed out; so let's keep heading north." And so we did, passing Banff (pretty but not really inviting for the climbers in us), then Lake Louise ("Wow! Look at Temple's North Face! Did you read the account in the AAJ by one the Lowe brothers about their ascent up it a few years ago?"). And we just kept chugging. But the tranny just kept getting worse. "God, the stick is pointing toward me. Is it in fourth?"

"Can't tell, might be third. It's in something."

"We're in deep shit. If we turn around we might make it back to Calgary."

"Don't think so. If we're lucky we can make it to Saskatchewan River Crossing about 15 miles ahead. There's bound to be a mechanic there."

"Then try not to shift. Slow down so you don't have to change gears at all for the next twenty minutes."

About a quarter mile from SRC Don gave up finding any gear that was left. But we were on top of a small rise that allowed us to coast almost the whole rest of the way. The last 50 yards I was running alongside pushing, and—luckily—we barely made it to the far side of the parking area of a touristy store. Just outside our door there was pitched a fake Indian tepee.

Don, inspecting under the car, saw at once that many bolt-nuts had disappeared and that the transmission was now hanging loosely below the engine housing. Our prescription: Don would hitchhike back to Calgary to obtain the metric bolts needed, while I would bide my time here awaiting his return. Don got ready and he was off.

Meanwhile, I made myself as inconspicuous as possible and, in darkness, entered the tepee to lay out a ground cloth, foam pad, and sleeping bag. I passed a decent night. In the morning I awoke, but was in no hurry to do anything. About 9:30 a.m. I heard a car drive up and stop some 50 feet away, and then the patter of small feet. "Mommy, a real Indian tepee!" I lifted my head to see a pair of small eyes peering in through the partially open flap-door. Then I heard the footsteps running away: "Mommy, there's a real Indian sleeping in the tepee." Discretion motivated me to move myself and my stuff out and away.

Reader, be patient! We will get to Alaska. But these stories must be told!

Don did get back and, after a primitive job of re-bolting, we realized we had no option other than that of returning to Calgary for the pros to install a wholly rebuilt transmission. So, with two of the four gears restored (we weren't sure which), we headed back to Lake Louise. We had a week to kill. What better way to spend our time than going up that spectacular north wall of Mt. Temple? In another chapter I describe that exciting ascent. After that, two days of waiting during the installation of a rebuilt tranny in Calgary, and then we were able to resume our long, long drive north.

Passing by Jasper, we ogle-eyed the fabulous line that we had climbed the year before up Edith Cavell's north face.

And then, a stopover with our intent to ascend that dreamy snow-ice Kain Route up the north face of Robson. Unfortunately, Bugaboo weather was still on our tail. Just like the year before, we were turned back by rain—after that long, dreary hike to the base of the climb. Two times rained out in two years! Damn. Well, Mountain Gods, revenge will be sweet. Heading my list of climbs to do in my next reincarnation is the Kain Route on Robson. So there!

**The Bugaboos (British Columbia's Interior Ranges) are North America's closest thing to the Alps, with their mixed, multi-day climbs. Here, Don rests at the summit of Snowpatch, with the Howser Spires in the background.**

Back to the car. Onward. We reached the border with Canada, where immigration officials gave two hoots about any possible contraband we might have been carrying. "I told you so, Katra."

And then, the endless bumpy curves of the Alas-Can Highway.[2] Don and I, sobered after having almost lost the tranny on the 40-mile dirt road to and from the Bugaboos, now knew that any existing bolt on the car was at risk. At every gas station (after our obligatory fill-ups) we took out our wrenches to tighten any bolt in sight. Worrisome was the fact that in a few places empty bolt holes stared us in the face, and no store or shop we passed even recognized the meaning of "metric." Proceeding, we kept an eagle eye out for any auto junkyard, where we would discreetly step over barbed wire fences to locate any foreign car in order to attempt the removal of any metric bolt we might find. I wrote "attempt." Years of corrosion made this operation difficult, if not impossible, in many instances.

We just kept driving, curve after curve after curve. For fourteen hundred miles, human habitation was visible at only the infrequent gas-station outposts that—perhaps in their majority—we duly visited.

One day we were impressed by how, within a half-hour after a rainstorm, heavy machinery miraculously appeared (out of nowhere?) to scrape off the road's fresh mud cover, fill in the ruts, and level it all again. Spectacular.

Another day—actually it was at the end of a long driving day—we, with a thirst for beer and a bar, pulled up to a tavern in a very small roadside community and had a human experience that—in retrospect—seems to belong more to the pages of Jack London or Robert Service. Occupying a pair of empty bar stools, we quickly became friends with a lumberjack-type young man, already tipsy with drink. The pleasant presence of his recently arrived girlfriend then acquired draconian undertones when one of his male rivals entered through the doors. (Reader, have you seen this melodramatic movie before?) Knives were drawn—we were not uninvolved. Only with difficulty did we extract ourselves from that explosive and unpredictable entanglement, welcoming once again the boring peacefulness of the road. The whole situation helped us to define our own—shared—perspective: that while we did not eschew danger in the natural wilderness, we wanted nothing to do with explosive human dramas emerging from a wilderness setting.

The next mini-drama occurred at the Alaska border—we were finally returning to the "good ol' U.S. of A." Don, at the wheel, got himself ready with the whiskey bottle in its desired position. "Hello, boys," said the beady-eyed border employee in a starched uniform shirt—and with a pastiche smile glued to his face. He inquired, and we explained, about our climbing plans for the next month. Did we look that suspicious, with our unshaven faces and ratty non-climbing clothes? Were we the only climbers or mountaineers he had ever let pass through his frontier gate? "Could you kindly step out of the car for a moment?"—again spoken with a huge institutionalized smile on his face. (Don's bottle! In my mind the situation could become hilarious!) Getting out on the other side, I could only imagine their reaction upon seeing Don's contraband trophy. Then, Don (sans bottle) and I stood to the side as Mr. Beady Eyes and an assistant gave a once-over to the mounds of equipment and food we had piled in the back. I didn't even notice their inspection of the cigarette-ash receptacles embedded in the car's doors.

(What was happening?) He then ordered Don to follow him to one room while an assistant led me to another. "Sir, what's this all about?"

"Young man, in the ashtray of your car we found roaches." Ashtrays? Neither Don or I smoked—anything. In our two weeks of ownership we hadn't even thought to open up or inspect the car's ashtrays. "Kindly take off all your clothes." (What??) "Turn around and bend over.... Pull apart your cheeks." (Are you kidding? Am I in a Russian concentration camp or a gay hothouse?) Here the reader has to realize my befuddlement, my naïveté, and perhaps ignorance, because over the past three years I had dedicated 100 percent of my time to just two things: climbing and studying, with no time for *anything* else. My thought today: perhaps I was the only young male from Berkeley, California who didn't recognize immediately what he was talking about. (Roaches? What? Cockroaches? Gads, are they going to fumigate us?) This is precisely what was running through my head.

Over the next 90 minutes the situation became much more clarified. Finding Don's bottle, our clean-scrubbed FBI-like agent was now imagining a much bigger prize. They ordered us to take everything out of the back of the car, piece by piece. That would take a while. The situation turned ludicrous when we pulled out two huge plastic bags full of granola. Mr. Beady-Eyes opened each one and methodically poured every small particle of roasted oatmeal through his separated fingers. (Ugh! The scent of this horrible man on my breakfast? The situation might have been funny if it had not been so perverse!) Sitting on the curb with a ring-side view, I continually had to stifle a caustic laugh. Finally, he pulled Don's sleeping bag out of the stuff sack, which had hadn't been washed or cleaned over five years of consistent weekend use. Turing it inside-out, Mr. Jeepers spied a piece of lint (probably intertwined with musky toenail clippings), grabbed it between his thumb and forefinger, and then held it up to the light. Then he moved it to his nose and gave it a whiff. His gleaming eyes emitted a sparkle. (Was this really happening? Were we in a Mel Brooks movie?) I couldn't contain it: the semblance of a laugh erupted from my innards. He looked at me with a dagger face. In an icy voice, and aiming his piercing glance on me: "You're the type of person who makes my day complete." Glacial irony. You can bet that I shut myself up and tried to shrink my body right there at the curb.

At some point, we moseyed over to converse with a tearful young fellow, also detained, who told us that yes, they had found a stash of pills he had hidden in the upholstery of his car. Now he knew he was in deep shit.

It must have been a disappointing surprise for the guards, that they didn't find any illegal substances mixed in with our equipment and food. (Duh.) They then mentioned the possibility of continuing their search by pulling back parts of the car's interior wall linings. Luckily, something about us must have convinced them that this, also, would be a waste of time. And luckily, the amount of mojo contained in the few roaches they had located did not constitute a sufficient amount to warrant detaining us. Finally they told us we were free to go. We repacked, got in, and gladly left the border unreality behind. Now on to Anchorage—at least one more day of joyful driving.

There, they told us of our good luck: we were oh-so-fortunate to enjoy the tail end of what might amount to Anchorage's only week that calendar year of uninterrupted sunshine—if this turned out to be a typical year. In that city we had the sole objective of connecting with Ludwig Ferche, a carpenter friend of Don's—but not a really dedicated climber—who had moved there shortly after the devastating earthquake a few years earlier to take advantage of the construction boom. Being the busy season, he decided to let Don and me fly in without him for the first of our two climbing experiences. Don and I, according to Ludwig, would have time to "scout things out" before he would join us for any serious undertaking.

The two of us arrived at the small Talkeetna airport and selected the equipment and food we would need for two to three weeks of climbing. Our objective was to fly in to the Cathedral Spires which are "technically" part of the Kichatna Region of the Alaska Range, located about 150 miles southwest of Denali (in the 1970s the latter was universally referred to as Mt. McKinley). We would fly in with Cliff Hudson, one of Talkeetna's legendary bush pilots (the other was Don Sheldon), whose small Cessna, outfitted with skis for glacier landings, could hold a maximum of two passengers plus a moderate load of equipment.

Dave Roberts, writing a few years before, had described the Cathedral Spires as "hidden in a southwestern corner of the Alaska Range, [they were] probably North America's closest equivalent to the towers of Patagonia. No other area combines heavy glaciation, remoteness, and bad weather with such an abundance of vertical walls, pinnacles, and obelisks."[3] Of note is the fact that even though this area belonged to the same "range" as their "big brother" Denali, it offered an entirely different climbing challenge: the Cathedral Peaks are at relatively low altitude (under 8,700 feet) and have near-vertical rock faces.

Ours would be the fifth visit ever by "modern" climbers. We would copy the Roberts party in establishing a base camp on the Glacier of the Shadows, from which we would attempt routes up two unclimbed peaks:

Gurney Peak and Peak 8520. The party led by Royal Robbins a few years before us had chosen the Tatina Glacier, as did the DeMaria party that had preceded us (but did not attain any summits) by a month.[4] We went prepared for the legendary bad weather. The Roberts party—a half-dozen years earlier—had had to endure a snowstorm that "continued for twelve straight days." Similarly, almost continuous rain had limited the Robbins party, during their visit of about 25 days, to reaching only two summits![5]

A digression about equipment. From the fragmentary information offered by articles written by the leaders of both of the aforementioned parties, Don and I made crucial equipment choices. First, we brought along skis and skins that immensely facilitated our approaches on the gently sloping glacier. They certainly shortened the hours involved and energy expended in our two successful climbs, each of which took us a single day to approach and then climb, then another day to descend and return to camp. In contrast, Roberts had written about his party's continual "tromp through thick snow" and their "exhausting" six-to-eight-day climbs. Robbins, in his turn, admitted to "plodding and trudging" through snow as major causes of their generally frustrating experiences.

A second issue with regard to equipment was our possession of twelve-point crampons. It's interesting to note that neither of the two articles written by previous climbing parties mentioned, or even alluded to, this obviously important issue. If memory serves me faithfully, the early 1970s witnessed a radical upgrade in ice-climbing equipment and technique for all American climbers. Most important, during that period the 12-point crampon replaced the—until then—standard 10-pointer (the additional two prongs protruding horizontally in front of the boot made front-point ascending possible).

A third equipment issue: Don and I possessed Chouinard ice hammers. This was a revolutionary tool for its time, combining a hammer for pitons (used by all serious climbers back then) and a short ice pick.[6] A word about the latter: before the advent of the Chouinard tool, the most audacious of climbers, equipped with only the traditional ice axe and the primitive cork-screw style ice screws, inevitably would feel extremely nervous or even suicidal if positioned 500 feet up and unprotected on even a 40-degree hard-snow slope (and this is much worse on ice). I can testify that one whack with the pick of my reliable Chouinard ice hammer, connected to my waist swami with an appropriate length of half-inch webbing, added instant, and bomb-proof, protection. This added safety would come to motivate myself and other climbers to attempt more risky ascents.

In 1966—the year of the Roberts party—the Chouinard ice hammer was not yet available. Could it be that awareness of the severe limitations of their old-school crampons and axes influenced key route decisions? For example, on one peak they chose to ascend a "vertical wall [requiring two days of direct aid instead of] a 1600-foot snow couloir, steep all the way but unbroken, that led exactly to the ridge."

**A Peruvian friend obliged me by displaying the best "ice tools" available for North American climbers in the 1970s: a short ice axe (left) and a Chouinard ice hammer (right).**

Both previous parties had prioritized forging very difficult routes up the two most majestic, as well as highest, of the (as-of-yet) unclimbed peaks in the area: the Roberts party on Kichatna Spire and the Robbins party on the south summit of Triple Peaks.[7] Don and I knew that we didn't even come close to being in the same climbing league as Royal Robbins. But in the previous two years we had gained confidence through a few successful ascents in the Bugaboos and the Canadian Rockies. Now, we welcomed a new adventure, but lacked total confidence about what we would be able to ascend in this new area.

We had read closely the two parties' route descriptions with the USGS map in front of us. Taking all the limited information into account, we had tentatively chosen Gurney Peak, still unclimbed, as our first objective.

When Cliff Hudson flew us in, it was a rare sunny day, offering exceptional photo ops of Foraker, McKinley, and the multiple glaciers and peaks of the Cathedral Spires. Thanks, Cliff, for veering toward those first two giants and your extra loop around the Cathedral Spires before ski-landing at the head of the Glacier of the Shadows. We unloaded our equipment onto the snow-covered ice and made ready to pitch our tent. He instructed us about operating the radio in the case of an emergency and hanging the wire antenna between two skis vertically thrust into the snow. It turned out that our one attempt at using it was frustrated by what Hudson later explained was an extremely rare sun-spot event. (Forever after Don and I have wondered if he was on the level about that.)

After Hudson left us, we had a chance to study our setting carefully. Roberts had not exaggerated: to the east and west we saw nothing but "jagged, clean" walls hemming in the glacier. It felt as if we were at the bottom of a pit (a sensation I would later feel—but for different reasons—in a back-country campsite of Glacier National Park). Looming over us was the intimidating west flank of Kichatna Spire and—somewhere—the start of a route abandoned by the Roberts party. Butterflies fluttered in my stomach. Seeing no inviting ridge or gully, I immediately realized that Don and I had no business—and no desire—to attempt an ascent right here. Had the Robbins party, with a base camp located three glaciers to the west, initially experienced a similar sense of dread?

Partial relief came by turning our heads to study the terrain directly to the south. There, above the glacier's headwall, loomed Gurney Peak, whose north buttress looked much more inviting: an irregular Bugaboos-type summit cut by a few gullies. Yes! Our preferred type of mixed climbing! Within an hour Don and I, acutely aware of our good fortune in enjoying a sunny day, hurriedly put on our skis to scout out a possible route. Already we had decided to be off early on the morrow and to forget any idea of sitting around waiting for Ludwig!

At first light, and without hesitation, we got on the route we had spotted the afternoon before. We ascended the steep icefall, where we enjoyed a privileged view of our Glacier of the Shadows down below, extending directly to the north and on to the horizon. The early-morning sun, shining through the sawtooth line of the east ridge, cast a long and jagged shadow down its whole length. Had any member of the Roberts group seen this majestic sight, surely one fit for the gods? I doubt it, because their (accidentally appropriate) baptism of the glacier's name was due—in their own words—to the "gloominess" they had experienced camping on it. But we, Don and I, visually feasted on that most incredible view of shadows—up and down and up and down—extending along the whole length of the glacier that was stretched out before us.

Now roped up, Don and I continued what we had come there to do. In truth, there's little to write about the "physical" side to our experience, other than to provide a rather standard description of the route. This "mixed" route required crampons the whole way. We belayed each other on a steep traverse over hardened snow, putting in a pair of ice screws for protection. Then we carried the coiled rope over our shoulders as we scrambled up over snow, rock, and ice in a shallow gully. On belay again, we huffed up the route's crux: a difficult, icy, 300-foot chimney that—fortunately—provided good placements for pitons and nuts on the rocky sides. Attaining the summit ridge, we were still looking for the "tough ice pitch and a direct-aid wall" that had turned back the Roberts party some seven years before. Our route required 15 hours on the ascent, a bivouac at the summit, and eight hours to descend the same route as the previous day.[8] *Veni, vidi, vici.*

Am I the same person? Because when I write about that experience of some 45 years in the past, I retain no memory of how that young individual, who bore the same name, must have *felt.* The passage of time has erased from my memory what must have been his elation and sense of accomplishment in attaining the summit of a mountain never before trodden by the footsteps of man, and surrounded by a remote and hostile wilderness. Might the (adopted) words of the Polish-English writer, Joseph Conrad, assist? The experience was like a "flick of sunshine upon a strange shore.… By all that's wonderful it is the [mountain], I believe, the [mountain] itself, or is it youth alone? … [W]asn't that the best time, that time when we were young … and had nothing, on the [mountain] that gives you nothing, except hard knocks—and sometimes a chance to feel your strength?"[9]

Worthy of note: During our long shivering stopover at the summit, and in moments of at least partial illumination, I was able to detect landmarks and imagine skirting around peaks and venturing onto crevasse-cut glaciers, to navigate the 27-mile hike to the Rainy Pass Lodge—that is to say, our only path of salvation if our pilot were to abandon us here. With perfect weather, and throughout the frigid, starry night, we were able to enjoy special views of the moonlit spires surrounding us.

It took most of the next day to descend the same route. Somewhere around noon we heard, but could not see, Hudson's landing and then departure. Approaching our pitched tent, there was Ludwig, pissed off that we had not waited for him. But with the good weather holding, the three of us made immediate plans to depart early on the morrow to ascend our second objective, a peak fairly near us on the west side of the glacier, marked on the map as "Peak 8520."[10]

Its east face, overlooking the Glacier of the Shadows, is an impressive array of towers and gullies. From our base camp it appeared to be a moderate climb up to the summit via the ice and snow on the north slope. At the head of the glacier we left our skis, put on crampons, and began ascending an icy tongue to gain entrance to a smaller glacier which lies on the western side of the peak. A snow couloir that requiring 3rd and 4th-class climbing ended at the north arête, which joined the snow ramp visible from our camp. There we had political problems: Ludwig, a climber from the old school, must have held in admiration the 1903 feat of fellow German Konrad Kain, who had chopped over six hundred steps in his first ascent of the route that now bears his name on Mount Robson.[11] I can't remember specifically, but it was entirely within Ludwig's "character parameters" to have ignored Don's prior insistence that he replace older 10-point crampons with newer 12-point ones. He stubbornly insisted on chopping steps. Needless to say Don and I were royally pissed off. In out-voting him, the two of us went first and at least granted Ludwig the safety of an upper belay. The higher stretches of the route required ascending hard snow, a bit of ice, decomposed rock, and steep hard snow again. In all, the ascent required 12 hours up, a bivy at the top, and a 10-hour descent over the same route.

Another first ascent. Today, writing these paragraphs in April 2018, it makes me proud to read—in the 1973 issue of the *American Alpine Journal*—about a dude named William Katra, accompanied by two rope buddies, who put up the first route in human history on—an admittedly obscure—Peak 8520 in the out-of-the-way Cathedral Spires area of the Kitchatna Mountains, in the southwest part of the mighty Alaska Range. Something to be proud of. Hmm, I wonder if my grandchildren will appreciate this—what for the youthful Bill Katra was just one more mini accomplishment in a long trajectory as mountain climber.

Our climb up—and down—Peak 8520 was not all glamour. Early in the pre-dawn light, when we were bleary-eyed after having shivered away the whole night just below its summit, a very heavy dew added to our discomfort. Then, during the descent, it started to drizzle. Halfway down, none of us wanted to call it other than rain. Our good luck with the weather had ended. When we finally reached our tent, we were drenched.

During a lull in the rain two days later, Hudson was able to land to ferry Ludwig on out. Don and I stayed, still nurturing the illusion of at least equaling Royal Robbins' feat of attaining three 8000+-foot summits here. We were going to wait for the next stretch of decent weather.

But that was not to be. It just wouldn't stop raining. Lethargy set in as, day after day, we would venture outside of the tent only to relieve ourselves and fill the cooking pot with snow. After a couple of hours, the same once again. And again. A week later, with our patience exhausted, we thrust two skis into the snow, stretched the antenna between them, and attempted via radio to instruct Hudson to fly in and pick us up. Was the radio equipment dysfunctional? No contact was made. We continued in groggy inactivity for several more days. We had read all our books. There was absolutely nothing to do but listen to the constant pitter-patter on the tent's exterior. Finally—on the designated date—Hudson came in, we dutifully packed and loaded our gear, and he flew us out.

Back in Anchorage we were more than rested, so Ludwig, Don, and I drove 40 miles south to Girdwood, whose small airport serviced climbers bound east, over the sea-water inlet called Prince William Sound, and toward the Chugach Mountains (and—possibly—the western fringes of St. Elias National Park). Following Ludwig's advice, the three of us would fly over the impressive, winding Radcliffe and Harvard glaciers, then on up to land at the highest possible point of the Marcus Baker glacier, whose head lay just west from the summit bearing the same name. This peak of 8000+ feet is the highest and "most prominent" of the Chugach Mountains.

Any sane person would consider our intent to have been crazy, at best. Following Ludwig's (very mistaken—as it later became obvious) advice, we would fly in to land high on the glacier and pitch our tent by early afternoon. Then, starting in late afternoon and hiking by flashlight, Don and I would proceed by crampons on up to the peak's summit. Ludwig's tall tale was that a year earlier he had attained that high point without removing his skis. So, this time his plan was to accompany Don and me only for the first hour, and then leave us to continue the stroll up the snow

**The small plane, outfitted with skis, left us at the top of the glacier, with the summit of Marcus Baker in the background. Only to an enemy would I recommend repeating our day-long ski descent over hidden crevasses.**

slopes to the summit, and then down. The master plan was that, in the morning, all three of us would then ski on down the relatively safe glacier. Then, at the pre-arranged hour of 6 p.m. our pilot, upon viewing the large orange-colored plastic that we would spread out upon the glacier surface, would land to fly us out.

In our attempt to live out this "wishful" plan, Don and I were not entirely disappointed. In fact, how many times in a lifetime is one privileged to witness a truly magical display of Nature's magnificence? It happened at least three times. First, during the 40-minute flight we were treated to an incredible view of the miles-long glaciers, in serpentine form, that twisted and flowed together below us. Then—the second time—upon landing high on the pristine glacier, bordered by picture-perfect *arrétes* (broken ridges) and satellite peaks, and all under an intense summer sun. Our third "magical" experience occurred a few hours before midnight, while the three of us, in crampons, were marching upward toward the summit: a thick mist, blowing in between us and the pale sun just above the horizon, illuminated the whole western sky. It was a scene prepared either for or by the Mountain Gods, and we were the privileged spectators! During that last special minute I snapped a photo, and I was later able to verify that my camera had been able to capture, at least in part, a suggestion of that glowing-sky miracle.

Unfortunately, however, the rest of the night's activities fell far short of the expectations that had been fueled by Ludwig's skewed information. As planned, the latter turned back to the tent after ascending an hour with Don and me. When the clouds moved in—and then the encroaching darkness—the two of us continued, but now guiding ourselves by flashlight and the inclining slope. Once every 20 or 30 minutes a light wind would momentarily lift the haze to afford us a hundred-yard view in partial light. It was spooky—luckily the fairly easy terrain did not inspire fear—but we continued, soon passing the four-hour mark, which was the bullshit estimate given by Ludwig for getting both up and down. Then five, then six hours, and conditions did not improve. Our worries grew, not over the ascent, but over the risk of losing ourselves in unknown and unseen terrain on the way down. Light snow was covering our crampon tracks within minutes, and we had not thought to bring along wands to mark our way. Nor did we carry compass, map, or altimeter. And given the near total lack of visibility, it was impossible to guide ourselves via known landmarks. Reluctantly—and with eternal regrets—we turned around before reaching the summit. In truth, we had no solid idea as to how much distance, or how much altitude gain, we had yet to travel.

And luckily, the walk on down offered no unforeseen difficulties or surprises (Don's and my "lucky star" continued to shine). In the early morning light—still unable to distinguish "ground" from "clouds" and still an hour away from the pitched tent—we heard the roar of a plane. Our pilot landing? Why so early, and why up here, instead of way down the glacier—as we had planned? Our hurried pace had no effect: within ten minutes we heard the plane take off again.

Finally arriving at the tent, we found a note from Ludwig: without our knowing, he had left instructions for the plane to pick him up early. The unconvincing explanation he fed us later was that he feared a new storm front would prohibit the plane from landing later that afternoon. The pilot had insisted on leaving us a ten-pound bag of food that, when added to the weight of the tent and our own gear, turned out to make very unwieldy—and dangerous—our task of skiing down the glacier that day.

In other conditions, that might have been a joyous experience. But my homemade ski-mountaineering bindings (cables adapted for climbing boots) proved to be quite inadequate for downhill skiing. Several times my slip-turns made the cables uncouple. It was more than awkward. In fact, it was nearly impossible to ski down in a normal fashion. Those difficulties were compounded by the fact that—due to the heavy glare—I was unable to distinguish minimal rises or depressions in the snow directly underneath me. On the other hand, Don, an accomplished skier with the proper equipment, was having few problems of his own. Both of us—whether foolishly or not—gave little attention to the inherent danger of skiing unroped over the lightly crevassed glacier. It was a full day. By early afternoon we arrived at an ideal level area, spread out our orange plastic, and had to wait only an hour for the arrival of the Cessna and our return to civilization.

Neither money, enthusiasm, nor time permitted yet another mountain experience, so we made plans to head back home. But—almost predictably—we fell victim to yet a new mechanical problem with our ancient Volvo: its generator had ceased to function (when the Swedes produced that car, had alternators been common?). Find a rebuilt one in Anchorage—or even a workable substitute? We tried. But forget it. Our advice to anyone thinking to copy our experience in travel to and from Alaska: choose an American car. We brainstormed: what to do? Luckily—again—Don found a solution (remember, he was no "ordinary" person). We removed the useless generator and disconnected all electrical connections minus the cables running to the starting motor and the distributor. Then we purchased and installed a new, super potent battery from Sears.

As it turned out, we had absolutely no unexpected problem during the whole five-day drive—without windshield wipers, lights, or radio—back to Seattle. Every day at the break of dawn—when headlights were no longer needed—we would start driving and not stop for anything other than bathroom visits and gas. In the waning rays of sunlight we would find a gas station to give a quick charge to the battery,[12] lie down in our sleeping bags beside the car, and wait for the disappearance of the stars that signaled the coming of a new day. Again, without headlights, we would commence, once again, the daily ritual.

It worked! We made it back—with neither a driving mishap nor an unfriendly intrusion by the Highway Patrol. But, unfortunately for Don, he crossed back into Washington State bottle-less (he had learned not to cry over spilt whiskey!) Hours later he summarily dropped me off at my parents' house in Seattle, and then made ready to suffer yet one more day of the same to arrive back at Berkeley—just in time for his fall classes.

All in all, it had been quite a summer, with a boggling series of adventures. "Twas so good to be young then…." Heck, even now I'd jump at the chance to do it all again.

## Chapter 4

# Camping Sauvage in the French Alps

It was the summer of 1976—I am sure of the year because I had been working painfully on my doctoral dissertation for a few years and it was then approaching completion. A fellow student: "Bill, you've got to be kidding. A climbing trip to France right now? You've got to finish it up. How about your last chapter? And it'll take time proofing and typing. You're crazy!" But there was the charter flight deal, hard to turn down. Its low price also attracted my young wife, Sara, who also began planning to take along her mother—both would carry nothing but backpacks. They would youth-hostel it in Barcelona and perhaps other areas of Spain (they were native Spanish speakers)—like Sara and I had done two years before—and then would make their way to Chamonix to join me at the end. It sounded like a good plan.

There we were, arriving at some strange airport outside of London, where we got on a train to Paris. We arrived at the Gare du Nord and went our separate ways: they to the south and me to the east. A taxi carried me and my heavy duffle bag to the Gare de l'Est. After I located the train whose final destination was Geneva, I learned I had a three-hour wait.

Nothing to do but look around. Hmmm. *There's a couple of lads, similarly equipped with large bags—could they also be climbers, bound for the same place? Just possible.* How nice it would be to find out from them some basics, because I knew absolutely nothing about Chamonix—like where to camp or the nature of the climbing there. I went over and began conversing with them, impressed by their heavy English accents. *Yes, they were climbers. Obviously British. But they didn't invite me to join them. Understandable.* Finally—toting my bag—I got on the last car, and they the second-to-last.

All the seats were sold out: standing room only. Not a problem, I thought: I'd be able to sit on my bag. Six hours later the train arrived at Chamonix, the historical center of mountain climbing for the French Alps. It was late afternoon, an hour before darkness. I was just shouldering my heavy duffle bag when I spied the same two guys up ahead. They seemed to know where they were going—so I decided to follow them at a short distance. After two blocks I caught up and excused myself, asking that they not get offended, but that I wanted to follow them to the camping area. No problem, they said, but if I really wanted to go to the "official" area, then I had to go in another direction. Pete and Andy—they introduced themselves[1]—had the plan of joining up with a few other friends from their hometown. That, in brief, is how, for the next six weeks, I became a member of a group of climbers from the old industrial city of Sheffield.

How nice it would be to find in one of the several Chamonix books in front of me (now, in 2017) a street plan of the small city, because memories now are so vague. We must have walked a half-mile from the train station, mainly uphill. I remember passing by the Mer de Glace tourist-train station, then we rounded a corner and entered onto a faint, unmarked trail leading into the woods. A quarter mile in, we came to a semi-clearing where they cheerfully greeted a couple of friends standing next to a few pitched tents. For them, this was all pre-arranged; they—and other friends soon to arrive—were quite familiar with everything. I looked around: we were surrounded by trees, we were literally in the middle of the woods. There was a primitive campfire area. I asked about relieving ourselves, and they told me that I simply had to find a tree or go 40 yards into the woods and dig a shallow hole. I inquired about showers and they explained my two options: walk a half-mile and pay to use the town's public bathroom; or wander an equal distance down through the woods to a small, almost hidden stream. I asked if it was safe to leave stuff unattended in our tents, and they answered that there were few if any reports of stolen equipment. Whew! Just in case, I would follow the normal practice of placing my passport and hundred-dollar bills in my front pocket—regardless of the pair of pants I would be wearing. I asked about other climbers. Their response: there were a few other Brits a hundred yards in, and a group of Polish climbers in the other direction and just down the wooded gully. Not many others. The whole scene was quiet and isolated, all kind of nice. They told me: "This is camping *sauvage*. Coming and going we have to be discreet. Even though it's officially not permitted, the gendarmes here are a bunch of wusses: they'll probably leave us alone."

(2017: Thumbing through the mint-condition Kodachrome slides usually stored in my basement, I see photo after photo of the beautiful peaks around Chamonix and a few taken on the five and a half climbs I ended up accomplishing. But—because I must have been committed to being a climber and not a tourist—I had taken only one shot of our campsite, none of different places in the village of Chamonix that I'll mention here, none of the spectacular *téléphérique* line [gondola] or Mer de Glace tourist-railroad, and only a few of the entertaining people that I'm going to treat in this chapter. But I do have perhaps forty slides of mountain scenery that I took while actually climbing. Funny, my different priorities, then and now.)

A few weeks into my stay, I did have the opportunity to visit the "official" and legal campsite of the area: *ugh*. It was a rest day, meaning a rainy day. We had to walk a soggy mile to get to a huge muddy grass field, bare and wet. Frankly, it was ugly, with no trees or even bushes. Several miserable tents were pitched in one corner. *Poor tourists.* It seemed to me that any real climbers would avoid the place at any cost. It was so unappealing that I didn't even inquire about other, potentially positive features, such as bathrooms or showers or nearby food stores. I never went back. End of that story.

So, whether they wanted me or not, I became a member of the Sheffield climbing community, camped together in the middle of the woods. Within two weeks we would number about 14, which included a few non-climbing girlfriends. Did I write "climbers?"—most of them were also "teddy boys" which, translated to American English, means "delinquents." Every night, just for sport, a few of them would go out raiding. A pair brought back several long three-inch-thick sausages. Do I also remember chocolates? Not sure. The only prizes they seized a few nights out were stupid touristy knick-knacks. But the best yield was the four-by-eight feet sheets of corrugated metal roofing material that they lifted from construction sites in the small city. My buddies knew well what they were doing: every third day it would rain, so all of us would benefit from a shelter. At first, they hid the roofing sheets in the woods near our tents. Ten days later, when a gendarme visit motivated us to move our camp to a protected flat spot up the hill (more on this below), there were enough sheets to protect all of us, sitting cramped together, during a whole day of piddling rain.

All of us males were there for serious climbing. I learned that Britain has its crags and rock outcroppings, but no real mountains. So for most of my Sheffield friends the dreamed-of summer excursion was a trip to Chamonix. This is where it all began, and this is where it couldn't get any better. Chamonix: the alpha and omega of the climbing world. I, a humble Yosemite devotee, had to admit: this place rivaled the Valley with the honor of being one of the most beautiful places on earth.

I wasn't the only visitor to know this. I had read accounts written by some of the most skilled free climbers in the world who had visited here to put up memorable, awe-inspiring routes. Heading this short list were two Brits, Don Whillans and Joe Brown (I'll end this digression with my own anecdote about the "Joe Brown Crack.") They were living legends who were still hanging on, but their respective moments under the climbers' sun were already behind them.

Other climbers? I admit that the relative isolation of our forest camp meant that I would not get to know too many other mountain enthusiasts. After my six-week visit I was convinced that the Brits, from different parts of the Isles, were the most hardcore of all the climbers in the range—and especially on ice routes (they had the formidable "teradactyles" that made any ice-climbing equipment available in the USA seem like children's toys). Truthfully, the few French climbers I did witness were attempting only mediocre routes (I was convinced that the glory days of Gaston Rébuffat and Lionel Terray belonged to a long and almost forgotten past). Americans? I soon learned that the only Yank who had left his mark there was Royal Robbins, with his scary route on the Dru. Had Chouinard—the French-descendant American who was one of the most outstanding climbers in the world and the manufacturer of state-of-the-art climbing equipment—done anything significant here? Anecdotes then about him were non-existent (and the few printed climbing guides available to me today as I write these words make no mention of him). Yet I do know that during the 1970s he performed an undeniable service to all us aspiring American climbers in disseminating information about the best ice-climbing techniques that he had learned from the Europeans (probably the British, maybe not the French).

***Opposite:* While on belay, I free a hand to point the camera down at my buddy Bill and the impressive ridge we had been ascending since first light (Mont Blanc de Tacul, French Alps).**

In actual fact, during my six or seven weeks in Chamonix, American climbers were noticeable for their absence. The only other American I ran into was Ben, the son of an American ambassador! A summer or two later I would run into him again in Yosemite Valley, when he would invite me to be his partner on a super-difficult route up Clouds' Rest. I would politely refuse, knowing that I was out of his stratospheric climbing league. But one afternoon I did accompany him to the elegant entrance of the Ahwahnee Hotel (where two decades earlier President Eisenhower had slept), where he scavenged some two dozen long cigarette butts, that is, enough to feed his smoking habit for a week!

(I have to stay on task: back to Chamonix, 1976.)

We were there to climb and, as soon as we arrived, plans were put into motion. Thank goodness for me, my Sheffield buddies had English-language guidebooks. Moreover, a few had spent time in Chamonix before so they knew about several appropriate or desirable routes. Also, they had extracted beta from friends.

Almost immediately they set me up with Mike. And two days later we followed Pete and Andy up the Ryan-Lochmatter Ridge of Aiguille du Plan[2]—a good warm-up climb. More so, it was a fabulous introduction to the Chamonix area. The day-long climb and early-morning jaunt across the summit ridge provided unique views of the impressive granite spires piercing the sky in every direction. To the south was the rounded snow summit of the mighty Mont Blanc (15,872 feet—Europe's highest) which, unfortunately, was almost always engulfed in clouds (in six weeks I never saw the regional giant clearly enough to warrant even one photo attempt). Berg heil!

This first experience was also a wonderful and needed—and dry!—introduction to the style of climbing that I would be doing over the next five weeks: without exception, all of us climbed with heavy, leather (usually Italian) climbing boots with Vibram soles. Climbing rope, of course (I probably had my white nylon 150-foot REI). Hammers with pitons all the way (I think I remember that even my British friends carried the newly standard Chouinard chromoly[3] pins)—and only a few of their (much less expensive) soft-steel European cousins that we might be forced to leave as anchors on an emergency rap descent. (We might also have carried a few homemade chocks or newly available commercial "nuts." Can't remember.) Twelve-point crampons and short ice axes were standard—we lashed them to the outside of our climbing packs when not in use—because nearly all routes involved glacier approaches and delicate bergschrund crossings. (Below I'll discuss ice tools for our hands.) And on almost every climb we had to carry bivy equipment: a down jacket, mitts, a pair of dry socks, and a coated-nylon or large plastic bag as protection from wind and rain (we would sit on the rope for "insulation" and "protect" the feet by jamming them into the rucksack).

Each climb usually required two bivouacs: one just before we would need to rope up at the start of the difficult climbing, and one at or near each summit. This meant that on each climb we'd suffer little or no sleep for two consecutive nights on two night-long shivers. Did I do any climb that did not require two bivies? Don't think so.

It was essential to be in rhythm with the weather, which appeared to offer a four-day pattern: one day of rain (when we stayed dry in our camp shelter), one day of transition (when, in the afternoon, we would hike up to the beginning of the climb and pass our first bivy), one day of sun (for going up the route, with the second bivy just after rounding the summit), then another day of transition (for descending in—hopefully only a—

**I'm at the right, alongside of two Sheffield buddies, Pete and Charles. The gendarmes (the police) never found our "savage" campground among the trees at the base of the French Alps. A warm sun was drying out the clothes and equipment that would be used for yet another climb on the morrow.**

light rain). After all that, we would spend a few days in camp resting, drying out equipment, and making preparations for the next climb. Figure it out: one climb per week was about as good as you could do. (As it turned out, my six weeks there allowed me to complete five climbs which—you have to believe it!—was one more than what any other buddy in my group was able to accomplish!) This doesn't include the fiasco at the end. (Noble reader, give me time! I'll get to this below.)

As a rule, the approaches were long. This was even more so for us, because my Sheffield climbing buddies didn't have a surplus of money. A ride on the *téléphérique* up to its halfway point[4] would have saved us two or three hours and a few pack-caused agonies on at least three of our approaches. But for Pete and Andy, money spent riding up would have meant fewer coins left over for savoring their treasured Guinness every Friday afternoon at Le Nacional—the only British pub that side of France. Guinness always took highest priority. As a result, our very long approaches—of perhaps 2,000 or 3,000 feet of elevation gain—made us, by the end of our Chamonix stay, in better shape than almost any of the other climbers we encountered.

Before leaving this topic, it was our relative lack of money, in addition to an ascetic climbing ethos, that led us to scorn those tourists (and tourist-climbers) who made their way, and then spent dearly, to stay overnight in one of the dozens of high-altitude chalets or lodges interspersed throughout the Alps. Maybe this was a generational—or perhaps class-based—thing. I say this because the route-guide book in my possession, written by the world-famous French guide, Gaston Rébuffat, makes constant mention of the early starts he would make with clients to climb virtually the same routes that we were then visiting. His must have been a golden age of climbing: he and his (aristocratic?) clients would slither out of their sleeping attire, sip warm cocoa, ingest hot oatmeal, and then venture out to the start of the nearby route. That wasn't the way it was with us. For us, all began with a—usually soggy—bivouac, shivering with cold and with butterflies in the gut. Then—if our lucky stars showed a clear sky at 4 a.m.—we would choke down some dry food and freeze our hands pulling on boots (I can't remember well, but on a few climbs we might have brought along sleeping bags for that first bivy which, when stashed at the beginning of the route, we would recover on the way down). On one occasion I remember spending the first night fairly close to a hut: the advantage was their supply of fresh water. But beyond that, we—in our entire time there—had nothing to do with hut-related Chamonix climbing-tourism.

My second ascent—the Vaucher Route on the Peigne—was also with Mike. He, upon finishing, had to hurriedly gather up stuff and head back to England.

There I was—in the early morning sunlight—at the side of my home-made impermeable-nylon mummy tent, eating, sorting stuff, and reading. Given the ideal sunny day, all the rest of my camping buddies had scurried off hours before to get on a route. It must have been about 8:00 a.m. To my surprise, in marched six gendarmes (city police), eager to shake tents and startle the whole group of delinquent British campers out of their drunken slumber. There was nobody to catch! All had taken off with climbing packs an hour before dawn. Witnessing this farce, I controlled my laughter. The gendarmes were not amused. Luckily, they had little interest in a lone American: they "wanted the blood of an Englishman." They left me there, but not before pulling out tent pegs and flattening all the tents save my own.

Most of my buddies straggled back to camp before darkness. It was then that we decided to move our camp up the nearby tree-covered hill. Which we did. We found a relatively flat plateau to construct our structure, covered by perhaps six—and maybe nine—sheets of corrugated roofing—that is, their raid trophies. From then on—each time—we were careful to approach our hidden camp from different directions in order to not create an obvious trail. At no other moment during our entire stay did the late-rising gendarmes demonstrate any willingness to climb the hill for a visit. To this day I wonder whether our primitive cooking structure is still in place.

On that rest day I made my way to the nearby station to pay my money (far less than the *téléphérique* fare) and take the tourist train to the Mer de Glace. For the first hour I was surrounded by pedestrians oohing and ogle-eyeing the broken topography of that rapidly receding tongue of ice. But my primary objective was to follow the trail about a kilometer further to the Argentière Glacier, where Pete and Andy had passed much earlier that morning. They were ambitious: their objective was to follow a route up the mighty Walker Spur of the Grandes Jorasses. About that route and that peak, I could only dream: the lengthy approach, the scary first-ascent history, and its overall majesty simply intimidated me. But if I were to return, a few years hence, transformed into a super-climber or

a hardened Warren Harding type, then a route up it might be feasible. Meanwhile, I just wanted to catch a view from afar.

But I had an additional objective. Since the first day all of us at the Sheffield camp had been boldly talking about doing at least one ice route during our visit here. The most obvious objectives were various routes up two peaks—Les Courts and Les Droites—whose ice faces rose up from the same glacier I was then on. In the next two days Pete, Andy, Deek, John, and I shared the same opinion: that the low snow accumulation of the previous winter, when coupled to the above-average seasonal heat of the summer, made it so that ice was too scarce on either peak for any satisfactory—or safe—climbing. But if per chance a storm were to temporarily alter those conditions…? Yes: suspension marks in our minds. (Have I adequately anticipated your curiosity about what will follow, dear reader?)

Poor Pete and Andy. They were out-of-step with the weather: their sunny approach was not followed by an equally fine day for their climb. In late afternoon the next day, thoroughly soaked and walking miserably in the drizzle, they came straggling back into camp, having abandoned the route and their Walker Spur dream. They must have experienced a close call, because for the rest of our time there it seemed that they couldn't get back on track for successful climbing.

That same long, boring day—as the rest of us listened to the pitter-patter of the rain—we kept mostly dry under our corrugated roof. If there was a highlight, it was a person reading aloud from the hottest number of the camp: a paperback, torn in the middle for a double circulation—*Death to the French* by E.M. Forster—whose title captured our party's imagination more than the actual narration about British sea-battle victories in the age of Napoleon.

And meanwhile, I had found another rope partner: Bill Wayne—another Brit, but from a London neighborhood. Our chosen shake-out climb was the Vaucher Route up the Aiguille du Peigne (rated TD—*très difficile*). Not too much to report, except that we climbed wonderfully together. What impressed me was Bill's almost "anal-retentive" insistence on adding his own new half-inch webbing loop to every rock anchor for every rappel. Safe we were.

Another memorable moment that I snatch now from the vaults of near-forgotten memory: One late afternoon we wandered down through

***Opposite:* Three constants about climbing in the French Alps: majestic topography, physical challenge, and uncertainty about the weather.**

the woods to the encampment of a group of young Polish climbers. It still mystifies me how they had been able to leave their Iron Curtain country (in the pre–Perestroika era) in order to partake of this wonderful climbing paradise. Unfortunately, communication between us was not ideal. A few of their number spoke some French, and I did also, so a minimal exchange of ideas was possible. Mostly, though, it was the warm energy that radiated between and among a whole throng of committed climbers: we knew that all of us belonged to the same exalted brotherhood. One of the Polish lads took a guitar in hand and played song after song from his Beatles repertoire—each and every one of his songs rendered in a very broken English. At one point he asked me, "Lit eet bee"—*Qu'est-ce que ça vous dire? Qu'est-ce que ça vous dire*?

Then Bill and I executed the climb of my dreams: the Gervasutti Pillar on Mont Blanc de Tacul (also rated TD—*très difficile)*, which can be described as a long day of sustained 5.7—easily 15 pitches—climbing up a ridge of majestic granite spires. (At least twice a year I enter a jewelry store at the O'Hare airline terminal in Chicago [just entering the H corridor] where I feast my eyes—yet one more time—on the enchanting glass-illuminated photo of this marvelous line.) Both of our bivies—before and after—were spent in the frigid *téléphérique* station at the top of the Aiguille du Midi. Before dawn on our climbing day we trekked for an hour up, down, and across the high 3,700-meter (12,000-foot) ridge, sinking in snow up to our knees. Getting onto the route, we knew we had to climb fast. We saw a party easily two pitches ahead of us and, a few hours later, were able to detect yet another party four pitches below (as it turned out: poor dudes!) Toward afternoon, the thunderclouds, thickening overhead, motivated us to accelerate our climbing pace. Topping off and attaining the snow ridge (and an easy and safe way down), we wondered how the party below us was going to deal with the added danger of falling snow. Even hustling our butts, we got back to the *téléphérique* station just as flashlights began to feel needed. In all, it had been a full day of wonder, with majestic gendarmes (the rock peaks, not the police), ever-present danger, high-angle challenges, and our own contribution of well-executed teamwork. What other superlatives could I add here in order that the reader appreciate our climbing joy?

Early the next morning, our frigid gondola descent. By early afternoon Bill had left me to return to his own tent and campsite, and I was to have yet another memorable "cultural" experience. There I was exhausted, grubby, dirty, sticky with dried sweat. With towel and clean clothing in hand, I took the ten-minute walk down through the deserted forest to the small stream at the bottom of a wide, three-meter-deep gully. I stripped down, waded up to my thighs, and was shampooing my hair, when voices surprised me. Up there, standing on the gully edge, was a foursome of gendarmes! I saw the gleam in their leader's eyes: he had finally caught one, and in the act of violating a known ordinance. They let me get dressed, but carefully retained my dirty tennies in their hands—obviously to keep me from running away. In single file, they escorted me for the 20-minute walk down to their station. When I pulled out my American passport, I saw the disappointed droop of the lieutenant's face. The English Teddy-boys had eluded him again! Dutifully, he wrote up (or pretended to write up) my data in his log book. It was obvious they then wanted to dispense of me: I was not their intended prey. Without fining me, without a word of reproach, they escorted me to the door. And I walked back to our campsite, unable to decide whether I should feel mirth or concern.

The next day, a cold front came in, accompanying a fierce summer storm that lasted at least 48 hours. The first of those stormy days I put on my raincoat, wandered down to the highway, and hitched through the Mont Blanc tunnel to the first Italian town. I was worried about the growing holes in the tops of both of my climbing boots: could I obtain a decent replacement pair in a shoe or equipment store there? I had a 40-minute conversation with a salesperson—me talking in Spanish and he in Italian. He then surprised me with the astonishing question—in response to our obviously belabored conversation: if I was from Southern Italy? (Was he wondering if I were the son of a Sicilian mafioso?) Interesting.

The second storm day was Sunday and—if I remember right—we descended *en masse* to pass the long afternoon and evening hours in the Nacional, surrounded by warm, dry, and intoxicated British climbers.

Seeing the huge, unseasonal snow/hail accumulation, all of us from the Sheffield group were silently wondering: Could all this possibly affect, in a positive way, the condition of the ice routes? Sure enough, an exploratory bus trip the next day demonstrated this to be the case. So we all made ready.

Three teams from our Sheffield encampment had independently decided on the route of choice: the Swiss Direct of Les Courts (according to Rébuffat, it consisted of "an extremely steep ice slope"). The next day all of us—Pete and Andy, Deek and John, Bill W. and I—left camp about noon to make the long approach under a light drizzle, up to the Argentière Glacier and then to a semi-protected site for our bivouac just under the steep glacier toe. This was the exact site where, with the first light of the morrow, we would have to rope up and put on crampons. It was a typical, uncomfortable bivouac. About three in the morning, I glanced up. *Yes, there were stars.* The clouds had disappeared. *Yes. God existed. It was going to be a sunny day.* About an hour later—again in total darkness—I glanced up again and saw that the stars had disappeared, meaning that it was almost dawn and that the moment had come for us to get started. We forced dried food down our throats, pulled on cold (but thankfully not frozen) boots, and strapped on crampons.

In the palest of light, Bill and I were ready first, so off we went. Belay on. Going down, then climbing up the steep frontal glacier wall was not fun. But the stomach did not tighten, having little inside. The two other Brit teams—each with teradactyles in their hands, were following close behind (I had my trusty ol' Chouinard ice hammer in one hand, and a [very deficient] short ice axe in the other). Once on the glacier, it was icy and "steep"—the guidebook description had not lied. From start to finish we belayed. Three pitches up Bill Wayne and I realized that the other two parties, either less courageous or more prudent than ourselves, had turned back, refusing to venture onto the route.

I don't remember the details, and I won't make up a heroic story. We climbed and climbed, almost mechanically. At the end of each pitch the leader had to struggle to get in a pair of ice screws: the ice was either too thin or too inconsistent for firm placements. All this took time. For me the entire climb was an exercise—like a few other very hard routes I've done—in repressing fear and concentrating on what had to be done. After the first two pitches, we realized that turning around and retracing our route back down the ice wall would be even more dangerous than continuing to go on up. So, as light was fading, and after an extremely long and nerve-racking day, we pulled ourselves onto the summit block. We were not elated, but incredibly relieved. There we bivied. The next day all was easy and safe: we rappelled down the rocky south face. End of that story.

Well, not quite. After that experience on the Swiss Direct, I never again—during my whole, long career as a climber—ventured onto another steep, dangerous ice route. I had seen displays of how the best-driven ice screws bend—at best—when they catch a long fall. And I had heard stories and had seen first-hand how difficult it was to place the perfect screw (what with the variables in ice quality or depth). After months of nightmares after our day on the Swiss Direct, I came to the realization that safe climbing would be best guaranteed only when placing my pro into cracks of rock and not into ice surfaces.

All of our Sheffield buddies congratulated Bill and me upon our return, and stories were muffled about why the other four had turned back. Were we admired? We were certainly praised. But that didn't compensate for the burnt-out feeling experienced by us both. The end of our time there in Chamonix was approaching, and we felt done-in—both physically and mentally. We were ready to return to our respective homes.

But we did still have a few more days, and the good weather seemed to be holding. *"Just one more route? A shorter one, one with no bivouac?"* Hmmm. "Here the guide shows the West Face of the Blaitière—it's long, but we're climbing strong and can do it in a day." Hmmm. *"A Joe Brown Crack? Sure, he was good. His first ascent of this route was in 1954. Anything the best of that breed was doing back then would be a piece of cake for us today, right? It's got an easy approach under the first tram of the* téléphérique. *Let's go for it. Okay?"*

The next morning, after a short, easy glacier approach, we started out on the rock face of the Blaitière. It was a marvelous, sunny day. After a fast three pitches up, we saw two parties just ahead of us. Bummer. This is one of the most unpleasant of all climbing experiences: having to wait behind (what we first considered to be) slow ropes above us on the same route. Ouch: not one team, but two, ahead of us. They were stopped. Now so were we.

But we had caught up to them, stalled before the famous Joe Brown Crack,[5] and not—what we had previously imagined—by their timidity or lack of experience. We had to wait in line. From the first party, first one climber, then the next, gave it his best to get up the 70-degree-slanted, flared, jam crack. It was too wide for any possible aid (anyway, who carries a 7-inch chock? Nobody). There were no real hand holds. You had to get your foot and leg in and then lean back and/or jam with the upper arm. Then you wiggle your way up. If you can. But there's nothing to grab on to. Everything is rounded.

The two climbers of the first rope spent three-quarters of an hour trying, then finally gave up and rapped on down. Here, how can I represent with feeble words the time very slowly passing, our tedium and frustration, and the cold creeping into first the bones, then the spirit? Then came the turn for the two climbers of the second rope, while our own desire to continue climbing was dramatically cooling. Their attempts? It is only necessary to say, "ditto"—the same as what had happened 45 minutes before. Finally … finally it was our turn. I scurried up the thirty feet to the beginning of the crack and tried, backed down, then tried again. (I could write the word "tried" as "tired" without misrepresenting my reality at the time.) Then I descended to Bill's level, who was still on belay. It was his turn. I took his place at the anchor and he went on up. He tried, and he tried again, then he came back down to my level to go back on belay. I went up again. And I tried. Then Bill took his turn at a second try. No way: neither of us could get up it. There was no way to cheat by aiding it. Worse: there was no alternative route to go around it. You've got to hand it to Joe Brown: his ascent—a half-century earlier—had been formidable. "You're a better man than I am, Gunga Din."

The only direction left for Bill and me: to go on back down. So we did three routine raps (with "anal" Bill leaving a new piece of webbing at every anchor). In an hour we were down, standing on the snow, with ahead of us (what appeared to be) an easy snow-field slope down the couloir that bottomed out onto the glacier below. Our first inclination was to coil up the rope to carry it over my shoulder, turn to face inward, and kick steps downward into the hard snow.

Bill, a bit above me and some thirty feet away, called out, "Hey, it might be easier descending this first part facing out with a shoulder rappel. Just this first part. Can you throw up the end of the rope?" I had been busy coiling it, and was ready to defer to super-safe Bill in making this call. "Sounds great to me." Bill: "Here, I found a ski pole that we can use as an anchor. I'll pass the rope around it." Bill, overly prudent Bill, was taking the initiative, setting it all up, so I didn't pay too much attention. Then, with thirty feet of double rope around his anchor, he started tensioning on down. After fifteen small steps, he was now slightly below my level. Suddenly he shouted and disappeared. That is, he fell … and hard.

Turns out that what we had taken for a somewhat easy snow slope immediately below us turned out to be the upper lip of a bergschrund that neither of us had seen nor imagined to be there. Bill, arriving at its upper edge, with the rope only draped over his shoulders, slipped in. The ski pole might have held him, but he—unthinking—had threaded the rappel rope through the weak leather hand strap, which had broken with his

**I've always felt that pro in rock is preferable to pro in ice.**

violent tug. He fell thirty feet straight down, hitting against the rock at the bottom of the crevasse.

Carefully, I made my way down to his side. He was in terrible pain and his leg was bent at an obscene angle. It was a no-brainer: I had to descend to get a rescue party. After cramponing up and out, it took me 30 minutes to goose-step down the glacier and cross to the mid-station of the *téléphérique*, where they let me use the telephone. In broken French I explained what had happened, and they said that in 20 minutes they'd be able to dispatch a helicopter. But arrive where? They asked if I could get back up there to signal to the pilot? Of course. Huff, huff, running up hill on the softened snow. Forty minutes later, I was exhausted. But then the chopper came, and it hovered while one person slid down a rope ladder to stand beside me. Then, after that, the personnel in the chopper passed down a stretcher. Then they flew away, yelling that they'd be back when we were finally ready and able to send them the radio signal.

The rescue man and I then lowered the stretcher to the bottom of the bergschrund and alongside of Bill—who was by then crazy with pain. He put a pain-control thing into Bill's mouth who, after wheezing in deep breaths for a minute, communicated to us that the pain was easing. We strapped him in. Then, it took all our force, added to a rope belay, to push, lift, and pull Bill-plus-stretcher over the lip of the crevasse and secure it/them to the sloping surface. My rescue-buddy radioed for the chopper to return and we slid the metal stretcher, containing my agonized buddy, a quarter mile down to a less-steep section of the glacier. There, the helicopter landed and we loaded Bill in. Did I want to go down with them? Of course! Within twenty minutes we landed at the Chamonix hospital.

A day later I visited Bill, with his leg now in traction. He would have to stay in the hospital for days—perhaps weeks. In the best of cases he would wear a cast up to his chest for the next six weeks. That meant that there was no way he would be able to mount his cycle, cross half of France and then the channel, and then return to his parents' home near Oxford. He understood clearly that he would have to find a place to store his cycle somewhere in Chamonix until the next year and, within a few weeks, return to London via the train. We clasped hands. It was as intimate a gesture as I have ever given to a buddy who had shared such dramatic moments at the other end of my rope. We said good-bye. Best of luck, good buddy.

Now, writing almost a half-century later, I believe it appropriate to mention two more "casualties" of that eventful month climbing with *mi tocayo* Bill. We knew we had accomplished something bordering on greatness in having risked life and limb going up that ice route of Les Courts. Therefore, at his hospital bed, we both agreed to select the best five slides from the photos we had respectively taken, copy and send them via the mail to each other. Back home in Michigan, I went through my own slides, selected the most outstanding five, and sent them off in the mail to be copied. I never saw them again. And I felt apologetically guilty when I received his five in the mail some weeks later and had to write that I had nothing to send him in return.

Well, the second "casualty" has been my three attempts, over the past four decades, to make further personal contact with Bill. In the early eighties, a returned letter must have signified his change of address. Then, during a library research visit to Oxford in the mid–1980s, I attempted to travel to the last address he had given me on our elapsed correspondence. I was not successful, mainly on account of the confusion experienced with the mixture of British wards, districts, parishes, and postal zones. The third occasion: yet another failed attempt, only in the past year, to have my new letter fall into the hands of a family member or remote acquaintance—I had written on the front of the letter, "Please forward if his address is known." No luck. Old friendships, like old memories, "never die, they just fade away."

Back at camping *sauvage*, all of us were making final preparations to depart. But we had to have one last celebration. All of us—minus Bill—chipped in: it would be a chocolate fondue extravaganza. Pete and Andy had to sacrifice their last week's Guinness allotment for such a worthy cause. There it was: a pot full of hot, melted chocolate, and a plate heaped with ripe fruit pieces. We had enough for a royal pig-out—for all eight or ten of us. We began. The first dipped piece: "Delicious." The second, hmm, "Quite sweet." The third, "Well, it's OK." The fourth: "Don't know how much chocolate I really want to consume." The fifth: "Hey guys, I think I'll pass this turn." The sixth: "Guys, I'm already feeling a pain in the gut, so I guess I'll have to stop." "Me too. That stuff is really too much."

I don't know whose pot it was, but he ended up with it ⅔ full of chocolate which, I'm sure, must have hardened within a few hours. Chocolate and Chamonix, I'll love you both forever.

## Chapter 5

# Canadian Rockies Redux[1]

I made a fabulous choice for my 2014 end-of-summer climbing junket: the Canadian Rockies. The 200-mile stretch between Banff and Jasper—along the western boundary of Alberta—is simply marvelous, with a new breathtaking alpine scene at every curve in the highway. With the exception of Yosemite, there is no more spectacular region on the entire North American continent.

My vehicle was ideal for the occasion: a small pickup truck with a topper, under which I spent my nights. A fold-up chair and the lowered tailgate provided adequate furnishings for rest days and cooking.

I was traveling in time and space to an unfamiliar culture. What I did see is recorded in the following pages. But right here it is appropriate to list a few things that I did *not* see: ugly billboards; straight highways or signage going through cities; available tent sites in designated areas along the highway after 2 p.m.; highway patrol cars; dirty public bathrooms; cheap food or low fees for trail overnights; thunderstorm-free afternoons; a Canadian person opposing shale-oil, natural gas, or pipeline development; campground Nazis; a young generation of climbers getting off the beaten track.

I chose "redux" as the title for this chapter because I was returning to peaks that I had climbed some forty years ago with my legendary partner, Don Fredrickson. The two of us had successfully ascended several difficult north-face routes. My idea for the summer of 2014 was to return to the most memorable of those peaks, but this time I would scamper solo up easier routes to gain those same summits.

In a pamphlet entitled, "A Scrambler's Guide to Mount Temple," published by Banff National Park, Mt. Temple (3,543 meters; 11,621 feet) is described as "the prominent triangular-shaped peak capped with ice and snow that towers above the hamlet of Lake Louise. While there are technical routes up the main face, a moderate scramble (elevation gain 5,543 feet) is hidden from view on the southwest side of the mountain."

**I had a weird experience during the few weeks spent writing this chapter: I dreamt that Don's spirit was attempting to communicate with me. The italicized paragraphs below present my best effort to capture his messages.

*Don: Remember: we had just come from a frustrating, rainy week in the Bugaboos, and our decrepit Volvo losing its transmission forced a week layover between Calgary and Lake Louise—we were on our way to the Cathedral Spires in the Alaska Range. We both remembered vague details from the Lowe brothers' article about their new route up Temple's north face in the previous year's issue of the AAJ. We ditched our sleeping bags and packs at Lake Annette (where the chipmunks devoured our packs' shoulder straps!) and ventured into the prominent gully, crossing our fingers that the loose rock or ice (from the hanging glacier above) would not choose that moment to pulverize us with an ill-timed avalanche. Remember that horrifying traverse west with crampons over verglas on a high horizontal ledge, that we pretended to protect with a tied-off Lost Arrow?—in those days we climbed only with our trusty sling of pitons. Then, higher up, a strenuous mixed-climbing pitch over snow-covered ribs in the middle of the glacier. That long day ended with an epic bivy in soft snow just short of the summit ridge. Come morning with trepidation we threaded our way between cornices on one side and an unseen drop-off on the other—in total whiteout—to the summit, then to a secure descent along the scree-covered southwest ridge. It's no surprise to learn that only a handful of teams have chosen to repeat that route since.*

The walk-up route of the southwest ridge was on grey, dry rock the entire way: what a dramatic contrast to the snow and ice-covered north face of decades before! But this backside route was ideal for familiarizing myself with the weather and getting my legs and lungs ready for whatever I would ask of them in the days ahead. A very helpful employee at the Information Center had shown me a new book—*A Scrambler's Guide to the Canadian Rockies*—and then gave me a folded, one-page, colored handout with the scamper information specific to Mt. Temple. For better or worse I was going to go up an advanced tourist trail. It departs from the luxurious tourist lodge (frequented by buses full of free-spending Japanese and Chinese tourists) on beautiful Lake Moraine. A surprise trail regulation was the prohibition of any party numbering less than four as protection from the bears! The trail to Sentinel Pass is superb, passing through exquisite alpine meadows and, with the clear day, we enjoyed views of the majestic glaciated peaks to the south. Fortunately, by August—in this epoch of global warming—enough snow had melted that I and the half-dozen others near me needed neither ice axe nor crampons. The day was long and exhausting due to the 5,543 feet of elevation gain that we then had to descend. But the path was hard to lose, given that hundreds of young adventurers every season choose this unique route to gain the summit of a most impressive peak via a path that—surprisingly—is devoid of technical difficulties.

After two days of R&R I found myself ninety miles to the north at the Columbian Ice Fields, "a magnificent field of ice" winding some 140 miles on a wide plateau, feeding eight major glaciers, spanning the Continental Divide and the boundary between Jasper and Banff national parks. With crampons (purchased at the end of the 1970s for a second rain-aborted attempt at Robson's North Face) and ice axe, it took me three hours to thread my way around crevasses, up alongside dramatic ice falls, and then out onto the upper plateau, before prudence—in reaction to the sight of snow-covered hidden crevasses—dictated that I not proceed further without a partner and a rope. In all, it was a neat, dramatic jaunt.

**That's me; I'm on belay in the Sawtooths. Each mixed ascent required ice axe, pitons, and hammer.**

The next day I was off to Mt. Athabasca (3,491

meters; 11,450 feet), the spectacular peak just to the south of the Ice Fields' tourist center. The peak's large glacier descending the north face, visible from the highway, offers some of the most popular and accessible snow/ice outings (and photos) in the region. My choice was the North Glacier Route (grade II) that follows up the center of the glacier then traverses right up under seracs (overhanging surfaces) to the north side (in August this rocky rib is bare of snow) and onto the summit ridge.

*Don: Back then we also did routes on Andromeda and Randall. We used our primitive ice tools: a trusty Chouinard ice hammer and a short ice axe whose pick we ourselves had notched to have it stick better when swung deep into the ice. My memories are now vague: didn't we climb a line to the left of Chouinard's North Face Route—a line not represented in the guidebook now in vogue? I remember kicking steps up firm snow, without any real ice to speak of. That must have been early in the climbing season, because I understand that in recent years by mid–August parties will be climbing on a lot of hard, slippery, ice.*

Like every climb this trip, I went alone. My new mountain religion insists on eating a substantial breakfast and leaving the car-camping site with sufficient natural light to avoid route-finding problems. This was significantly later than our customary get-going hour in the 1970s. Why be masochistic? I calculated—rightly, in every instance—that a brisk pace would get me to the summit and down again with ample time to avoid the afternoon thunderstorms. Two other parties, with less experience, had departed hours before me and had roped up at the bottom of the glacier. But I assessed there to be almost no danger of hidden crevasses due to the lateness of the season. With my well-honed scampering skills, and going super light (not having to carry rope, pickets, or screws), I simply delighted on the traverse over the snow-covered glacier and received a slight adrenaline rush kicking straight up to avoid a few small crevasses and gain the ice and rock of the north ridge. In a whiteout I met at the summit a party of Canadian Army trainees; gods forbid that these inexperienced novices would constitute the rescue party if I were to have an unfortunate accident. Thankfully, those same gods lifted the clouds for four minutes to provide all of us with a fantastic photo opportunity. The other climbers chose to go down the scree-covered west ridge while I elected to reverse my path and descend the way I had come up. This would not have been a wise decision had the day been sunny, because soupy, heavy, snow might have added danger to the descent.

Two more days of R&R and my legs were ready for the third of my four main objectives: the mighty Mt. Edith Cavell (3,363 meters; 11,031 feet), another 60 miles to the north of the Ice Fields and some 10 miles south of the small park-village of Jasper. "The typically snow-covered north face [of this], the highest mountain in the vicinity of Jasper, dominates the southern skyline from the township."[2] Applying my personal definition that a worthy mountain "inspires both majesty and dread," Mt. Edith Cavell leans heavily to the latter. In the second of my two rest days killing time in a Jasper parking area, I intentionally avoided letting my gaze fall upon its ever-visible profile, not wanting to add psychological weight to the difficulties that I knew I would experience on the morrow.

*Don: Its north face was definitely one of the most demanding—both mentally and physically—of the hard climbs we did back then. With bulky headlights we climbed unroped up the loose fourth-class rock under the glacier, then traversed left on a fragile ledge to our ridge, where we finally starting belaying. It was a long day of sustained mixed climbing. At dusk we punched our way through the summit cornice and then fumbled in encroaching darkness down the west-ridge descent. The last stretch in complete darkness along the road and back to the car were the longest two miles I have ever walked. We were so fatigued that it was only hours later that our bodies were willing to accept more than a sip of life-restoring water—and any food had to wait till daylight. It was a glorious climb, one of the finest lines anywhere in the Canadian Rockies. What? Bill, you're telling me that today, after four decades of global warming, the route has almost no snow or ice on it, that it—to all appearances—is no more than a sustained 5.7 rock climb? That blows my mind! Well, I continue basking in personal glory, knowing that some 40 years ago you and I climbed in great style one of the greatest, I said greatest, climbs in the whole range.*

The East Ridge Route is rated III, 5.3. As on all three other climbs, I was dressed only in a nylon bathing suit, a white long-sleeved cotton dress shirt (I can govern body temperature by rolling up or down the sleeves or opening its front buttons for greater ventilation), a baseball cap, and light approach shoes with non-slip soles. In the pack I carried a tight-fitting fleece vest, a stocking cap, wind pants, a wind jacket and a light down jacket (never used, for an emergency only). I had a minimum of food and water. Oh! I've discovered a wonderful new trail food: a small easy-open can of whole-kernel corn that is sweet, moist, and filling.

Rating 5.3? In no way is the word "scamper," for me, a euphemism for free, unroped climbing. I would be very reluctant to do a solo scamper up the exposed Upper Exum on the Grand—of similar technical difficulty—but a 5.3 *ridge* route in the Canadian Rockies is much less dangerous. Most of the way up is 3rd class, and there are only a few 5th class moves, most of which have minimal exposure. Knowledge about many individuals previously not roping up for this route added to my confidence.

On the way up the lower part of the route I decided, correctly, that my own route-finding skills for scamper routes (that I had honed on Owen and Nez Percé in the Tetons) would provide me with a more solid and interesting path than the well-trampled, loose-scree stretches of the regular route. I chose my own path, being careful to place about 30 small personal cairns to mark my way if I were to choose to down-climb the same path (this type of marking proved indispensable in the Tetons, where I had learned—almost the hard way—that route finding while ascending is far easier, and safer, than while descending). Later the inch accumulation of hailstones led to my decision to go down the same route. Even so, while descending that immense south face, I had trouble locating my cairns. As a result, I almost got onto dangerous terrain, and me without a rappel rope or slings for anchors. Yes, the "dread" was still in force. Lesson learned, but thankfully not a costly one.

Otherwise, the climb went quite well: I took no crampons or ice axe, and neither was needed for the snowfield leading up to the col above the tourist-destination lake. And the 5.3 moves on the upper part of the route were few, even though they were airy. (Another personal lesson: I must keep practicing down-climbing technique on every visit to Devil's Lake: safely descending easy fifth class is perhaps the most difficult part of scamper-climbing.) At about 11 a.m., after I had climbed the hardest part of the route and with the summit still about 20 minutes away, I took my eyes off the spectacular views on three sides and happened to glance backward. Uh oh. I saw a very dark weather front that was advancing rapidly. It was a no-brainer to turn around immediately in order to get down the fifth-class moves before everything became slippery-wet. Now, weeks later, I regret not having passed on to the summit and then continuing that same line descending down the other side. Oh well. But still I felt that I successfully completed what I had set out to do. Morally, if not physically, I had done the climb. Agreed? Well, any other opinion on this issue does not really count.

Descend I did. Delicately down-climbing the exposed 5.3 moves, it took me a half-hour to return to the exposed plateau and my pack before the horizontal rains hit. Freaky—and a bit scary—was the buzzing I heard all around me: static electricity? With no bomb shelter near, I could only hustle my butt. Mentally I celebrated the fact that I carried no steel hammer or rack of chromoly pitons—as I surely had had with me forty years earlier. Finding a large boulder on the ridge, I scooped away rocks and wedged myself in just as the thundering rain turned to hail. I took off my dripping cotton shirt and slipped into the fleece vest. With it against my torso, cold—luckily—was not an issue—as long as I was continuing my descent and generating body heat.

Two hours later I was on relatively safe terrain. The renewed sunshine had already dried the cotton shirt, again covering my upper torso. But new dark clouds convinced me that only with extra hustle would I avoid getting drenched a second time. So after finally gaining the trail, I found it preferable to prance rather than hike on down. With a flushed face, I slid into the car only seconds before the deluge. But how to explain the behavior of a dozen crazy tourists who chose to ignore those ominous black clouds?

An hour later: what a joy to "talk shop" with a pair of young climbers over hamburgers and fries back in Jasper—but my hot-wired body still balked at any refueling with beer. I had met them on the summit ridge, and even with my problematic route-finding descent, I had beat them down by a half-hour. After another lonely parking-lot night, I drove back to Lake Louise to prepare for the climax climb of that year's August climbing junket: Mt. Assiniboine (3,618 meters; 11,867 feet).

"Mount Assiniboine is a most striking mountain with a certain resemblance to the more famous Matterhorn in Switzerland."[3] Or Alpamayo in Peru. It is one of the most photographed peaks in the whole range, and—because of the 23-mile approach from the Alberta (east) side—it is also one of the least visited.

*Don: Bill, your talk of ["redux"] gives the readers a false impression: back then we never climbed that peak. You only wanted to climb it. Every trip to the Canadian Rockies we fantasized, but never felt sufficiently committed in order to suffer the long hike in. Finally masochism won out over pragmatism?*

As it turned out, no. There I was, again within thirty miles of that peak, after a 40-year hiatus. I got to thinking: if I don't climb it this time… Inquiring, I found out that for $150 I could fly to the tourist lodge on day one, make the climb the next, and on the third begin (put a stress on this last word) the purgatory hike out. Although the price sounded reasonable, there was a complication: how would I get my fatigued body, after 23 miles, back to the car?

Another visit to the helpful Information Center provided another, and this time more favorable, alternative. A two-hour drive west from Lake Louise, half of which was on a dirt road, would take me to a seldom-visited trailhead, from which a hike to the climbers' hut on the skirts of Assiniboine would take only seven hours! The perfect solution. So within an hour of finding this out, I called in and reserved—for $25—a bunk in the climbing hut for the next night. I still feel a bit guilty: this was the only time during the entire trip—and perhaps during an entire climbing career—that I have paid for overnight privileges at a hut.

So I was off to the mountain of my dreams. Rains in the previous months had eroded the road, so I had to park 1.5 miles from its end. Arriving at the official start to the almost unmarked trail, I saw that other adventurers, after having parked their two 4x4 pickups there, had wrapped the car undersides with chicken wire to protect against voracious porcupines that prefer brake lines to power bars.

After a few hours, the climbers' trail took me past a beautiful secluded lake, then another mile up to the carved-out valley where my Cro-Magnon ancestors probably had to walk on ice. I finally put on my crampons for the high glacier, on which a thunderstorm caused a quarter-inch sheet of water to run down its entire width. After a nasty 15-minute scamper up sliding boulders, I gained the col and was able to see, down below, my destination for the night: the Canadian Alpine Club's hut. Four other climbers were already there: a guide plus client who had climbed earlier; and two other individuals whom I would join on the summit the next day. From the hut, there was a perfect view of the normal North Ridge Route (II, 5.5), and its start was only twenty minutes away.

The next morning I had only 3,000 vertical feet to ascend. Mentally, I was ready to negotiate the dark grey mass above me, even though it hardly resembled the snow-covered triangle of photo-memories (and dreams). I made the summit in less than three hours. The fifth-class moves—mainly to get through two bands of harder rock near the summit—were a bit more airy than on Edith Cavell. On the summit ridge, which dropped off vertically to the southwest, I experienced stomach gyrations looking straight down upon the hanging glacier a thousand feet below. And with perfect weather, the neighboring peaks, along with Assiniboine's gendarmes, made for fabulous photos. I was finally here.

An indication of the seriousness of down-climbing the same route was that it took me the same time as its ascent. I was at the hut before noon, and I reached the car before six. For those who read this and might be inclined to venture here, the ten or so slings protecting the route's harder portions would make this an ideal easy route for roped fourth-class or simul-climbing. But be warned: the loose rock on the lower part of the route could be treacherous with another party above you.

*Don: Bill, you are in an ideal position to reflect upon how the passage of forty warming years has changed these beautiful peaks and the nature of climbing them.*

*Bill: It's interesting to note that these days, in early August, all four summits are remarkably alike: the slightly corniced snow ridges curve and then fall vertically down to cover the upper part of spectacular north faces. But you can walk safely along rocks on the south side of each of those ridges where the snow has totally melted. I would predict that any August in recent years one could summit from the backside of most peaks in the range without touching snow or ice. I've already suggested that in no moment on any of these summits did I experience sufficient cold—except when I was damp from thunderstorms—that made it necessary to pull my windbreaker over my thin cotton shirt. I have just reviewed the slides I took 40 years ago of our climbs on Temple, Randall, Athabasca, Andromeda, and Edith Cavell. Immediately apparent is the abundance of snow everywhere. Back then, we did mixed climbs, moving primarily on rock with either hard or loose snow. Today, with so much melting, many routes in the early season might require passage over kickable hard snow. But by late season you will probably find no such snow, only ice—hard, slippery, dangerous ice. This is true for Sky Ladder, for Andromeda, and for north-face routes on Athabasca. I also remember how necessary it was, 40 years ago, to carry a cagoule and a down jacket for the icy winds that whipped you at the cols, on the ridges, and certainly at the summits. Today, forget all that. With accurate weather reports, and with consistently warm temperatures at high elevations, you can get by with significantly less.*

Four summits were enough. Any more would amount to overkill. Or I would suffer the law of diminishing returns. On all accounts, this was a quite successful trip: I faithfully accomplished what I had set out to do. But I have to admit not feeling the elation of before. Was it the accumulated fatigue of four scamper climbs? Was it the predictably blasé reaction to OD'ing on too much mountain beauty? I suggest yet another important reason: I missed the wilderness experience. That is to say, my gymnastic achievements were performed in a civilized context, what with huts, worn paths, detailed route descriptions, reliable weather reports, and shared summits. Redux climbing, I realized, can only be a pale reflection of past adventures.

Or had I aimed too low? The area deserves a return trip. Awaiting are scores of impressive peaks equally aesthetic but far less civilized. And I still leave Mt. Robson unclimbed (two attempts foiled by rain in the 1970s). Thank the gods we'll never run out of mountains. Berg Heil!

## Chapter 6

# Huascarán

One of the greatest joys of this 71-year-old climber has been to revisit the scene of former exploits. There we were in Huaraz, Peru, in October 2016, for five days of tourism and investigation. Only 30 kilometers away was Huascarán, the highest peak of Peru (at 6,768 meters, or 22,208 feet)[1] and the gem of the country's Cordillera Blanca.

Every step along the streets of Huaraz, and during the day-long hike out of the small indigenous village of Shilla, my mind echoed the wonderful memories of the seven or so weeks I had spent with my two climbing buddies between June and July 1974, going up routes in the northern range and culminating with six exhilarating days on the East Face of Huascarán Sur.

Chronological order? Jim Milne and I met in Ann Arbor, Michigan, where he, of New Zealand origins, was an assistant professor of math, and I a graduate student beginning my doctoral thesis in Spanish/Latin American studies. I ignore or have forgotten what brought us together, but there are few serious climbers anywhere in the Midwest, so perhaps our encounter was eventual. After frustrated attempts through our contacts in the USA to interest another pair of climbers to climb with us in Peru, a desperate Jim wrote to a fellow Kiwi, Mike Andrews, who was mentioned in some climbing magazine, and who was then residing in Peru. Surprise of surprises, the letter made it into his hands and he answered affirmatively, under the condition that we would bring for him an ice axe and a pair of crampons. Arriving at Lima's international airport, there was Mike waiting for us, sporting a beard, covered by a wool Peruvian cap, and smelling like a llama.

Jim deserves most of the credit for researching the Cordillera Blanca and our possible routes and for contacting H. Adams Carter, of the

American Alpine Club. Following the latter's advice, we decided to spend most of our time in the northern part of the range, near the much-photographed Alpamayo where, we decided, we would attempt only first ascents. (The *AAJ's* 1971 issue provided us with a fine map.[2]) Then, we would return to Huaraz for R&R before culminating our Peruvian trip with an attempt—it would be the second ascent—of the ANZUS Route[3] on Huascarán Sur's mighty, two-kilometer-long East Face. As it turned out, our freedom from health problems (almost all the international parties during that climbing season reported serious cases of hepatitis), good planning and weather, and the benevolence of the Mountain Gods, made it so that we were able to accomplish almost everything we attempted—and in magnificent style.

Over the first two weeks spent coming and going out of Huaraz that were necessary for acclimatization, we made three important decisions that were to impact favorably upon our plans for the rest of the trip. First, in an early excursion to a south-facing glacier I routinely thrust my ice-axe shaft downward before taking the next step and received the shock of my life: visual evidence that two of us were standing on the fragile surface of a bottomless cavern which was totally unmarked by the usual surface-level indicators. From that moment on we made the (possibly life-saving) decision to avoid or limit whenever possible any glacier travel. Period. That meant our future routes would have to follow perilous corniced ridges and very steep (with irregular snow-ice consistency) south faces. Doing this, at least we would be able to see and therefore rationally assess the objective dangers.

The second fortunate pre-climbing decision involved our stoves. In the three years of climbing experience since my near fiasco on Aconcagua, I had come to the conclusion that only stoves burning white gas, or an equivalent, could produce the necessary heat intensity for the long, drawn-out task of snow melting at high altitudes. Adams Carter had informed us that via John Ricker (one of several Americans then assisting in the establishment of the Huascarán National Park—and spending considerable time compiling information for his excellent guidebook), residing in Huaraz, we would be able to obtain our needed supply of gas. So from the USA we brought with us two stoves: my trusty white-gas-burning Primus, and a new multi-fuel MSR, which (Jim believed) would serve our needs in Peru. Zzzttt the latter: on our second day burning regular gasoline, the MSR never again would stay ignited. This meant that the success of all our climbing endeavors over the next six weeks would depend entirely on the proper—and consistent—functioning of my ol' trustworthy Primus.

Trustworthy it proved to be. Climb after climb. But only I, knowing its idiosyncrasies, was able to light it (I had become expert in using a few gas-whetted scraps of toilet paper on the tank top to pressurize it sufficiently so that it would send forth vaporized gas). Old faithful—at least up until our last, and hardest, climb up Huascarán. There—about 30 minutes into every cooking episode that always involved the endless melting of water—the fuel cap, which doubles as the pressure-safety valve, would begin to fail, and hot ignited gas would shoot forth from it in a flaming plume. For a few days a hard breath would extinguish this and permit a continuation of our snow melting. But halfway into the climb that remedy proved insufficient, and we wisely chose to run the stove for only 15 minutes before turning it off to cool for a quarter hour. By the last day even this was insufficient. Luckily, we had a surplus of gas. We would light the stove and place it at the bottom of a half-meter hole in the snow (certainly five meters from the tent) and cook or melt over both the regular flame and ever-growing plume of ignited gasses sizzling out of the safety value—until the liquid gas inside its small tank was depleted. Luckily, we suffered no explosion, but our thirst deficit increased by the day. (Lesson learned: On any future extended climbing trip, pack and carry an extra, small [one-inch diameter] pressure cap for the Primus fuel tank.)

Three other pre-climbing decisions—all proving to be fortuitous—were about food. Jim, Mike and I knew (either vicariously or through previous experience) about the nauseas experienced by ravenous climbers at high altitudes. This problem was compounded in Peru, due to the impossibility of obtaining some particular foods (and airplane weight restrictions prohibited us from bringing common mountain foods such as sugar drinks, chocolate, gorp, granola, or candy bars). We did pack about four days of freeze-dried meals that, in our wisdom, we saved for the long six-day traverse of Huascarán. But for the rest of the trip: heavy decisions.

The first involved food for dinners, i.e., with protein, which would have to come from local stores. Sardine cans, okay. Cheese: okay for the first few days out. Hmmm. Other protein foods? Can't remember any other protein sources at this temporal distance. As it turned out, the main source available to us was canned fish—a Peruvian staple—so we dutifully but not enthusiastically obliged. Dinner after dinner. The reader can readily imagine that after two or three weeks of that, I could not even contemplate the consumption of any type of fish for about the next five years.

Carbs? Of course we planned for a few dinners with spaghetti noodles—they are available everywhere except on the moon. Specific to the Andean nations were sun-dried potatoes, available in the form of hard granola-sized kernels or flakes. They proved to be easy to pack, inexpensive, and tasty. (Their preparation involves soaking in water for a day.) Forget the available bread, that came in one-inch-thick, six-inch-diameter disks: none of us liked it fresh and, after a day—even in a plastic bag—it turned hard and unappetizing. Nowhere in Huaraz did we find the equivalent of Wonder or "bubble" bread, even if we had desired it.

Experienced trekkers and climbers will instantly recognize what could become a major problem: what to eat for lunches. Here the Mountain Gods (and Mike) once again smiled on us. From the Monterey Hotel kitchen we borrowed the largest metal pot they had—it must have measured 50 cm across and the same from top to bottom. Following Mike's recipe, we purchased flour, raisins, sesame seeds, honey, dried milk (and who knows what else—a small quantity of baking power?). I recollect no peanuts and very few other "nuts." Using milk, we mixed it all into a stiff dough. Then we located a bakery that would rent to us their wood-heated oven for four morning hours (they almost always bake their bread at night). So there we were—to the utter amazement of the oven owners and workers—patty-cake, patty-cake, shaping about 200 wallet-sized rounded flattened biscuits, then sliding them into the oven on four-meter-long wooden spatulas, then out and piling them into two half-full gunny sacks. Over the entire seven weeks these biscuits proved to be magnificent. Their relative hardness meant no wrapping or squishing while packed. Even when high-altitude nausea rejected every other available food, gnawing on one was always a pleasant experience. I have to conclude: the success of our climbing endeavors was due mainly to these make-do, homemade biscuits. Thank you, Mike—eternally—for your inspiration.

Our last food choice—equally memorable, but only for me—involved breakfast. It was a one-minute decision, because majority ruled: the two kiwis have known only one breakfast throughout their lives: porridge. Do Americans, do my readers, really know what porridge consists of? To educate those readers: not much—runny, water-boiled oats. No sugar, no salt, no milk, no raisins. For me: ugggh! Thankfully, my two companions fudged with our strict group rules: they let me carry, throughout the trip, a softball-sized plastic bag of sugar to help me get my share of breakfast down the hatch.

Our first objective, following Adams Carter's advice, was to climb nothing but new routes up peaks in the northern part of the range. (I am a fluent Spanish speaker, so throughout the trip we would have no problem whatsoever with transportation issues or in obtaining food, fuel, or information.) We hired a man with a small pickup (two of us rode in the open back and on top of the equipment) for the eight-hour trip north from Huaraz, around the top of the range, and then south to the Safuna Basin[4] via a dirt/bog road. When our driver proved unwilling to proceed the last kilometer over dubious terrain, we lucked out locating a local farmer, whose mules carried our equipment and three weeks of food the rest of the way. All this proved so uncomfortable and inconvenient that we determined to walk out at the end.

We had only one definite goal, Pucarashta Este, at 5,550 meters (18,209 feet).[5] Ricker had given it the distinction of being one of the last unclimbed peaks in the whole range, which meant that previous parties had considered it either too hard, or too unimpressive, to climb. The latter seemed to be the case, and its appearance from our camp 1,000 feet above Laguna Pucacocha earned it the nickname "Pucabumpa." So confident were we that, when we left next morning, we were carrying gear more suitable for an easy day in the Alps. To our dismay our route from the west turned out to be the typical Andean ridge—a very sharp rock formation covered by meters and meters of unstable snow. Our progress involved bulldozing up unconsolidated white mushrooms and removing huge quantities of snow to cut a path up a four-meter vertical wall. The final part of the ridge maintained our excitement by slab-avalanching on the south and being heavily corniced on the north. All in all, a slow, dangerous, and spectacular climb.[6]

Darkness caught us about 40 meters below the summit. On a relatively flat place we kicked out a small shelf, popped down two sleeping pills apiece, and drowsed into a twelve-hour shiver. The monotony of the long, cold night was broken only by Jim sleepwalking into a crevasse a few meters below, but fortunately self-arresting himself with the ice axe he had had the good sense to grab. All this taught us a lesson: the size of the mountains, the shortness of the days, and our reluctance to move before

***Opposite:* In Peru's Cordillera Blanca, Mike snakes his way up the glacier toe.**

being warmed by the rays of the morning sun meant that never again would we climb without taking light sleeping bags and bivouac tents with us. The Andes Gods, in their turn, were kind to us: we never lacked for a good bivy site.

A case in point: after 6½ hours of hard climbing on Tayapapampa's north face (5,674 meters; 18,618 feet), we found a large, perfect, horizontal shelf about 15 meters west of the summit. A second example: after nine hours on Pucahirca Norte III's north face, we stumbled upon a bergschrund only 20 meters from the top that provided protection and space for our three tired bodies. Virtually the same would occur three weeks later when the fading light would surprise us with yet another small crevasse high on the scary 70-degree East Face of Huascarán Sur: a perfect dream-creation of nighttime accommodations for three desperate climbers. Yes, definitely: The Andes Gods had willed for us to succeed.

Our base camp for those first three weeks was a cabin maintained by the governmental agency in charge of controlling the water level of the high-altitude Safuna Lake. This was of particular concern because four years earlier an earthquake had triggered the release of a huge mass of water from a nearby lake that shot down the valley and completely destroyed the town of Yungay and its 20,000 residents. Aided by my fluent Spanish, I developed a friendship with one of the employees stationed there, who shared information about that disaster. I eagerly listened to his explanations of the social changes then occurring in his agrarian community under the guiding hand of the country's progressive president, Juan Velasco Alvarado. To this day I regret not having been able to make the ten-hour horse ride to observe first-hand his and his neighbors' experience with the historical agrarian reform.

In a published essay (1975), I provided technical details about what we climbed.[7] Luckily, we were in rhythm with the weather: when dismal, we were holed up comfortably in the Electro-Peru cabin; and when decent we were putting up new exciting routes. Mostly, it was going up 70-degree flutings—that is, channels of hard snow—on southerly faces. Being that the Cordillera Blanca is "one of few ice-clad regions within the tropics" (Ricker), its short, hot days melt snow surfaces and its long, cold nights freeze them hard. So, during our climbing, if one fluting began to show bare ice we simply had to move another three meters away to find a more desirable snow consistency. As a rule, we practiced simul climbing, with our rope protected at any one moment by two pickets—we carried about a dozen of these 90mm aluminum, 1¼-inch-diameter pipes—and an occasional ice screw. The single thrust of a Chouinard ice hammer would provide instant, and nearly bombproof, protection. In the other hand each of us carried an old-style ice axe. Fortunately, the occasions were few when we had to rely on its pick for solid protection. Experienced ice climbers today would shudder if they had to rely on these tools. But—truth be told—at no time did we experience significant fear or face undue danger. On the contrary, every day offered magnificent new challenges. One of our best—but certainly not atypical—nights: "Every good climb deserves a bivouac such as this. After the intense physical challenge and mental absorption of the climb, we were able to relax, suspended in the darkness near the top of our face, and meditate. It was a marvelous night, too special to pass away in sleep, as I intentionally woke myself at times in order to gaze out over the vertical landscape, reminding myself that I was really and fully alive."

Being that our time was running out for the northern segment of our Cordillera Blanca visit, we made plans to hike out. Our path would take us about four kilometers due south from the Laguna Safuna cabins, down and then up over the pass between Pukarashta and Alpamayo (moderately difficult), then another six kilometers down the Quebrada Arweigocha to the stream at the base of the huge Quebrada Santa Cruz (moderate-easy). Then, we would walk west down the latter for some 19 kilometers, through thigh-deep bogs, slippery-surfaced stream beds, and any sort of rocky terrain (easy but tedious). Remember: no adequate maps yet existed. The distances I have just written are estimates taken from the map, now in front of me as I write, that was probably drawn (by Ricker himself) several years after our visit. In the days before we departed, our Peruvian friends at the Electro-Peru cabin had estimated that our total distance would be about 10 kilometers, taking about eight hours. We should have doubted their feigned certainty, being that we had even better maps than they. But we took their word on faith. Accordingly, we accepted their offer to make radio contact so that a taxi from Huaraz would be waiting for us at 6:00 p.m. at the nearest road the next day.

We gifted all the remaining food to them and, early in the morning, set off carrying packs full of our equipment. All was straightforward until the Quebrada (valley) Santa Cruz. Walking through the bogs, my water-filled double boots became so heavy that I removed the outer shells and tied them to the outside of my pack. For the remainder of the long hike they flopped with every step, driving home the certainty that the leather-sewn inner boots I continued to wear would suffer irreparable damage. But the main problem was time. The endless and trail-less *quebrada* offered no real obstacles. (Judging from recent maps, this route now is a frequent destination for many trekkers.) We knew we had to hurry, so rest stops were out of the question. By six p.m. there was not the minimum sign of human presence. Continuing our speedy hike, we convinced ourselves that the taxi would wait for at least a few more hours. By eight, we fantasized that we would soon arrive. By ten we were walking in near darkness. By eleven we would periodically hear the barking of dogs, which meant that we were passing by darkened homesteads. Fatigue and hunger played with my mind: I convinced myself that faint cattle or llama paths were actually human trails. By now the three of us were spread out and unable to communicate. By midnight, we were still blistering on down, now hearing continuous dog-barking. By one o'clock, I was deliriously convincing myself that mine was the shortest path. About two I simply gave up with the idea of arriving. Almost sleepwalking, and with near rigor-mortis legs, I felt a furrow with my foot, spread out the plastic cloth, crawled into my summer-light REI bag, and instantly fell asleep. A few hours later it was the smell of the fresh cow dung directly under my head that awoke me, along with the first glow of a new day.

By late morning we three were seated together in the town's plaza. We had ample time to relax. There, I tried my first drink of homemade *chicha* (a fermented corn drink). Discreetly, my encrusted fingers removed two floating dead flies and, the rest of the afternoon, I fretted, awaiting the first indication of "the runs." By three I knew I had escaped, as we boarded the only scheduled transportation leaving from that village: an open truck. With our packs, we climbed up to stand alongside a dozen other passengers. I lucked out, being privileged to sit on a bag of potatoes, next to chicken cages. A few hours later we got off at Huaraz's central market.

Now, R&R for three days, before we would set off for the mighty East Face of Huascarán. Ah, the comforts of Hotel Monterey. Then, in the morning, off to visit the city and attempt to appease our monstrous appetites. There we were, unshaven and zombie-bronzed (i.e., with white eye sockets on tanned faces), and jump-walking down civilized streets as if we were on the surface of the moon. I have to add: saliva must have been dripping from our mouths because we were ravenous for beef. I personally had experienced a wet dream the first night back in a real bed, that

**We failed to anticipate the difficulties of our first ridge ascent and the short hours of daylight, meaning that we had to pass an unplanned and uncomfortable bivy-night just below the summit.**

had been fueled not by thoughts of a beautiful female, but of juicy steak. Loaded down with breakfast, we waltzed down the streets, intoxicated by the fragrance of cooked food. I eagerly stopped at the first *chifa* in order to consume a Chinese sizzle-fry steak. Thirty minutes later, out on the pavement again, I oozed over yet more meat fumes. I was not able to resist, in spite of my stuffed stomach.

Three, four, five hours later I was still bloated, and now miserable. What with all that canned fish we had consumed for three weeks in the Safuna refuge, had my system lost the ability to digest beef? It is an understatement to say that I spent a horrible night. By morning, I was faint as I crawled to the Hotel Monterey kitchen seeking a jar of mustard. My induced vomit nearly filled a three-liter pot! With thoughts of suicide, I could barely move as my two buddies went out to purchase the supplies we would need for a week on Huascarán. Over the past forty-some years this experience has acquired the status of folklore: with ironic exaggeration I have called it one of the two closest calls I have ever had in a lifetime of mountaineering (the other was my attempt at crossing a swollen glacier-melt stream on Aconcagua.)

Next morning I remained miserable. A taxi carried us two kilometers past Shilla to Llipta. (The fine road that—today—continues up the Quebrada Ulta, passing Punta Olímpica, and on to Pompey on the eastern side of the cordillera, did not yet exist.) The first hours on the trail were sheer misery. Bent over while painfully shouldering my now-loaded pack, I dutifully followed my two comrades. Then, the Gods sent us a huge tractor that carried us for a half-hour, before we descended and hiked north toward the Matará Glacier. We passed by three young girls in felt hats, sitting on a low stone fence, whom I eternalized in a prize photo. By this time, I was beginning to feel okay. By dinner, I was my ol' self. Long live the Spartan conditions of the wilds. The cure for any of my ailments: just get started on another climbing adventure.

We experienced astonishment gazing out at the two-kilometer-long, imposing East Face, that I could not capture in a single photo. There, left of its center—in spite of the distance—we could eye-follow our route whose upper third was a right-bending snow-strip "sleeve" that ended just below the rocky summit crest.[8] And just before us the east-face glacier, a topographical nightmare of crevasses that—somehow—we would have to traverse in order to get to the beginning of our route upward.

The first indication of our streak of luck: without retracing a step we successfully (and perhaps miraculously) threaded our way through that maze of crevasses to the avalanche cone. The second: in the waning light we hustled our butts safely up and then out of an avalanche chute. The third: with butterfly stomachs we goose-stepped down through ice-chilled air and onto the flat bottom of a huge crevasse: it proved to be an ideal bivy site because—in spite of the constant swirl of snow or ice particles—we were totally protected from snow avalanches or rock and ice fall from above. On the morrow we easily walked out the other end of the crevasse to continue up the same type of 70-degree ice flutings that we had come to know so well over the past month. Up and away—the whole day long, simul-climbing while methodologically placing a new picket every half-rope length. The weather was ideal.

Our fourth lucky find (already mentioned above): the crevasse, high on the East Wall (just before the start of the right-slanting snow/ice strip), that provided for another perfect bivouac.

The next morning—our summit day—I put myself on belay to protect my two buddies who, in exiting from our magnificent bivy cave, had to perform a scary, front-pointing horizontal traverse before resuming

**Darkness had been setting in when the Mountain Gods saved our butts, high on Huascarán Sur's steep East Face, by surprising us with this small bivy cave. I'm in front-in the life-restoring morning sunshine, and Jim is in the shadows behind.**

an upward direction. Then, the equally scary diagonal traverse on the right-bearing crescent-shaped band. By now it was late in the afternoon, and we had long since entered into the cold shadow of the mountain, Where had the hours gone?—no time to rest. Then, our exit onto the dangerous loose rock of the summit ridge. (Reading the first-ascent account of the ANZUS team, I realize today that we had chosen a fortunate path because—unlike their experience—our ascent over that rock was devoid of technical difficulties.) I went first since I would be the least likely of us three to dislodge a loose rock. We must have remained roped up (I can't remember now, at the time of writing)—even though we had no need to belay. Nearing the top of the shit-rock, the wind picked up. Daylight was fading. Even though the cold began to bite, there was no stopping to put on our jackets. We did that only when we reached the safety of the snow on the summit ridge. After another forty minutes—in near darkness and a raging wind—we realized that in no direction did the terrain continue upward. We had arrived.

I can't think of too many enjoyable summits in my long career as a mountaineer-climber, and this was not one either. We had to lean against the high winds that lifted our ropes into the air. Caray! In the two minutes of faint glow that remained of daylight we were able to see, way down below, Huascarán's shadow stretching toward the horizon! Then, darkness—except for the dull red glow reflected from the white snow. I distinctly remember fumbling with frozen fingers in my massive gloves in order to snap a summit photo. What a pleasant surprise—weeks later—to see that the wide aperture setting and slow shutter speed magically added sufficient light to the photo so that—unlike what my eyes had seen—my two companions came out in faded colors.

We had to get out of the high wind, and fast. Again, the Mountain Gods looked down on us with sympathy. In near total darkness, one of us found a functional flashlight to help us plod five minutes to discover a flat protected spot, where we eagerly got into our bivy gear to pass a welcome, but hungry, night. The only victim was Mike who—in the morning—reported to Jim and me that he had suffered a mild case of frostbite on some fingers.

The next morning, I'm not sure whether we even roped up to crunch-step down the easy slopes of the south summit, heading for the top of the Garganta—that is, the upper part of Huascarán's normal route. We arrived at a point where, high above—and with perfect visibility—we were able to peer down at the gentle-sloping glacier far below, that was speckled with perhaps forty tents housing dozens of international climbers. Between us and them: the dangerous ice fall. All those people down there must have been patiently waiting for their hired guides to complete fixing the ropes that they would use to get up the problematical ice blocks. How long had they been there: days, weeks? Our first reaction: "Oh God, they don't have the ropes fixed, so how are we going to get down?" (Suppress panic). A second reaction: "*We*, the three of us, are the first to reach the summit this season!" A third reaction: "Could they, down below, see us? Is anyone looking up and wondering how we made it to here?"

Present tense. Here, in my computer study, the year is 2017. I read in the two guidebooks open before me that the few previous parties that successfully ascended the East Face have had to spend yet another bivouac right here, above the ice fall, due to the inevitable difficulties and high danger involved in its descent. But—fortunately (and all hail to the Mountain Gods)—that was not necessary for us in 1975.

There we were, stopped, and wondering how we were going to accomplish the ice-fall descent. I looked from left to right, studying the steep topography below me. Several minutes passed. Would it be possible? Over there to the right, on the north side of the ice fall? Did I see a continuous line? Two dozen guides down below obviously had not seen it, so I was probably mistaken: from our perspective I could not see what to them must be an obvious, impassable cliff or a crevasse gap too wide to cross. But was it just possibly "a go"? Gads, we would have to descend half the distance just to find out and, after encountering the yet-unseen obstacle, our exhausted and famished bodies would have to ascend back up here again. Not fun at about 6,500 meters (20,000 feet). Jim and Mike, initially, were not even interested in my suggestion. Squint. Squint. I kept thinking: to the right of the ice fall: it's just possible. I start out. "There's a chance it will go." Would my buddies follow me? I keep descending. They're still not moving. I'm 50 meters ahead and keep moving down—unroped. Drop-stepping into ideal snow, I thread my way here and there, following the possible path. No obstacle visible—yet. I yell back at my companions, "Follow me, it seems to be okay." They begin to move. I continue. Not even dangerous enough to rope up. They're moving behind me. We proceed. *It goes.* In the short period of 15—or was it 90?—minutes we have completed the entire descent and are standing on the safe surface of the glacier. The highest of the tents are just ahead. *We made it.* Hard to believe.

In that fast and easy descent I don't remember gazing across to see if a guide or a team of guides was hanging from ropes or treading carefully in crampons in an attempt to screw in yet another anchor for fastening yet another rope across and up the broken ice blocks.

On the super-safe, gently sloping glacier, the three of us just kept walking on down. Passing the multitude of tents, I don't remember speaking to anyone. (Were they all inside, asleep or bored to slumber?) Not even a friendly "hello." Perhaps not even one person saw us descending our own safe and easy route to the left (if you're looking up) of the ice fall. Of course, we were hardly of the disposition to socialize. So we kept striding on down. The path over the glacier was well worn and easy to follow. Then the dirt-gravel trail, then—hours after nightfall—we arrived at what must have been the village of Musho. We were down and out.

Fast forward to October 2016, Huaraz, Peru. My wife and I had just spent five wonderful days in Huari—about five hours away, on the eastern edge of the Huascarán National Park. (That is to say, if you draw an imaginary west-to-east line stretching from Huaraz, across the now-existent

**Roping up provided us only an illusion of protection on the Cordillera Blanca's (Peru) ridges, given the deep, unconsolidated snow and hidden cornices. Pictured here are Mike Andrews and Jim Milne, on our first ascent of Mushac Shipash.**

Huascarán National Park, you will find the small, delightful city of Huari.) Now, we had three to four days for my primary, if not only, mission here: to get up to date about the Cordillera Blanca range, and in particular its queen, Huascarán Sur, but especially the East Face routes.

I made the rounds of the different guide agencies that were most visible. (Remember, I speak excellent Spanish.) In every case I came away with the impression that for any of them, and their associated guides, the Quebrada Ulta or the East Face of Huascarán didn't even exist. Understandably, they wouldn't advertise their guide services to take novice climbers up such hard and demanding routes. I heard several anecdotes—a few even tragic—about avalanche dangers on the regular route up the ice fall to the Garganta. But nowhere, including in the most famous "mountaineering" restaurants and equipment agencies—and even the headquarters of the national park—did I see even one photo of that mountain taken from the Quebrada Ulta side of Huascarán Sur, or of its majestic and dread-inspiring East Face.[9] That, in spite of the new road passing underneath it—as alluded to above—that would make any afternoon jaunt up to the toe of the Matará Glacier easy to accomplish.

An ego-padding anecdote: at the Huascarán National Park headquarters they must have believed that I was some sort of *personaje* (celebrity), because its director interviewed me for a half hour and then gifted me a precious 150-page, full-color book that commemorates the fortieth anniversary of the park's founding. Interestingly, all the photos in that book taken of the mountains before about 1980 are in mediocre black and white. I instantly realized that I myself possessed, stored in my La Crosse, Wisconsin, basement, a treasure trove of perfectly preserved Kodachrome slides of our seven weeks climbing in and around Huaraz. Already I have begun the tedious operation of digitizing many of them to share with the dedicated staff at the national park. I'm sure they will appreciate them.

In and around Huaraz, I was also super interested in learning about the existing maps of the range. Nowhere did I find, either posted or stocked by guide services or equipment suppliers, a copy of the very decent Ricker maps of 1977.[10] In fact, good maps were almost nonexistent. In one equipment store I viewed under protective glass a copy of what an employee argued was the best map available, which was of German manufacture.[11] I left with the distinct impression that most tourist-level climbers or trekkers have to make do with the one-page xeroxed diagrams given to them by the agencies, and that serious international climbers have to arrive with their own maps, which—I assume—they have no problem obtaining.[12]

The last few paragraphs suggest the major disconnects existing between climbing communities, but especially between the climbing scene in Huaraz and the different climbing networks in the northern hemisphere. The first example: for every significant Cordillera Blanca route the Ricker guide makes reference to first-ascent information published in perhaps 25 different regional or national alpine publications—and in dozens of languages (pp. 131–2)—eternal thanks is due to the author for this outstanding research effort. This means that—for example—only the most diligent of the young German climbers in the 1970s might have been informed about what their climbing colleagues from Italy or Harvard might have accomplished in previous years. A second example: in my recent visit to Huaraz, I met no one who was familiar with, or had access to, the yearly issues of the *American Alpine Journal*, which contain accounts of the most important first ascents in this range. (Perhaps the last will and testament of a generous north-hemisphere climber can designate the library of the Huascarán National Park headquarters as recipient for a complete *AAJ* collection.)

And of course, while in Huaraz, I inquired about the ANZUS Route, and any other lines up the East Face of Huascarán Sur. In equipment store after equipment store, in guiding agency after guiding agency, I learned nothing. Absolutely nothing. It was as if that mighty East Face didn't even exist. This means that serious international climbers would still be making their arrangements completely independent of the different local agencies. No surprise here: we had done the same forty-some years ago (and we hadn't wanted an extraneous third person to come along and tell us "*no*" to any—even the most minor—detail of our distance-concocted plans). Here was, potentially, yet another of the existing disconnects.

Other East Face routes? Both Ricker and Sharmon describe three: the 1971 ascent up the southeast ridge (its left skyline: TD—*très difficile*); the ANZUS route I have described earlier, for which we did the second ascent (in the face's left-center: TD+); and the 1972 Austrian line up "a great sweeping ice field" perhaps a hundred meters to the right (north) of the ANZUS (ED—that is, *extrêmement difficile*). Sharmon includes two

**A Huascarán (Peru) summit shot of Jim, Mike, and the shadow of my awkward, gloved hand. This is the only instance of "trick photography" in this book: a slow, open aperture shows much more light than what, at that moment, we were able to see.**

others: the Spanish line up the northeast ridge (the right skyline: TD+), and the desperate 1979 Austrian Direct line (ED) that begins between the ANZUS and Austrian routes. All routes require multiple days—and bivouacs—steep ice technique and gear, and passing over dangerous loose rock near the summit.[13] Were I to return to climb, I would definitely choose the same line we had selected 42 years earlier.

But—after my short 2016 visit to Huaraz—I remain with the nagging question: How has this alarming aspect of global climate change affected the climbing routes on Huasarán and the other Cordillera Blanca peaks? More specifically, does the very substantial melting of permanent snow/ice fields mean the disappearance of much of the climbable steep ice and, therefore, an increase in the distance over which a party would have to go up dangerous loose rock? Are the Austrian and ANZUS lines even climbable still? Perhaps an informed reader can provide me with relevant information.[14]

The disappearance of ice and snow in the region has alarmed all informed individuals. One source reports that glaciers in the Cordillera Blanca have receded, between about 1980 and 2010, some 37 percent.[15] A specialist, visiting the Huaraz region, recently reported that all the Cordillera Blanca glaciers are melting "at an alarming rate," and that some are now smaller than they have been for the last 6,000 years. What's more, he predicted that the Pastoruri Glacier would probably disappear within ten years.[16] This rapid disappearance of centuries-old ice could have dramatic, and indeed tragic, consequences for all of Peru, but especially for the millions of indigenous people residing in mountainous areas who will face a growing scarcity of water for their life-sustaining agriculture.

## Chapter 7

# Crossing the Line in the Tetons

Nowhere more than in the Tetons have memories intersected: those of the gristly scamper veteran that I am today with those of me as a novice mountaineer. So, it hardly need be stated that this mountain range has played a central role in my career as a climber. Here—in writing this—I feel inventive: I'm motivated to project a different class of remembrances. I'll write about the downside of my experiences in the Tetons—let's call them the misadventures or the screw-ups. There are at least a few.

So, we go back to the year 1965, my first season as a climber. I had met Peter Craig, to whom I'll be eternally grateful for introducing me to the sport. In my first week as a college freshman at Pomona College, we immediately hit it off. He was the son of two Swiss-French parents who had taken climbing classes in both the Alps and California's Sierra Nevada. I, in contrast, had to my credit a few trekking experiences and some crevasse-rescue practice in Washington State—but no roped climbing.

A few days after meeting him, we drove his beat-up old Volkswagen to Highland Outfitters, in Riverside, where I bought my first Austrian-made klettershoes. Then, a week later, we spent the weekend at Tahquitz Rock, located above an alpine-like community called Idylwild, just across the mountain from Palm Springs. This would be the first of many thrilling weekends, as we strained and struggled our way up the easiest trad routes there, protecting ourselves with a rack of the newly introduced Chouinard chromoly-steel pitons (I continue musings about Tahquitz Rock in Chapter 13).

On other weekends we visited "Big Rock,"[1] where I registered several important chapters of "cutting my climbing teeth." It also fell upon us, with our medium-level skills, to put up a few new routes. A random memory: at the end of a sweaty climbing day I carelessly left on the top of the car my first rope—a 150-foot, white nylon, REI three-strand—that slipped unnoticed off the top of the car when we drove away. (Goldline would be on the market only a year later; and Perlon was yet a decade into the future.)

A few years ago, while visiting Southern California, I heard rumors that the area had been flooded when state agencies created a reservoir; I also heard that with special permission some willing climbers could still gain access to the area. It would be neat to go back and relive old memories.

On weekends during that first year, I was emerging as a committed climber. Peter and I worked out hard—we knew we had to be in great shape. Spring vacation that first year would be dedicated to early-season climbing in the High Sierras. I distinctly remember our long drive up U.S. 395 to Big Pine—on the eastern escarpment of the Sierras and about 50 miles south of Reno. What a chilly drive with us already bedecked in our Terray down jackets, what with the defunct heating system of Peter's old VW! After driving over snow to reach the trailhead, we put on skis, outfitted with skins, and spent two days winding through the trees to reach the Pal Glacier and our campsite for the next four nights. Boy, were we hearty! From there we reached the summits of four nearby peaks via moderately easy mixed climbs.

Now—finally—the Tetons. Come summer, Peter and I were off to that beautiful range with an ambitious list for two weeks of climbing. First was the Nez Percé's North Face (rated III, 5.7).[2] This would be my first experience in (what for me were then) large, intimidating mountains. I remember how my shoulders hurt carrying our climbing gear and overnight equipment up the tedious switchbacks leading to Garnet Canyon. Early the next morning we roped up for the first hard pitch. Peter, the more experienced of us, took the first lead. I was seated on a secure slab as he started out by reaching out to place a pin about ten feet up. Then, it happened: on a quartzy rock he slipped, turned in the air to fall face out, but the rope through his biner was in the process of twisting him back in when his foot landed. A broken, or at least severely sprained, ankle. Removing a few straight metal supports from his pack, we made a splint. Then, using the rope, I lowered him about a hundred meters down to the steep scree, and then helped him crab-walk down another 300 meters. There I left him, cheerful but in sharp pain, to hike out and seek a rescue party.

They found him in darkness and got him down with the assistance of a wheeled stretcher. He explained to me later that every rock on the trail resulted in a stab of pain. A day later Peter was back in climbing camp, a cheery cripple with a cast and crutches. He was resigned to hobble around for the duration of our planned outing, while I had to slum it out finding other people to climb with.[3]

A word about that historical climbing camp on the south shore of Jackson Lake—nearby today one can find the headquarters for the Teton Guide Service. But then, it was a rustic tent city, where fellowship with other climbers and ambitious trekkers was the rule. I was green, I was the neophyte. I especially remember a communal campfire where some older tourist-climbers brewed up a bucket of Teton Tea (red wine with anybody's other alcoholic contribution, flavored by clove tea), and each of the twenty of us dipped in our own cups and partook. It was a sublime moment. Could the Tetons have ever been better than that?

One other distant memory: we were there two weeks. Please tell me where—if anywhere—a climber could get a good hot shower. Against the posted rules, Peter and I, early risers, on at least a few occasions snuck down to the Jenny Lake shore, stripped, and rubbed accumulated sweat and grime off our bodies, making sure not to use any contaminating soap. I'm sure our example, when multiplied by a thousand, ended up serving as an adequate incentive for the American Alpine Club, pushed by the Park Service, to seek an in-park alternative to the historical climbing camp.[4]

Jump forward exactly a decade to the summer of 1975. To celebrate my tenth anniversary as a climber I made my second visit to the Tetons. But this time I arrived alone—with my trusty ol' rack of pitons (a standard rack for me was 15 pitons of different sizes, the largest being the 2" Chouinard angle). Other climbers, seeing my rack, discreetly demonstrated their scorn: the sport, at least in the Tetons, had already jumped into its clean-climbing phase, with serious climbers newly committed to using for protection only "chocks" and other assorted "nuts."

Over the previous decade I had become a much stronger and more confident climber. My regular, and constant, partner was Don Fredrickson: together we had gotten up difficult routes on Edith Cavell and Temple in the Canadian Rockies, and had climbed neat routes in the Bugaboos,

***Opposite:* I put my buddy, Tom Burns, on belay, and he begins his lead up the new route we were climbing on Mt. Teewinot in the Grand Teton National Park, Wyoming.**

Cathedral Spires (Alaska Range), and Yosemite, culminating with the NW Face of Half Dome and El Cap's Salathé Wall. If it had been Peter who introduced me to climbing, it was Don who toughened me up as a climber. His silent confidence helped me control my tremble before any hard pitch. Over the previous seven years rare was the route we had had to abandon before reaching the top.

I was also high-altitude tested, having just returned from Peru's Cordillera Blanca—where two Kiwi buddies and I had experienced several climbing successes.

An end result was—in August of 1975—my new disposition vis-à-vis the Tetons. Unlike a decade earlier, they no longer intimidated me. This time, the loaded-pack hike up the Garnet Canyon trail no longer cut so painfully into my shoulders. I ended up climbing with confidence.

This was to be my most productive Teton visit ever. Long live, and be ever blessed, those climbing partners who were willing to accept into their team a stray third such as myself. Bless you Tom Burns and Joe. It must have been in the common cooking area of the new AAC Climbers' Ranch when they, recently arriving, invited me to join them. Tom, initially, was apologetic: he explained his activities as a caver, which meant that his normally white nylon rope temporarily had a dark-grey color. "Don't worry, this dust from bat shit will fall off after the first few rappels." That was a new one for me.

The three of us proved to be an efficient team. After successfully scaling Irene's Arréte on Disappointment Peak and the North Face of Nez Percé, we set our sights on something more ambitious: the mighty North Face of the Grand.

In our cockiness we didn't consult the normally unreliable weather reports. After no real problem crossing the bergschrund, there we were—in mid-afternoon—weighed down with bivy packs on the lower part of the route. Two pitches up, when it started to rain, we abruptly realized that our route line followed the drain channel for the entire face above us. Difficult to put on a cagoule when roped up and perched on six-inch ledges. Water gushed down over our bodies and drenched the packs. I began a violent shiver as the rain continued: 90 minutes of immobilized misery. In the fading light there was only one possible direction: rap down on soggy ropes. Forget the drenched flashlights. Not fun crossing back over the bergschrund, but it was the last point of serious danger. Movement neutralized cold. We stayed on the long trail down only by the feel of our feet. By two in the morning we almost cried with relief as the key was inserted into the car door lock, allowing us to pull on dry clothing and slip into chilled slumber.

In the morning we headed to a laundromat in Jackson for the long, slow drying of down sleeping bags and jackets.

Throughout all this, Joe, severely asthmatic, had refused to take his medications, and a severe attack meant several days in the hospital. With tears in our eyes, Tom and I said goodbye to our buddy. Two days later Tom and I were back on the North Face. Revenge would be sweet.

But Miss Serendipity had not ended with us yet. There we were, high on the face, with the pendulum pitch behind us. One more rope length to go. I was on lead when I heard thunder and looked at the dark clouds engulfing the summit of Owen—only spitting distance away. I thought: a typical late afternoon in the Tetons. I yelled down, "Tom, can you keep dry?" I heard affirmative as I tip-toed to the extreme right to hang the hammer and all the iron, and then delicately returned to my own mini-cave on the left. We would have to wait it out then proceed over wet rock. Not nice, but in the expected order of things. *Crack!* Lightning. I put on my cagoule and wedged my butt inside: with little wind, only my head and feet were going to get sprinkled on. Could be worse. *Crack.* One minute later: *spiiiit.* Ouch! Some goddamn insect just bit my lower back! I looked down to see if it, now dead, was flittering down to my boots. Hmmm. Nothing.

Then I realized: gads, *electricity*. Really? What else could it have been? Good thing my pitons were over there. What else might have happened? Hmmm. The bod still felt okay. No problem continuing my perch on the small holds. Also, the hair on my head was intact. End of anecdote—it makes a good story.

It was inevitable: everything else that Tom and I would do after the historical North Face would be anticlimactic. A few days later, it was boredom on Teewinot's west face that tempted us into the previously unclimbed Chockstone Chimney (III, 5.8) a route that—to our honor—is described in the super-thick 1996 climbing guide.[5] Then, a few days later we went off along the (then maintained) trail around the west side of Leigh Lake to ascend Moran's Black Fin route (IV, 5.8). After delighting on its first half, the climbing angle eased off considerably, meaning that the climbing became quite boring. We simply had lost the desire to belay up the last two incredibly easy 5th pitches. Our desire to loaf in the sun and consume a whole pack of Oreos won over whatever previous aspiration we might have had to continue up the very, very, long hike up to the summit.

Fast forward three decades to 2006. I'd missed climbing, I'd missed the Tetons. In the intervening years I had gotten married, had two children, and I was … well, doing okay. The itch just got too great: I wanted to reboot my climbing skills. Therefore, I bought my first harness and a string of hexes to supplement the older stoppers. (Pitons, never again!) And there I was, once again, alone and eager in the Tetons' Climbers' Ranch. I was somewhat physically fit, and two weeks of day-on, day-off mountaineering would leave me buff. But I had my doubts: would the verve still be there for leading? There was only one way to find out: go out and do it.

Like usual, I had to hook up with other climbers. Ann was free for a day on Teewinot's East Ridge and Black Chimney. Then, Thomas (from Canada) and I got together for the Southwest Ridge on Storm Point, and the Upper Exum plus Petzoldt Direct on the Grand.

The descent of this last route offered a valuable learning experience: it's no fun to climb any route on the Grand carrying in your pack that second rope you'll need for the long rap to descend down the ugly Owen-Spalding line. Well, I had what I thought was the perfect solution: my spaghetti rope, left over from our mini expedition to Peru some 30 years earlier. The only problem was its twirling around the thicker climbing rope when set for the long rappel. Again, the Benevolent Gods intervened: another party, 150 feet below us, was able to untangle our two rope ends so that we were able to accomplish our safe and speedy descent.

On rest days I freely used my new Golden Eagle card (the lifetime pass for national parks that one can obtain after one's sixtieth birthday) to come and go. Between Jackson Hole and the Tetons: what a magnificent playground. First, the Mexican restaurant to "recarberate" after an exhausting climb. Then, the new bolted sport wall and the Monday-night folk-music Hootenanny, both within shouting distance of the park's Moose Junction entrance. Finally, the teeth-grit river jump, some 10 miles past the campground on the Gros Ventre road. It's hard not to dream of next August's return visit.

In 2008: yet another visit to the Tetons. With Danylo, I climbed Baxter's Pinnacle and Guides' Wall, and then the two of us forged a short new (and unrecorded) route on the extreme left edge of the Snaz Wall (II, 5.8—

Cathedral Peak). Another day, when we blundered by crossing too high on Teewinot's east face, we failed to find the start of the unique Tunnel Route (I simply must return to follow that amazing line!).

Then, the banner year of 2010, climbing with John Young. We began with yet another mini-blunder. How could I not remember that one passes Symmetry Spire—our initial destination—in the first ten minutes of hiking up after the boat crossing of Jenny Lake? As a consolation, we hiked all the way up the valley, crossing the east side of Mt. Owen, and settled for putting a new line (unrecorded) up the SW Ridge of Ayres' Crag 5 (II, 5.8). Two days later: celebration. In grand style we weathered two bivies to waltz up the magnificent East Ridge of the Grand. Praise is due for Brother John. Since he had attained the summit of the Grand two times in the previous few weeks, he had no trouble leading us down to the rappel ledge, where his extra-long rope (80 meters) proved essential for our descent.

All the above is a summary of the roped climbing I accomplished over those three Teton visits. Now for what I was beginning to do: unroped scamper climbing.

Finally I'm getting to the paragraphs where I was sort of "crossing the line." It was not entirely my fault. With every succeeding year there were fewer and fewer solo, unattached climbers showing up at the AAC Ranch looking for a partner such as myself. In fact, anecdotal evidence has me somewhat convinced that young male athletes itching to do knock-you-down-and-drag-it-out Teton-style climbing (that is, long-approaches, long-day, heavy-pack, exhausting trad mountaineering—as opposed to belay-from-your-bumper sport climbing) is a disappearing demographic. You tell me the reasons. But there I was, year after year, showing up at the AAC Ranch and finding fewer and fewer prospective partners.

You don't know me if you think that, without a partner, I'd just stay all day sunning myself and getting fat eating decent food at the climbing ranch. I admit it: some rest days I'd transform myself into a touristy pedestrian. But the days with a partner: best. Without a partner: only okay. It meant changing expectations. Also: it meant forging a wholly new ethos regarding equipment, safety, and objectives.

The Tetons is where I honed my scamper skills (in those same years I did similar low-difficulty routes elsewhere: Canadian Rockies, high Sierra Nevada): the Hourglass Couloir on Nez Percé, Koven on Mt. Owen, East

Face on Teewinot, East Face on Buck. This was a whole new dimension of climbing!

And meanwhile, my "relationship" with the Teton Climbers' Ranch was disintegrating. The place was becoming less and less appealing: the hard, wooden sleeping surfaces; the stuffy cabin air and—horror of horror—a snorer; and the absolute prohibition of campfires. The last one is the worst: what will you do after dinner? It's great to spend a few hours silently reading in the AAC's fine library, but you do so at the expense of stifling your urge for fellowship. In truth, in the after-dinner hours the place becomes a "ghost ranch" because most single adults drive either into Jackson or to the Moose-entrance bar to pass the evening hours. Hooray for the Ranch's director in 2009: at the risk of losing his job, he allowed a whole group of us (we were really grooving together and most would leave on the morrow) to build a specially protected platform in the middle of the gravel patio (between the cooking structure and the office), to build a discreet fire and to have an amazing time with guitars, songs, stories—and even a bucket of Teton Tea!

Meanwhile, the undesirable sleeping conditions inside the Ranch's cabins launched me on a trajectory that began with me fudging with existing regulations, and would end with me banished totally from the area. Under the cover of darkness a summer before, I would dutifully pay my fee and store my stuff on a hard wooden bed inside one of the cabins. But come sleep time, I would grab my stuff, walk toward the darkened meadow, and position myself on the ground out of sight on the other side of a tree. In the morning, no problem, since I've always been an early riser.

Stage two: a year later, accompanied by my wife, we were in agreement that the accommodations of the Ranch were not groovy for couples, so we drove out of the park and pitched a tent in the nearby Gros Ventre campground. There we were able to enjoy a wonderful campfire every night, but without the company of other climbers. With my Golden Eagle I could enter and leave the park at will.

Year three, I returned to the Tetons and Gros Ventre without my wife: my desire for a nightly campfire now outweighed all other considerations. The friendly note that I placed on the campground bulletin board attracted absolutely no climber-companions—neither to share the campsite nor a rope. Without a partner, scamper climbing was what was left to do. And on rest days I would return to the Climbers' Camp at dinnertime in order to maximize my possibilities for hooking up with a partner for the next day (does that sound sexual?).

Stage four (the year of Katra infamy), on yet another Teton trip, I did not even go to the Gros Ventre campground, and instead arrived at the Ranch at dinnertime. I did not register and pay for space in a snorey cabin. Nevertheless, there I was in the cooking area, engaged in the increasingly futile effort of recruiting a climbing partner. Days later I would return—I'll explain more below—to coordinate with fellow members of the Chicago Mountaineering Club—the CMC—for our pre-arranged ascent of the CMC Route on Moran.

My nights? Being a frequent visitor to the park, I had discovered a place where I could pass the night in my closed pickup, both undetected and undisturbed. But on the third night, I made the mistake of choosing to pass the early evening in the Ranch library instead of at the Moose Junction bar. The Ranch director that year proved to be very unfriendly (and fully living up to the folklore of "Nazi" campground chief). She, seeing me there, made it more than clear that I and my type were not welcome, so I left post haste. (More and more, events were pushing me toward that "rogue" line.)

Now, details about the CMC. Back in Wisconsin I do top-roped climbing with them at least a dozen days a year. With fully two months of anticipation, I had signed up to go on their "western outing," which objective that year was to make a fortieth-anniversary ascent of Moran's CMC route. At the time I naively believed that by signing up, and even by showing up for a "practice weekend," I would be guaranteed a climbing partner for the historic anniversary ascent! Wrong. Four months before, the rope teams had been assigned and no subsequent changes would be tolerated. Inflexibility?

Regardless, I drove out to the Tetons thinking that I'd have four or five days to snag a non–CMC partner for the group-climb. Or—I figured—I could pass my time before their arrival in scamper activities and be in super shape for when they arrived. About not "belonging" to a rope team, I nourished the vague idea of accompanying them to Moran and independently scampering up—unroped—that somewhat easy 5.6 route. At worst, I could beg to tie in with one of their ropes for perhaps the most exposed pitch.

But in my rendezvous with them at the Climbers' Ranch, I learned that they had made no alteration in their months-old rope assignments.

Experience had taught me that three-person ropes are incredibly slow, and that four rope teams might cause a dangerous bottleneck if even one part of the route were to prove unexpectedly difficult. With visions of the recent Everest fiasco flashing through my mind, and wholly aware of my "outlier" status with the club, I "buttoned my lip." But I immediately decided that under no condition could I climb with them. An additional reason: they had already excluded me in their arrangements for a canoe approach. So it was a no-brainer: however I might accomplish either the approach or the climb, I was on my own. My very vague plan was to go in a day after them—following a yet-to-be-determined land route. Then, I would join their group at the campsite halfway up. There, we would pass a night together—they having scaled the route that day and I just arriving with plans to go up it on the morrow. Vaguely, I convinced myself that their "beta" (precise information about the route) would be an adequate substitute for a belaying partner. I knew of the high possibility that, if conditions were not ideal, I would choose to abandon the scamper attempt altogether.

Vaguely, I was convinced that even this was preferable to being a third member of one of their teams, roped in and impatiently waiting our rope's turn to perform belay after tedious belay in climbing up the relatively easy route. Standing there before them, I envisioned how it would be, roped up with some of them ahead of me and others behind. Even under the best of possible circumstances, I would be chewing my fingernails, *impatient*, perhaps anxious, but definitely *antsy*—with shut mouth and gritted teeth—upon gazing out at the inexperienced personnel bottlenecking the route's easy crux. I would have to *stay calm and quiet*—and suffer. It would be akin to mental incarceration, after having yielded my liberty to another rope leader. No thanks. That was—absolutely—not my style. (God, why was I born so ornery?)

Things were even more complicated than what I have just described (bear with me, patient reader). Whereas they all had reserved canoes to approach Moran via String and Leigh lakes, I still harbored pleasant memories of my hike along the east-lake trail some 42 years earlier (goddamn memories!). Bull-headed, I wished instant forgetfulness for the description of that same trail in the most recent guidebook: a "dense layer of thatched logs and swampy areas … [which] will deter all but the most masochistic people."[6] But—if my own path to Moran would not be via the east-lake trail—would it be just possible, and perhaps even desirable, to approach along the lakes' west side? Hmmm. Hmmm. Studying the map, I did see a maintained hiking trail, about five miles long, leading from a parking area all the way along the two lakes' west shore and ending at a "patrol cabin" for ranger-volunteers. Might there exist a rarely used mountaineer's trail beginning there and continuing west along Leigh Lake's north shore? Might that trail lead me directly to the canyon that one must ascend to arrive at the CMC campground and then the start of the route itself? When I asked around, no one knew. So I decided to find out.

Now was when I decided to cross that line. As one would expect, a posted warning at the trailhead stated clearly that vehicles of any type were prohibited. Translation: "no trail bikes allowed." But, at the same time, the query of a rogue philosopher was reverberating in my mind: "If nobody witnessed it, did a tree actually fall in the middle of the forest?" The sassiest of the mountain gods were egging me on: in Jackson I found a stout kid's bicycle for the give-away price of $7, and for another $15 I was able to extend the seat up to a desirable height. I was going to do it: I was going to go in via bicycle, violating a sacrosanct National Park rule. (Which sassy god was it, seducing me with those naughty whispers in my ear?)

Just before dawn I drove in to the parking area, with the small bicycle in the back of my truck. It was dark. In total silence, total stillness, I mounted the bike and rode it in along a seldom-used horse trail. Reaching Leigh Lake and the end of the maintained trail, I scouted around to my satisfaction. Only a half hour had elapsed before—totally unobserved—I sped back on out (but I had left a faint tire track in places along that hiking trail). As a result of my investigation, I was convinced that my best Moran approach would involve brush crashing along Leigh's north shore.

Two days later, the CMC climbers' approach day came. Resolved to wait a day before joining them, I found an alternative activity in brush-crashing up the canyon behind Symmetry Spire. I hadn't planned it, but from those heights I had a perfect view. It was moderately late in the afternoon. *What?* Looking way off to the north, I observed five distant dots on String Lake that had to be their canoes making an incredibly late start. Had they slept in till noon? Had it been their intention to fulfill the worst of my silent suppositions about their incompetence? But—*oh*—then I saw some super-black clouds that were blowing in, which meant that the CMC group, not yet even out of their canoes—overloaded with equipment—were going to be hit by the storm way before they could arrive at the CMC campsite. Celebrating the fact that I was not with them, I hustled my butt down and arrived at the car just as the heavy drops began to fall. And the rain fell. It was a fierce storm—all night long. But for me—"what, me, worry?"—I spent a wonderful evening, warm and dry, sipping beer in Dugan's bar with new friends, listening to thunder and the tat-tat-tat of the severe storm blasting away outside.

I knew that Teton summer storms never last long. So before dawn I was mounted again on my trusty two-wheeled steed, this time carrying a bivy pack with my 150' spaghetti rope. Again, fifteen minutes to cover the five miles in, and startling only a young boy camper who had stirred from his tent to take an early leak. Just as daylight was emerging, I hid the bike some 100 feet from the end of the trail and, minutes later, began my frigid brush-crashing and shallow-wading trek across the north shore of Leigh Lake. Between the drenched bushes and the need to wade the edges of the lake in stretches up to my waist, I was quite wet. Not to worry, given the perfect weather, even as I trembled with cold. Finally within sight of the canyon I would have to walk up to get to the CMC campsite, I saw the beached canoes of my CMC buddies.

What's that? *Oh my God*, a mother black bear with her cub! *Danger.* I began talking loudly. Gads, my only option was to wade right across the spot where the two were stationed. Now I was shouting. *It worked*: she and the cub retreated into the bushes. But I was definitely more frightened of her than she of me. *Whew.* Adrenaline flowing. I hung two cans—my third day's food—from a tree, within spitting distance of the beached canoes and the bushed exit of mama bear. Then, in picture-perfect sunshine, I started walking on up.

A few hours later, I was anticipating my arrival at the Moran campground before midday. Towering a few thousand feet directly above me was the black dike near Moran's crest—now massive and imposing. The early morning chill had disappeared. It was a glorious day and I was in a glorious place. Lazily, I imagined the CMC group, at that very moment, basking in the sun, headed for the summit. There was not a wisp of wind, which meant that great weather would hold for my climbing day on the morrow.

Then … voices. *Oh my gosh!* It was the first of the CMC party—they were descending! One by one, they were choosing their footsteps carefully in order to avoid stumbling while making their way down the gravel-covered boulders. The sight of them returned me to realistic thought: their retreat, and now their blah-blah explanations, confirmed what I had surmised: that because of their late start they had ascended only about halfway up the canyon when the storm hit. As a result, all of them had been drenched by the heavy rains. It was not necessary for them to recount the soggy night spent at the campground. They explained that at daybreak a half-inch of snow-hail was covering everything, that this—in their morning powwow—served as their reason for abandoning the climb. They had judged that to continue proceeding upward would court undue danger. I silently nodded my head in (feigned) affirmation as I glanced about. In the bright sun I was able to see no more than a few BB-sized hailstones behind an occasional rock. They had taken a vote, and the nays had won: their group decision was that all would go down. My feeble voice, upon seeing the face of my only (somewhat) friend in the whole group: "Chris. Stay. Let's climb it tomorrow. It'll be beautiful." *"Can't Bill, it was a group decision."* Group decision? That's a downer. "See you guys back at Devil's Lake."

The CMC campsite was marvelous. Just me. And silence. And a pesky pika. And way over there a noble marmot. In the early morning light, also a deer. With a perfectly clear sky and an early morning chill, I got up, made ready, and marched up the rocky gully. Up toward the humongous black dike, whose shadowy vertical face fully filled the sky to my right.

But my route up did not lead directly to its base. Instead, the easy (walking) terrain ended at a pointed ridge that dropped off, in frightening verticality, on three sides. Looking to the right, about eighty yards separated me from the vertical wall directly underneath the dike. Below that, there was a huge steep glacier that dropped precipitously. This was the Drizzlepuss, where the first-ascent party, stymied as I was, became drenched as they paused to contemplate their options about how to bridge the scary gap to continue on up the massive mountain. Looking upward, I squinted to follow where my route up its side might go. But how to get over there? The whole view: the dike, the stunning verticality, the huge dimensions of everything: it was exhilarating … and … well … chilling. Superlatives don't do the scene justice.

Would I continue on? I looked around for a pathway down and across to begin the route. That small opening? *Gads*, I'd have to go straight down. The guidebook's language ("down climb the steep west side … wander down ledges") makes the whole thing sound like a Sunday stroll.[7] But it wasn't. *One slip* meant a 2,000-foot drop, touching nothing! My courage and scamper impetuosity simply disappeared. Or, I could make up a story for my caution-urging wife: "prudence won out." But I know that is only a part of the truth. The dark side of my being would say: I chickened out. But a more admirable voice would argue that there, right there, the majesty and dread of Moran's Black-dike Route simply overwhelmed me.

(A day after writing the above, I reflected: where else in the Tetons had I experienced a similar "tremble"—or dread? Or call it an "intense peak experience"—or a gush of "fear-sublimity." A few Teton places come to mind: The southwest-couloir descent off the Middle. Above the glacier, just before scampering up the Koven couloir of Owen. Emerging above the towers on the Grand's East Ridge. Yes, the Tetons have their g-g-grandeur. Mountain Gods: you've done well here!)

I'll leave it at that. Black-dike face: I'd really like to return. You deserve it. I do too. But I'll have to have a partner, at least for simul descending down that darn hole-in-the-rock at the Drizzlepuss, and then for at least the first two pitches on up. Hail to the mountain. All Hail.

Without a partner to belay, this "scamper" climber had to learn the art of taking a "selfie." But even more important: I had to get out and enjoy—once again—the smells, sights, and quietude of an alpine setting.

Every year, come August, the "climbing bug" began to bite. While the heat discouraged any visit to lowland areas in California such as Yosemite Valley, Joshua Tree or the Sierra Nevadas, summits (despite their long, hot approaches) like Mathes Crest (a few miles' hike from Yosemite National Park's Tuolumne Meadows), at 10,000 feet, offered a beautiful alternative. Here, Don Fredrickson is warming up in Tuolumne's hot summer sun, with Mathes Crest in the background.

A typical weekend away from studies took us regularly to Big Rock, Tahquitz, and, here, Lovers' Leap (an hour from Sacramento, California). Here, I belayed Mike, who wanted to challenge himself by leading this 5.9 crack that featured squeeze—chimney and body—jam moves.

Come summer, we were off to the high country. In the 1970s we made several mixed-climbing ascents in the Canadian Rockies. Three times we visited the Bugaboos (Interior Ranges, British Columbia). Here, Don is studying the possible approaches for the alpine routes we would accomplish on Snowpatch (to the right) and the Howser Spires (in the center).

Over the years I would visit my parents in Seattle and then climb in the Olympics, the North Cascades, or on Mt. Rainier (State of Washington). All these areas feature superb alpine meadows that we passed through on our way to the higher elevations.

In the early 1970s Don and I spent considerable time in Yosemite Valley—which culminated in our five-and-a-half-day ascent of El Capitan's Salathé Wall. Contrary to popular belief, climbers on this route find several ledges large enough for two sleeping bodies.

Before the advent of drones, a climber took most photos either looking straight up or down. On its upper third, where El Cap leans past the vertical, we had to drive in pitons every three feet for aid climbing.

About eight pitches up the Salathé, I am securely clipped in to my piton anchor. Don, a pitch below, is getting ready to jumar up his fixed rope, while I prepare to haul up the two sacks containing our water, food, and sleeping bags.

The Tetons in Wyoming (just south of Yellowstone Park) offer some of the most scenic and exciting trad climbing in the United States. We were standing on the summit of Teewinot when I snapped this photo of Tom, with Mt. Nez Percé in the background.

Tom and I were in a celebratory mood upon completing (on our second try!) the challenging North Face route of the Grand Teton (Wyoming). Tom's large climbing pack, which he is sitting upon, suggests the obstacles we had overcome: a difficult ice bergschrund, a bivy on the face, and an electrical storm near the top.

I prefer not to remember the dangerous idiosyncrasies of my climbing partner and the way we negotiated this big gap on our way to the summit of Mt. Randall in the Canadian Rockies.

That ol' Volvo carried Don and me to Alaska and back. Here's the famed "Indian teepee" pitched in the parking lot near the spectacular Columbia Ice Fields, in the Canadian Rockies.

The previous day the bush pilot had flown us in to the Cathedral Spires of the Alaska Range. With perfect weather, Don and I wasted no time establishing a new route up Gurney Peak. Not needing to belay, I looked down to snap the photo of Don, climbing up to join me, with the aptly named "Glacier of the Shadows" in the background. Perhaps one of those "dots" above and to the left of Don is our pitched tent at least a mile below.

Two days later, Ludwig was fuming as we pointed out the line we had followed up Gurney Peak—visible in the background. The next morning the three of us set out for our two-day ascent up Peak 8520.

From the small windows of the three-passenger plane, outfitted with skis for glacier landings, we looked down on the lateral moraine separating two of Alaska's spectacular, serpentine glaciers.

A sudden storm surprises Vance and me on the south wall of Aconcagua. Tent pegs don't penetrate the rock and ice flurries chill to the bone. We're violating a cardinal rule of climbing: that if you're not ascending or descending, you're in the sleeping bag—melting water, heating soup, and trying to stay warm.

Mike Andrews carefully tests the strength of the snow bridge crossing a dangerous crevasse on our ascent of Huascarán Sur in Peru. On glaciers—whether in Peru or Alaska or on Rainier—we almost always roped up, because if you break through the snow crust you could fall several hundred feet straight down and into a huge cavern below.

Descending from our first Cordillera Blanca (Peru) summit, there were new dangers. Abandon an ice screw to anchor a rappel down and over the bergschrund? Forget it! The snow below appeared soft, so we risked an ankle injury by opting to jump. Jim Milne, who dared to go first, snapped this shot of me in mid-air.

Freaky conditions gave me this unique photograph of Ludwig and Don on southern Alaska's Mt. Marcus Baker, before we became enveloped in a total white-out.

Our Brit buddies, either more "chicken" or prudent than Bill and me, had turned back. Only two of the 15 pitches up the iced face of Les Courts (French Alps) offered "bomb-proof" protection. It wasn't fun, and I would choose to never do that type of route again.

**Luck was with us: before darkness we were able to thread our way through Huascarán's (Peru) heavily crevassed glacier. Tomorrow, we would begin the actual climb.**

In the Cordillera Blanca (Peru) we never lacked for an adequate camping site. Jim and I would cram our bodies into the single-walled red tent and Mike would weather the night alongside in his bivy sack. Here, the morning sun warms our fatigued bodies just down from the summit of Huascarán Sur.

A small bivy cave high on Huascarán's mighty East Face had saved our butts! Now, our first pitch in the morning involved kicking our crampons' front-points into the hard snow and traversing horizontally for a hundred yards before proceeding upward. Notice the picket we were using for protection. Also notice signs of my deficient belay—the risk I chose to run in order to snap this photo.

Had these kids in Shilla ever seen "gringo" climbers before? In the background is the mighty East Face of Huascarán Sur (Cordillera Blanca, Peru).

## CHAPTER 8

# Glacier National Park[1]

Who was it who said, "Old climbers never die, they just fade away"?[2] He was right—I think. Let me explain.

Here, I'll continue with the topic introduced before: the relationship between a climber's mind and body. There are three stages: First, in my younger climbing days I enjoyed a syncretism linking mind and body: I dreamed, then physically fulfilled, the mountaineering challenge to enjoy "a freedom of the hills." Second—the stage I'm now in—that of the "plucky ol' warrior"—when memories of former prowess produce climbing ambitions that the aging body fulfills only with difficulty or at high risk.

Then, there's the third stage that will be upon me in another decade (please Gods: might you make it two?). This will be when my body will simply not be able to deliver, and when the mind will be forced to reconcile itself to only sweet memories of past climbing joy. The Mountain Gods will have given up on me, and encroaching dementia will allow the mind to be seduced by the false promise of eternal climbing happiness.

No way would I want to speed up the mental/physical processes that will inescapably drag a resisting me to that third stage. How might I prolong my passage through stage two? That is what I was attempting to do—in great part unconsciously—during my 2011 visit to Glacier National Park (GNP).

Truth be told, I harbored few illusions when I chose Glacier for my August climbing excursion that year. I knew that there was very little if any high-quality climbable rock (the technical term is the prevalence of "shit" rock), being part of the Rocky Mountains' uplifted sedimentary area. But I knew of the park's formidable reputation among more pedestrian friends for unsurpassed beauty. And I was ever more aware of my status as a (somewhat) "over-the-hill" climber who should avoid rekindling the illusion that I can still do Alps or Bugaboo or North-Face-Grand-Teton type climbing that thrilled me so some forty years ago. Yet GNP still satisfied the thirst for mountain scenery, cool alpine air, proximity to active people similarly enraptured, and the physical engagement that mountains require.

Some useful lessons about GNP: it has extraordinarily benign weather. Not once during my nine or so nights did I need to even pitch a tent (I can't guarantee that this was typical). And it's warm. Car-accessible campgrounds are at about 3,200 feet, and even when I hiked in to "high country" camps I never slept higher than 6,500 feet. So GNP has this—in addition to its other qualities—to recommend itself: it is low and warm.

And forget technical equipment: no problem kick-stepping across snow fields without crampons or ice axe, or glissading down them in the late afternoon. Only one time was I inhibited from proceeding because I didn't have those ice tools, but my light pack made it worth the tradeoff.

About rock equipment: I never took it out of the car trunk. When the terrain got difficult, I realized that roped climbing was not an option. Imagine putting in dubious pro into shit-rock cracks. So a sad but necessary truth about GNP peaks: they are not the Tetons; their sexy-looking rock-ridged summits are not worth the risk.

And another general lesson about GNP: there are very few available high-country campgrounds, since most have been reserved for months. And they are not the most desirable places: many are bald spots cut out of the tree stands next to swampy lakes at the foot of high walls. For any hike-in campground, campfires are unfortunately prohibited. A recommendation for the next "climbing rogue": be prepared to spend an unscheduled—and very discreet—night out there if a climb turns out to take longer than expected.

Some useful lessons about myself: I have to admit that one of the goals of this trip was self-discovery. Is the running that I do year round in La Crosse, Wisconsin, adequate for keeping in shape for the high mountains? And the advance of years? Well, during the entire two weeks at GNP I felt strong, but only after having eaten an adequate breakfast. This means that I now favor later starts in order to nourish myself adequately at the beginning of the day. And I've learned that Spartan-like mountain grub belongs to the past; in the high country I have to carry palatable strong food: hard boiled eggs, Chinese-buffet chicken, Swiss cheese, and as tasty a bread as possible. Peanut butter and jelly sandwiches still go down. But primarily I have learned that my Teton-derived model of going super light and long doesn't work (any longer?) for me: simply stated, the bod just doesn't like to tack an easy summit—meaning an extra 2,000 feet of altitude gain—onto a 16-mile in-and-out day.

So the radical lesson for future mountain junkets: hike in for the first night with as light a load as possible, and then do my scamper-climb the next. And be minimally prepared to stay in the back country for a second night. For this style of peak bagging, GNP was (and will be) ideal. There, in a future summer, I can imagine passing okay nights in only a parka, booties, down pants, and a nylon envelope.

Oh, one other preliminary note: I had chosen GNP as my year's mountain playground with the concern that if I were to postpone a visit here for my next reincarnation, then I might not see any surviving glaciers. Well, surprise of surprises: with record snow falls this past winter, I heard absolutely no mention—by anyone, anytime—about the rapid disappearance of the park's glaciers. You, the reader, can judge the importance of this anecdotal evidence.

Well, after two long days of driving, I arrived at GNP with the immediate goal of minimizing my time as hiking tourist in order to scout out a few peak-bagging objectives. Early the second day I was off. I hiked seven miles in, putzed around a bit, and then hiked back out: I simply did not have the energy/enthusiasm to continue on up to a summit. But no regrets: I was getting into shape and feeling out the terrain. And I learned that altitude and weather were (until then) not serious concerns. One day rest, and then I was off again. I hiked a real impressive 11-mile uphill trail, surrounded by athletic tourists, and then I was able to ride the shuttle back down to the start. Great!!

I was feeling my oats. On the shuttle carrying me up and down the "Going to the Sun Road," I had a chance to study the approach to my first summit objective.

It is an impressive mountain with the poetic name of Heaven's Peak (8,987 feet), whose whole south side is visible from the shuttle window. According to the guidebook the legendary (of California's Sierra Nevada fame) Norman Clyde was the first to gain its summit in the 1920s: his approach was from the north side and, after staying alone on the summit to watch the sunset, he descended back to the river in semi-darkness. With this information I naturally assumed that the peak would be a good starter, with 3rd class scrambling to the summit and an easy descent down the other side. Viewing from afar, I was able to see a bench halfway up with a glacier at the foot of a near-vertical face. From years of experience I was confident that, upon approaching, the face would lean back to offer a manageable route to the ridge west of the summit.

But the most problematic part—I ascertained from a distance—would be the lower half, that is, the green skirt whose top was the glacier and whose bottom was the small river I would have to wade across. Lots of green could mean bad-news brush crashing that I had to avoid as much as possible. Luckily, not all was jungle green; also, I observed low-angle rock-outcropping ridges that were free of heavy vegetation. Also, the myriad of small streambeds carrying glacier melt seemed to offer a choice of possible, but not appealing, pathways.

Early the next morning I parked my car alongside the river and was off. Wading across, the river water came up only to my thighs. On the other bank I left my wet tennies and put on dry ones with the vain hope that I would have dry feet for the rest of the day. It took me three hours to get up to the glacier, generally following a streambed, sometimes having to go around or over boulders, sometimes having to climb out of the rock-lined gulley to avoid 20-foot vertical waterfalls. And sometimes having to enter into the much-feared brush—which meant pushing apart the one- to two-inch-thick branches of the viney trees that were growing horizontally five feet above my head. Sometimes, however, I could only fall forward with my body in order to open up a channel through the brambly jungle that left scratch marks on my bare legs. Upward progress also meant sometimes wading in a small stream passing over slippery rocks. Wet shoes: no way to avoid it. At times progress was difficult and ugly, as I had anticipated. But after an unpleasant five minutes, I would emerge to find a section of vegetation-free bare rock or a mountain prairie rib that provided much faster and enjoyable advancement. And finally, I pulled myself over a rock ridge to stand on the terminal moraine of the glacier, that soon became the lateral moraine leading to the face.

Would the route go? I had my doubts until I got within a hundred yards or so. Following the half-mile moraine I studied the rock blocks above me and sought out the most climbable gap between them. Uplifted sedimentary layers now formed sloping ledges leading up and left. This was the obvious—and only—path, even though Heaven's Peak was now far to the right. But about possible routes I could not be choosy. As I saw it, I would have to identify the least-problematical path up dangerous terrain, which would involve climbing through or over rocks to advance from one ledge to another. Near-vertical rocks. Looking up, I was able to see that on some of the scree-covered sloping ledges there were bushes—a good sign. So I spent the next two hours weaving my way up scree and rock and steering to avoid the high-sloping snowfields. I took care to make small cairns at key spots, knowing that route finding going down is far more difficult—and therefore dangerous—than going up. Everywhere, loose rock. Looking below I saw the ever-receding glacier at the base of a scary, vertical drop. I was convinced that few—or perhaps no one—in the mountain's history had been as adventurous or as foolish as I in attempting this route—that required confident scampering abilities and route-finding skills.

I decided that I really didn't relish descending by this same path, and I fantasized an easy Norman-Clyde pathway down the other side. Suddenly, happiness: some 50 yards away I saw a mountain goat! Hey! To get onto that face he must have followed a grassy sloping path up the other side. Visions of an easy descent flashed into my mind. Well, a half-hour later that Rocky Mountain high quickly disappeared when I pulled my head over the knife-edged ridge. Below: verticality, meaning dangerous terrain. And looking east to the Heaven's Peak summit: no way to proceed without a rope and a belaying companion. And maybe not even then, because where in that shit rock could you put adequate protection? It took me twenty seconds to realize that I could go no higher, that the only way down was the same route I had forged climbing on up. *Ouch.* Down climbing some of those stretches would not be fun. But there was no other way. So I turned around and started descending. Three hours later I reached level terrain and waded back across the river to my car. I was tired, but happy. Briefly the hope sprang into my head that one of my offspring, some day in the future, would feel as good as I did then—when and if they were to accomplish what I had just done.

Meanwhile, where in the park to spend the night? I continued practicing my now-familiar routine of inviting myself to share a campsite with another party. One night it was with three young bikers from Michigan. The next it was with a depressed middle-aged biker also from Michigan—weren't there any climbers here? A few bottles of Guinness, a neat campfire, good conversation (it's great to meet new people), and throw my tarp and sleeping bag on the ground. Perfect weather. Does it rain here in summer? Stupid question. But for me the Gods continued to smile: weather reports sounded great well into the next week.

In the days allotted, I was to make a second, and this time, final bona-fide ascent. The serendipity of events had a major role in our success. I say our, because when I was registering for my projected solo stay at a high camp near Mount Jackson (10,051 feet, one of the highest in the park) I met François, a 41-year-old physician from Switzerland, who became an ideal companion for the climb. The only campsite available in the area turned out to be undesirable: leaving it, we needed two uphill hours to traverse the map's one-half mile and reach the desired trail. But we were rewarded: following it, we passed through some amazingly beautiful terrain, over an impressive mountain pass inhabited by a hundred marmots, past another campsite that had been visited the day before by a mountain lion (!!!!), and then to the northern base of Mount Jackson. After stashing our equipment, for the next two hours we powered up the rather steep scree-covered sedimentary layers, avoiding the dangerous snow fields. Not a route for tourists. François, an accomplished skier, felt at home with elevation and verticality, didn't need Cheerios for his high energy, and was incredibly coordinated in ski-descending over scree and snow. With exceptional memory, François led us, and we threaded our way down without incident.

Beautiful views. A great summit in a great park. Yes, the highlight of my summer. And that night, even though without wine, rum, and food, we found a removed spot to share with the local moose, where we were able to camp and dry our socks with a discreet campfire. A great sky, a warm night, a superb 360-degree view. Hard to beat all that. Mountaineering at its best. What more can I say?

Hey, is there anyone out there who might be tempted to join me for next August's mountaineering junket? Do get back.

## CHAPTER 9

# Momo's Wonderful (Almost Nightmarish) Day on Orizaba

Someplace I have to get in here a few pages about my climbing experiences in Mexico. Personal and professional reasons explain my 30-year commitment to Mexico, that translated into spending, in and around Cuernavaca (in the State of Morelos), at least a few weeks every year. Throughout that time the country's high volcanoes exerted a constant attraction.

Memories are murky, but I am certain that it was the Y2K year when we transformed vague longings into action. Do you remember what the Y stood for? Not me. (Year?) Across the U.S. many feared that when computer calendars abruptly changed from 1999 to 2000 (the "2K") there would be a widespread digital breakdown of some sort (as it turned out: "much ado about nothing.") But with the uncertainty being real, we suspected—as it turned out, correctly—that airlines would be desperate to fill their seats for January 1. So that—in a (proverbial) nutshell—is how my son, Dan, and I arrived at Acapulco on New Year's Day, loaded with high-mountain equipment.

A few afternoons later, we got to Paso de Cortés—the 10,000-foot-high ridge running between the two huge volcanoes visible from Mexico City on a clear day: Popocatépetl (5,426 meters; 17,802 feet) and Iztaccíhuatl (5,286 meters)—their names in Nahuatl. Not wanting to have to carry overnight packs—and feeling totally "superior" to any possible altitude complications—we began walking up the nearest ridge.[1] It was a cool, moonlit night; we figured that we could proceed all night and then descend: all in one swoop.

Bzzzzt. Error! Wrong! First, we had totally ignored the need to spend at least one night at about 10,000 feet for short-term acclimatization. And second, even though the nearby city of Cuernavaca enjoys "spring-time weather" year-round, we abruptly learned that "winter" was still an issue in the nearby altitudes. In short, the bitter cold was what turned us back—and perhaps the beginnings of weakness associated with altitude gain.[2]

There is a consolation to this story: two years later Dan and I returned to go up the trail to the heights of Iztaccíhuatl.[3] A curious note about that trip: it was late afternoon, and we had just arrived at the campground down the way from Paso de Cortés, when I saw a "gristly" old (I mean *old*) gringo, covered with sweat and dust, who was just finishing the very long, tedious trek back from the summit. Immediately I realized that there was only one individual in the world who it could be—all my life I had read about his incredible mountain exploits, even though I had never seen him before. So I said to Dan, "Go get your camera and take a picture of him. You'll be able to tell your grandchildren that you actually met on the trails none other than Fred Becky!"

I've got to get back to Popo before introducing Momo. It just so happened that for the last several years the previously dormant volcano was coming back to life, producing what the tourist literature calls "explosions." Only weeks after Dan's and my failed attempt, the Mexican military panicked and ordered a temporary evacuation of all the surrounding rural villages in addition to a closure of the mountain to all climbers.

This is not the place to explain the fiasco related to this "official" hype. I write as a personal witness: my six years of part-time residence in a nearby community was just beginning at this time: from the roof of our house some forty miles away we could see the "plumarola" (a cloud of smoke and whatever rising thousands of feet high) that the mountain sent forth just about every morning between nine and eleven.

A year later: ditto. And two years later: ditto to the second degree. And there I was, patiently observing. I wanted to go up it. Then not so patiently. I was antsy, frustratingly waiting for the government to lift all restrictions. It became obvious to everyone but the government that Ol' Popo just wanted to let off some gas—nothing more. But they didn't lift the climbing prohibitions. Year after year.

Well, finally my patience came to an end. I figured: if so many Mexicans "illegally" cross the U.S. border—my border—then why do I have to restrain myself here? So I made plans. This time it would be in "real" summer—to avoid the (unexpected) cold of a few years back. Some friends drove me to Paso de Cortés and dropped me off a hundred yards from the checkpoint manned by two young dark-skinned soldiers. I instructed my friends to return for me in exactly 48 hours. So, with a light overnight pack, I simply walked through the woods totally unseen and, a half-mile up, turned onto the well-beaten trail.

Viewing the mountain over the past few years I had realized that a significant change had occurred: the disappearance of almost all snow and ice from the mountain top. This was due—I hypothesized—to the slow heating of the entire mass as a result of the minor volcanic activity. So I had assumed (correctly, it turned out) that neither ice axe nor crampons would be necessary. Also, scamper tennies would have been entirely sufficient. (Fortunately, my light snowboarding "moon boots" caused no heel-blister problems and proved to offer okay friction for balancing up the rock outcroppings.)

About the climb itself, there's not much to recount. I spent a superb night at 13,000 feet. The Mountain Gods had selected me, and me alone, to witness the immobile silence and stark desert beauty. But I also experienced a pang of sadness upon realizing that, given the lunkheaded prohibition, a whole generation of young Mexican adventurers were being denied the glorious opportunity that I alone had seized.

At dawn there was still no wind and the temperature was ideal. I took my time, not wanting to arrive near the summit too early. Sure enough, just before noon I saw above me the "plumarola" shooting forth from the top. No big deal—it was all totally expected. I found it easier to scamper up solid rock outcroppings than slip-slide in the steep sand. And I warily memorized bluff features, knowing that I would have to navigate away from precipices on the way down. Scrambling up the last hundred or so vertical feet, I noted that there were absolutely no volcanic particles or ash in sight. This, for me, was irrefutable proof of official exaggerations about reputed "eruptions." But still unanswered was the nature of Popo's frequent smoke or vapor emissions.

Then, I arrived close to the crater's edge. Ten feet below I could hear an extremely loud, steady roar. Its cause? My interest accelerated. When I thrust my upper torso up over the edge, *wrrssss*. The sound *smacked against my ear drums*. Surprised? Shocked? At once I lowered my head down two feet—just below the edge—and half the volume disappeared. My best description of the noise: what I would hear if I were to be suddenly dropped alongside of a fully throttled 747 jet engine on an airport tarmac!

Truly, the sound had scared me! My first reaction was the fear that a bona fide eruption had just began, and I hurriedly looked for the path to flee downhill. But wait! The sound was constant. Nothing was happening. There was no explosion nor rain of volcanic particles. My inner voice: *Calm down, Bill, nothing is happening.* So I didn't move. I was just under the crater lip, ready to shoot downhill, but waiting. With five senses observing.

I let several seconds pass: no change. The muted roar was constant. *God damn, Bill. Come all this way and you freak out! Get it together.*

So I got it together. With accelerated heartbeat, and ready to pounce downhill, I slowly stepped up again to raise my head above the crater rim. This time I was ready for the deafening roar. *Woosh.* But this time I didn't panic. Instead, I lifted my legs up and over the edge and sat down facing in.

With index fingers stuck in my ears, I realized there was no reason to panic. I began to observe. After snapping a few pictures I decided to take the time to meticulously observe everything about this incredible natural phenomenon.

Just below my body the crumbly dirt-ash crater-edge slanted down about 100 feet to a level surface that stretched to about a half-mile, or maybe three-quarters of a mile away. I rapidly dismissed the idea of going on down—although it might not have been difficult. I had seen something like this before at the summit of Mount Rainier (in the State of Washington)—but there the similarly huge, round, flat crater-top, inside a comparable dirt/ash shell, had been covered with snow. Here, I was viewing a black, crusty material—resembling the burnt surface of an apple crisp—with a dull red glow visible through its many cracks and lumps. It was a surface that almost invited being walked on—I would have obliged only if I had been out of my mind and wearing totally inflammable and heat-resistant boots. Within 200 feet I counted eight small air streams shooting up—and I surmised these to be the origin of the sulphur smell that predominated.

The deafening roar was constant. There was no visual evidence of its cause. To this day the mystery remains unexplained.

I pinched myself: the Gods had bestowed upon me a unique opportunity. It was my obligation not to hurry, even though my intense anxiety due to the smoke and roar never lessened. For five whole minutes I forced myself to methodological observation. Gazing out, starting at the left, I was determined to register every single detail. Then, moving my head slightly to the right, I began again. A vision flashed through my mind that I was a memory machine that would observe, capture, then archive all details—whether insignificant or super-important. In different time segments I shifted my head from left to right, peering at the cooled molten crust, the jagged crater wall rising above it, and the faint lines of gas squirting upward. Then, my curiosity was satiated. It was time to go. I got to my feet, turned away from the mountain, and stepped downward into the unstable sand. My descent was fast. Most of the way I almost ran, with long jumpy strides ending in sand slides. In about 15 minutes I was at the top of the dangerous cliffs, having just covered a distance that had taken more than three hours to ascend that very morning.

Carefully I navigated a path around and through the cliffs and on down to easy terrain. Then, I followed a well-worn path to the edge of the woods, which I passed through to view the van of my friends, who had been waiting to pick me up. I got in and we drove away, totally unseen by the unsuspecting uniformed youths a hundred yards around the corner.

It was in those very months that I met Momo, who was destined to be my partner in Mexican climbing escapades for the next few years. I was entering into a new stage of my life—details which need not be treated here. Suffice to say that I would spend considerable time in and around his home in a rural village in the State of Morelos.[4]

He might have been 15 years old. Middle school had left him behind, and he was not the most brilliant of carpenters after a year of trade-school instruction. For a few months he tried himself out as rural worker (at 70 pesos, or $6, a day), then as flunky employee for a garden center. Every night he'd return home to do his part in the struggling family business of pouring and carving spherical candles for sale in handicraft retail stores. No, Momo was not the most brilliant of my former climbing partners. But his smile was genuine and warming. And—as of yet—he had not been knocked by the penchant for alcohol that he had inherited from his family line. A mutual friend, María, appropriately pointed out, "Momo es muy noble."

In those days Momo was the only person to fully share my penchant for running up to the top of any one of the surrounding hills. What? There existed no map of the eight to ten geographic projections within sight of our village? What? None of the locals could even tell me the historical names of these bumps and cliffs? Inquiring in the three villages, and even in the library of the nearby small city, the result was the same: there existed only fragmentary information about local place names. Realizing this, I set for myself the task—for which I spent considerable time during two or three months—of interviewing the eldest, and hopefully wisest, individuals of the region to dredge the collective memory of almost-forgotten lore. The result? I drew, then made copies, of a large, framed map—one of which still hangs in the building of the county administrative center.

In carrying out the "exploring side" to this topographical task, I would put on my Salvation Army running shoes, and Momo—with no other choice—a pair of worn (and falling apart) leather dress shoes. Some days other members of the family would accompany us. We'd drive near the base of the chosen hill and seek out the best path leading to the summit. On other days, just the two of us—Momo and I would set off running. This was hardly the equivalent of crossing a golf course: there were separate *nopal* (an edible cactus) fields to cross, with irrigation ditches, fences, and sometimes protective rows of huge spiny cactuses. Worst of all, there were the *barrancas* (huge steep-sided ditches carved out by millennial torrents), now dry, brambly, and nearly impossible to cross unless one followed the occasional trail used by generations of peasant farmers. In the fresh morning air, Momo and I were invincible. We could be constant movement for as long as two continuous hours, running up long faint trails to puzzle ourselves to the top of yet one more "hill."

Several times I, with a "climbing chip" on my shoulder, would stand amazed at the fearless antics of Momo. Forget any idea of roping up for added protection in that setting. Going up the last—steep—twenty feet of crumbly vegetable holds on Cerro Tonantzín, Momo didn't even look down. On Cerro Las Mariposas (Zihuapipalotzín) he scampered up the 20-foot vine roots—a combination chimney-lieback—as if he had been doing that sort of thing all his life. On the 50-minute run around and over the top of Cerro Cuiyocuítlato he was indefatigable.

Then: our crowning achievement. We had delayed two years before reaching the absolute top of Tepozoco, because prudence dictated that we had to use a rope (which I had brought from my home in Wisconsin) to protect ourselves while getting around a vertical front to reach the base of a shoulder-stand stretch. Was it a first ascent? It's remotely possible that in the long pre-conquest centuries an energetic Nahuat youth had tread on that summit, but my vanity argues otherwise.

All this was a warm-up for our trip to Orizaba, Mexico's highest peak, at 18,491 feet—and a near-perfect snow-covered volcanic cone—that sits on the border of Mexican states Puebla and Veracruz. I used the same moon boots (i.e., snowboard boots) that I had worn on Popo, but this time they were outfitted with crampons. For Momo, I had brought from Wisconsin a tight-fitting pair of rubber boots over whose soles I strapped another pair of crampons.

After a few hours' drive we arrived at the town nearest the volcano and found a family that would "car-sit" our vehicle during our ascent. From there we were off, carrying light overnight packs. By mid-afternoon we had reached the Piedra Grande Hut, where we would spend the night. A few people were already there. At dusk two more teams arrived, having descended from the summit. We learned that on the morrow Momo and I would be alone on the mountain.

One has to have an idea of the topography of the Jamapa Glacier route that we would follow. In daylight, it's an easy walk, as the trail winds up gullies flanked by volcanic shit-rock cliffs, the highest of which are situated in the 800 vertical feet above the hut. Going up in the faint morning light there were no trail-finding problems, but I confidently patted the shape of our only flashlight inside my pack's pocket upon imagining possible difficulties in a nighttime descent.

Then Momo and I broke through to the sloping scree field. We reached the toe of the glacier at about 15,000 feet. Was it easier going straight up the 35-degree incline, or was it easier choosing an angled line? We tried one, then the other. Step after step, we gained altitude. At about 16,000 feet I began to feel the altitude. At 17,000, puff, puff, groan. Reaching 17,500, the elevation was taking its toll, forcing a short rest stop every five minutes. At 17,800, there was a bit of mist, meaning that the visibility was not great just ahead. My bod: it was hurting. That is, I was hurting. Not Momo, with his permanent grin and cheer.

At 18,000: very white. So white, in fact, that the position of the sun was indistinguishable. I thought to look around. The angle was dropping off—we had to be getting near. But there were absolutely no outcroppings or features to serve as landmarks. I glanced back at where we had come, only to see white mist. Looking down I noted how snow-dust blown by a light wind made our crampon tracks almost invisible. Drat! It would have been nice to have brought along some wands to mark our path up. My movement? Very, very slow. The moment was approaching when my mountain-forged will would wimp out.[5]

One hundred more feet—18,100: slowness and extreme fatigue. My chicken-shit will cried "uncle." Momo would have to continue alone to the summit. I would wait for him here. At that point I totally believed that he would join me again within an hour.

Two hours later: No Momo. Should I start on down alone? No, no.

Three hours: Still no Momo. My watch told me that I would have just enough time to thread through the dangerous cliffs in daylight. Reluctantly, I started down.

Daylight was waning as I approached the tops of the volcanic cliffs. I would not need the light. But Momo? I found a large boulder just to the side of the trail and placed upon it a light-colored garment that he might see, with the flashlight on top: Momo would need it.

And I continued on down to the hut to join a half-dozen other adventurers who would attempt the drudgery trek to the summit in the morning. I shared with them my worries about Momo.

Although hungry, I delayed preparing dinner with the hope that his arrival would surprise me. In deep shadows I traversed, and then returned, the 50 yards to fill our cooking pan and my plastic bottle with water.

An hour later, begging use of a neighbor's light, I prepared, then consumed, my own dinner. Then, leaving the hut and going out into the pitch-dark, frosty, air, I shouted for Momo—a gesture I would repeat every fifteen minutes for the next hour.

By 10:00 I reluctantly decided to crawl into my sleeping bag, resolved to go back up at first light in search of Momo. I had to assume that he would stop somewhere to not risk descending the cliffs, and would shiver away until dawn. There was nothing more I could do. I must have slumbered off to sleep.

*Bill! Wake up! We hear your friend over on the other side of the water spigot!* Consciousness returns. Completely dark. "What time is it?" "*Just before midnight.*" "You guys are still awake?" I didn't understand why, but that was their problem. Momo? Making it down? How? Way over there?

Indeed. That's what happened. Momo had—somehow—been able to return to the hut. But he hadn't come via the regular trail. He had found another way down, and he had done it in complete darkness. I couldn't imagine how he had navigated down through the cliffs. His path must have been at least a hundred yards to the east, where there was no trail. How had he done it? He must have discovered a way through a different gulley. How was it that he had not fallen over the near continuous cliffs?

Over the years I have witnessed mountain miracles. Well, Momo's descent that night surely heads the list.

## Chapter 10

# Ask Permission to Climb in Uruguay

How might a plucky ol' climbing warrior evaluate his young alter ego's decision to spend two Peace Corps years in Flatland? In retrospect, it definitely had been an experience of "character building through denial."

I can imagine the reaction of a zany climbing buddy: "Katra, so you're an expert on climber celibacy? You offer proof positive below: such sublimation causes unpredictable results—which can appear decades after the fact."

Uruguay has been a sort of second home for me—given my frequent research visits, then my marriage to Marta about a decade ago. On every trip to that flatland country I search out whatever could attract the attention of the long-tested climber in me.

For some years I had had my eyes on an impressive rock wall lying within a fine animal reserve near the coastal city of Piriápolis—which is near the five-kilometer-long rock outcropping called the Pan de Azucar. Being that there are few climbers in the country, I logically figured that whatever I might do I would be alone. Solo climbing? What a drag. Nevertheless, I packed my rope and some pro and—on the rainiest day in months—drove the 2.5 hours.

It was 90 minutes before closing time when I parked in the deluged and now tourist-emptied reserve and then strolled past open-air animal cages and up to the edge of a 40-meter-wide brambly jungle that separated me from the base of the 100-meter-long wall. Squint, squint. Hmm. A few possible routes. Hey, what was that at its extreme left end? Visible only if you were looking for it: from top to bottom a ribbon of metal steps cemented into the rock—obviously left by a granite-mining operation some 80 years before. A no-brainer: this would be my first climb on the morrow—and a relatively safe one—and all I needed was for a few of the iron anchors to have resisted corrosion enough to serve as tied-off anchors for my self-belaying.

I'll blame euphoria for my first blunder: on the way back down I stopped to inform the only employee still remaining about my plans, and I cheerfully invited her, at dawn, to take a phone-photo of my future exploit. I even nourished the illusion that she might be induced to send that photo to the iPhone of my wife who was waiting for me back in San José. It was a very brief conversation. At its end, I climbed back into my car and then I drove away.

In the early morning I was ready, with rope and a bit of climbing paraphernalia in the trusty backpack. Approaching the cliff from a different path, I emerged from the trees some 50 meters away *when* … egad: two cop cars and six uniformed cops were there waiting at the start of my proposed route!!! I immediately realized what had happened: the employee had contacted her supervisor, who had contacted the police, who came and now were there to tell me about the (unposted) rule prohibiting climbing in the reserve. Hmm. Instant decision necessary. *If they tell me no, then that's the end of my trip. (What would I do with myself for the next two days if they—as I expected—were to prohibit me from climbing altogether?) But if they don't have the opportunity to tell me no, then… And even if they might wish to say no to "climbing," that technically would not exclude "descending."* (Attentive readers might realize that my reasoning process—at that point—was still under the influence of the wine I had consumed the previous night.)

No way would I choose to end my climbing excursion now, at 7:00 a.m. on the first climbing day of my two-day excursion. No way. Hmm. The trail in the opposite direction? Luckily, trees shielded me from the uniformeds' gaze. Still unseen, I immediately made my decision. I would follow the other trail to the top of Pan de Azucar. Great! Off I went.

After a half-hour of following the alternate trail upward, I arrived at the top and the base of the summit's 40-foot-vertical cement cross. It really didn't interest me now. Instead, I turned to the east and gazed out over the quarter-mile crest of the Pan de Azucar that I would have to traverse: exposed granite islands, as if they were floating on top of a sea of chest-high brambles. But no trails. Not even one trail. Apparently, Uruguayan youth are not smitten by an unquenchable curiosity and are not impelled to read Jack Kerouac to escape from summer-vacation boredom.

In their eyes, nobody but a *gringo loco* would even think of traversing that crest. Even worse, I was a climbing-crazed *gringo loco*. Brambles? So what? I had suffered far worse approaches passing through horizontal vine-maples in the North Cascades and even struggling up a bushy jungle in Glacier National Park. For 90 minutes I carefully bulldozed my way through thorns and scrambled up and down slabs. I had to trust my navigation instincts, because the mean vegetation denied me any access to the long cliff's edge—and an orientating glance downward. Finally, with bare legs thoroughly scratched, I (somewhat fortunately) emerged exactly at the top of my route, with a panoramic view of the whole park below. The cops had left. Hooray.

My second blunder: in full view of anyone below chancing to look upward, I spent fifteen long minutes untangling my rope and setting an anchor to begin my descent. By the end of the first rap, the two squad cars had returned and a group of cops was down there again, waiting for me. Was it possible that they had taken the drastic act of closing the park to tourists? Then I saw the arrival of a fire-department rescue squad. Luckily, nobody began yelling at me that unsavory monosyllabic word. I continued my descent in great form, having to reposition the rope three times. I figure that the cliff, from top to bottom, measured about 140 meters.

When I finally touched ground, it was impressive how two of the cops blundered their way through the mini jungle to position themselves at either shoulder as I carefully coiled the rope. I figured that they wanted to make sure that their "prize" was not going to sprint away to avoid their grasp. Their droll interrogation was highlighted by the question—only in Uruguay—"*What is your number?*"

*What's my number? How about my name, my nationality?* A minute later I realized that they were really interested in my age—that is, the *number* of years that my "older" body had existed on this, Our Mother Earth!

As they escorted me down, they didn't see the humor in my offer to train them for performing cliff rescues. Upon reaching the car, they carefully studied my Wisconsin driver's license—the only piece of I.D. I was carrying. When, upon seeing my date of birth they were truly surprised upon realizing that I had celebrated my 70th birthday only the day before. "What? Why aren't you back in San José, celebrating with your family?" Then, their next question honed in on the real issue: "Where are your pills?"

Running through their minds must have been the question, "How was it that this 'older' man did what he has just done? Why is he not back home with his family, slouched in an easy chair, sipping mate, and watching the birds? Instead, he prefers to be out here, risking his butt descending this cliff—an activity that not even a young person, in a correct state of mind, would want to do?"

"I don't take pills," I answered them. *Aha! I then realized it: they must have believed that only a diet of nutritional supplements could explain why I was in better physical condition than any one of them.*

At the station they detained me for two hours, repeating several times that monosyllabic word which needs no translation.

But they did give me instructions about how to apply for permission to climb in the park at a future moment. Which I did. And I'm still awaiting the inevitable denial.

But this is not the end to my story. A week later I was off again, this time driving three hours, passing through the city of Minas to scout out the best-known, and perhaps only, legitimate climbing area in the country: the wall behind the Laguna de los Cuervos—the Crow Lagoon. There, I learned a sad truth that applies to most, if not all, climbing walls in the department (and therefore the country as a whole): the property owners or their representatives are very reluctant to grant you access given their possible liability if there's a climbing accident. I then learned that access would be granted only if and when I obtained the approval of the country's "Mr. Climber," Pablo Turielle. And I would find him in only one place: some 200 kilometers distant, in the capital city of Montevideo.

Three days later I made a special trip to that city and discovered, wonder of wonders: Pablo and a few committed associates were busily transforming an abandoned—and historical—electric-power station into a world-class climbing gym. His La Muralla Foundation—The Climbing Wall Foundation—was doing great things for troubled youth via their wall and high-rope activities. Furthermore, they were now in charge of an excellent summer-camp-like facility near the Laguna de los Cuervos—only a kilometer from where I had visited days before—which serves also as a second gateway to the only outdoor bolted sport-climbing area in the country. (Unfortunately, for me, the four-page guide shows only one route rated below 5.10a.) He turned out to be a real nice guy. Pablo explained that I would have to return to the climbing gym at a more appropriate moment in order to demonstrate—what I assume would be—proper rope and belay techniques. His personal "certification" of my skills—and those of any future partner—would allow climbing access to the routes he personally had established.

But his "guide" only shows 5.10 routes—which are entirely out of the league of this mediocre climber. Well, I'd have to satisfy my curiosity. It is remotely possible that a "5.10 route"—as rated by Pablo—would be of equivalent difficulty to a 5.8 at Devil's Lake in Wisconsin. Just possibly. But if it does turn out that all his routes are more appropriate for the superb athletic abilities of a budding climbing superstar, then ol' ornery me might just be motivated to scout around looking for easy alternative routes in the same immediate area. In the U.S. of A. I have been similarly pissed off when visiting new sport areas designed only for the young generation of star athletes: establish new 5.6 or 5.7 routes for future friends at my lower level.[1]

Like so many of my climbing friends, I sometimes know no shame: the idea keeps bouncing into my head that I should forget about all that permission stuff and simply sneak across Muralla terrain near the Laguna, carrying my rope and shoes, and accompanied by my future partner. I'd feel quite diminished if I had to return to the Kindergarten practice of raising my hand to ask, "Teacher, may I?"

# Chapter 11

# Patagonia[1]

January 2012, my big chance. After years of dreaming about Patagonia, my moment had come. The stars were in alignment, the money was there, time was available, the cold-weather push from Wisconsin, the summer magnet pulling from the Southern Hemisphere. It finally happened: 20 or so days in Patagonia. The fulfillment of a lifelong dream.

Well, perhaps better stated: I finally was able to confront Patagonian dreams with Patagonian realities. Not that I ended up having a bad experience, on the contrary. But simply that a lack of information and familiarity with the area had led me to create expectations.

Of course I had learned over the years to be cautious in venturing into new mountain areas. Decades ago a near stumble into a huge hidden crevasse was a sobering kick-in-the-pants that snow and ice experiences on Mt. Rainier would not necessarily translate into relevant experience for mixed climbing in Peru's Cordillera Blanca. And was it not the case that friction climbing on Yosemite granite was not the same as on Devil's Lake quartzite? And how about the realization that the only adequate preparation for Alps climbing was being there and suffering Chamonix's swing weather? So venturing to Patagonia, I knew I was going to experience surprises. But what type? And how to prepare for them?

What did I know about the mountains I would find there? First of all, I probably should have gone to the internet to identify, and then order via interlibrary loan, John Biggar's *The Andes: The Guide for Climbers*, about whose existence I have only recently learned. Instead, I had some vague memories from having read, years past, the account of Chouinard's first ascent experience on Fitzroy: ten wretched days in a snow cave in the middle of their summer, iced ropes, and a freezing ascent. Added to that were some very vague impressions about geography and climate, and the

**The Mountain Gods rewarded us with a rare unobstructed view of "Her Majesty," Mt. Fitzroy, in Argentina's Patagonia.**

impressionistic fact taken off the internet: on a given day in January—their summer—there usually was some 40 degrees difference in the air temperature from hot Buenos Aires—where my venture would begin—to chilly Ushuaia—the southernmost point in my trip. Ouch. Forty degrees! In retrospect, it is notable that in no moment did a written account by an American climber fall into my hands that would have given me solid information about where to go, what to take, and what type of climbing to expect.

Some other factors weighted heavily on my planning: first, my attempts at finding a serious partner ahead of time came to naught. Second, by age I am an unabashed over-the-hill climber and do not want to venture into super risky attempts. Third, over the past decade I have had several positive experiences in major mountains going solo, choosing scamper or mountaineering routes, and severely restricting equipment and weight carried.

So all of the above influenced to a great degree my selection of equipment: no rope, hardware, ice axe or crampons; only my "Teton tennies," only the lightest (and cheapest) bivy tent and sleeping bag available. And, not to be forgotten, I was nursing a slowly healing ("frozen"?) shoulder injury—from heavy work (*not from a climbing fall, you clout!*) that made carrying anything but a day pack out of the question. This also was the determining factor for me selecting a medium-sized suitcase with wheels: pulling it along, I would suffer far less than with a heavy backpack when performing the inevitable walking that accompanies air and bus travel. But what to take for the (expected) cold? Prudently, I packed medium mitts, a light down jacket and pants stuffed tightly in a bag—these items, it turned out, were not at all needed.

I will not write much here about the tourism side to the trip: how to get there, how much it costs, penguins, etc., because that type of information is readily available in the travel manuals available in any library. But I will say this: everywhere inexpensive hostels with communal kitchens are located within walking distance for all overnight lodging—a person must simply request this information—in English or Spanish—at any bus station. With regard to planes and buses, they travel full during the tourist season, so the spontaneous traveler will have to make reservations at least a few weeks in advance.

About where to go, this is easily answered. The distances are so great that only air travel from Buenos Aires (or perhaps Santiago de Chile) makes sense (your alternative is a bus ride of three and a half days!). Prospective trekkers or climbers will probably be most interested in one of three destinations: El Calafate and Ushuaia in Argentina, and Punta Arenas (near Puerto Natales) in Chile.

In the weeks and months before the trip several people cautioned me: "Patagonia? Be careful"—as if I were bound for the extreme boondocks. Wrong! At all times I was surrounded by European and Israeli young people, who had abundant information about these areas. On several occasions I requested from the Germans a half-hour travel book loan. Their information, with great maps, is by far the best and most detailed. These young people, with their huge backpacks, filled the buses (and I also encountered a few travelers my age too): in their vast majority, they were trekkers. Trekking—in the U.S. we might call it backpacking—outside of the United States, is a major sport. Who would have known?

But real climbing? Among the scores of athletic youth surrounding me wherever I went, I was able to count the number of climbers on the fingers of one hand. The one "sport" climber I met—from the U.S.—was without a partner and relegated to inactivity. The one pair of bona fide climbers I did encounter were British; they were engaged in ferrying loads for an El Cap–style multi-day attempt up the sheer north face of one of the Paine Towers. That's it.

Everywhere I went I inquired about published climbing guides, but they're not to be found locally. In my hostel in El Chalten (a 3,000-person town inside Argentina's Parque Nacional Los Glaciares, some 60 kilometers from El Calafate) I found xeroxed sets of topos: one packet of perhaps 200 (mostly 5.9+) sport climbs on the 40-foot walls within a short walking distance. The other packet showed perhaps 15 routes up Fitzroy and another 100 routes up the other surrounding peaks. These topos were hard to read, because the technical difficulty of a given route is not registered in the U.S.-standard Yosemite decimal system. Of note is the fact that the young Brits preparing to scale the North Tower had received their route information via the internet from the first-ascent team.

I shouldn't wait to admit the eventual: talking informally with those climbers and perusing those xeroxed manuals in El Chalten was the closest I got during the whole trip to climbing *qua* climbing. But while there I was not idle: I spent my first day hiking up a tourist trail to gain a view of clouds enveloping Cerro Torre. And the very next day I won the jackpot: the sun warmed us all the way to the lake and glacier at the skirts of the mighty Fitzroy.

If and when I return to Patagonia, my first priority would be a visit to the small town of El Chalten. With a rope and partner I'd love go to the climbing walls half-surrounding the small town and have a field day making a manual of those 5.4–5.8 routes that must exist, but which the more arrogant first ascenters did not deem sufficiently important to document in the existing route diagrams. And if perchance a Viagra-type pill would enable me to perform Alps-like ascents again (one or two bivies, max 5.8 or 5.9 leads), and if perchance I see benign weather again—like I saw on my Fitzroy day—I would consider going up one or two of the spires surrounding Her Majesty. Well, then again, maybe I'd have to study more critically what would be involved in making the daunting approach to even the easiest of those granite spires.

The second place of climbing interest is Chile's impressive Parque Nacional Torres del Paine—which you approach from Puerto Natales, a short day's bus ride from either Punta Arenas or El Calafate. Like its Argentine sister, this is a park designed specifically for trekkers, and nary a climber did I see. Nor could I locate any written information about the

**Las Torres del Paine is only one of a dozen national parks in Chilean Patagonia. If I'm reincarnated next time around as a super-climber, then I'd be tempted to return there with rope, gear, and a thick down parka.**

climbing routes up the mighty Paine towers which—to all appearances, would be of interest to only the technical (and masochistic) climbing elite. However, the approach to the towers from the north and east is straightforward: I personally followed a mountain path for two hours—beyond the established trekker trail—to arrive at a climbers' camp; from here it would have been another easy hour to touch the base of the Central Tower. These peaks are magnificent; it was a privilege to merely sweat alongside the trekkers in order to arrive at the lake that has replaced the Towers' lower glacier.

The third area of climbing interest in Patagonia is Argentina's Ushuaia, the southernmost city in the world. It was instructive traveling to and from it by bus: one crosses thousands of kilometers of desert-like Patagonian plains, whose sparse vegetation supports only scrubby sheep (the region's major industry) and the wild guanaco (of the llama family). Yet approaching within 20 kilometers, there appear beautiful forests and mountain-like lakes little higher than sea level. Skirting along the inlet shore, you then arrive at Ushuaia, with scores of glaciated mountains—each one a Chilean island—visible across the Beagle Channel. From this city's streets you can look south—across the channel—and see several whitened 4,200-foot peaks—Argentina's end to the Andes range. You see mountains everywhere—the scene is reminiscent of beautiful Victoria, B.C.

Yes, there are mountains on all sides, and few have ever been climbed. Their ascent would take mixed-climbing skills, because one would have to negotiate glaciers and ice falls (there are alarmist reports that if you wait 30 years these might not be a problem), and then an occasional wall of crumbly, shit-rock. The most formidable obstacle would be the thick brush that dominates the landscape for a thousand vertical feet before "alpine" terrain begins. It might be problematic gaining permission from the Chilean government—and then renting a boat—in order to attempt any peak on the Chilean islands south of the Beagle Channel. But think of the glory: a Patagonian first ascent! Inquiring in several places, I was not able to identify any published text of climbing routes. Nor did I find maps (à la USGS) to facilitate such wilderness ascents, although the Argentine military must have them, given the recent border disputes with Chile and the city's proximity to the British-occupied, yet Argentina-claimed Falkland—excuse me, *Malvinas*—Islands.

During my few days visiting Ushuaia I experienced my only real climbing (well, advanced scampering) experience. About ten kilometers north and east of the city one finds a glaciated peak about 4,500 feet high (I have not been able to identify it via the mystic powers of Google) in the Sierra Valdivieso. Packing super-light, I followed instructions from a British trekking guidebook that led me across some private property to a seldom-traveled trail along a stream (with beaver dams) and over a very interesting peat bog. Then the trail wound up through the woods to a glacier lake and then to the glacier itself. The rock became steeper and steeper on its east side as I wove my way between snowfields. Approaching the ridge between two summits, the clouds closed in and snow pellets flew. Not wanting to risk a 1,500-foot slide, I chose not to kick up a snow field near the top, so I turned back. I didn't reach the summit, but I have no regrets, because I had experienced the mountain's stark alpine beauty, a prolonged adrenaline rush, and the pride of having scampered higher on this mountain than any but a well-equipped climber.

The weather that day was typical for the summer season: there blew a constant light wind, the temperature required a sweater or windbreaker, and I repeatedly had to suffer 20 minutes of cold clouds in order to earn

30 seconds of warm sun. In spite of the low altitude, the alpine beauty of the terrain (vegetation, glaciers, moraines) was comparable to many other precious areas I have visited over the years in Northern Hemispheric heights.

*Viva Patagonia!* I'll return in my dreams.

## CHAPTER 12

# Mountain Climbing Junket, 2012

I can summarize my experience with the uniformed personnel in Uruguay—as explained a couple chapters back—as the clash between what others see when looking at me and what I personally feel.

This was not an exceptional experience. Indeed, situations are multiplying of I, myself, having a similar confusion. Upon looking in a mirror, I see what I want to see and what I truly feel: an unwrinkled face resembling that of Bill-the-young-climber. Then, *ka-bang*: my wife shows me a photo of the plucky old warrior that—in reality—I am becoming. So much for photo images; I prefer those in the mirror.

Is all this evidence of my encroaching senility? Or is it that some bitchy god is playing with my mind?

The following two chapters recount related experiences: when the "older" climber attempts to delight in, yet one more time, the joys of earlier climbing junkets.

First, August 2012. I left the Midwest in my car not really knowing where I'd end up: ironically, I had rejected the idea of taking along my route guides for Yosemite, the Tetons, the Black Hills. No, this time I was going to climb in new places and not return to my favorite old haunts. Wrong!

Eat your heart out, peons. I had at least a month of time while my wife was in Uruguay visiting her kids and grandkids. Being self-employed, I could arrange to have others cover for me during an extended absence. And money? Not a huge problem since the only significant expense would be the cost of 5,000 miles worth of gasoline. I welcomed a month of sleeping on the ground—it's free, and I'd enjoy the view of starry nights.

But where to go for this climbing junket? A friend recommended I go to (and around) Salida, Colorado. I should have suspected this suggestion from one who had given up climbing and had sold shoes, cams, and harness. Nevertheless, I headed to Southern Colorado with the only other fixed destination being that of Santa Rosa, California, where my son resided.

So after two days of driving, my seldom-used Falcon guide to *Rock Climbing in Colorado*[1] gave directions to the "Shelf Road" climbing area outside of Canon City, Colorado. Can you believe it? Not a climber there; nor were there campers. Well, not a great loss: how could I go woozy over a sport-climbing area with almost no routes below 5.7—that is, the only routes I'd be able to do? But the frizzling heat: who in their right mind would want to be there? Ditto for the red sandstone of Colorado National Monument and ditto for the steep cliffs of the Black Canyon of the Gunnison (where I delighted with mental images of desperate sieges by Pat Ament and Layton Korr)—other places where I'd fantasized climbing but, in the end, I merely passed through. With the insufferable heat, all rational climbers had fled to points at least a thousand miles away! But the city of Salinas had, at the very least, a fairly nice bar. There they informed me about the county road leading to the trailhead for the nearest 14,000 footer: Mt. Shavano, which I walked up the next day. At least the first half of elevation gain was through a pleasant tree-shaded valley. But with the first glimpse of the bare, bald summit, the voice of mountain majesty kept whispering to me that no "mountain high" in Southern Colorado was going to compare to what I would feel in the High Sierras of California.

So two days later, continuing south from Reno, I arrived at Bridgeport, the takeoff point for my next destination: the 12,279-foot Matterhorn Peak. The map reveals its location just outside the northeast corner of Yosemite National Park. That night I practiced my freeloader skills at a national forest campground on the shores of Twin Lakes. How monstrous: huge campers and several ATVs parked alongside one of the nicest trout streams anywhere. Early the next day, wearing tennies and carrying only a windbreaker and a minimum of water and food, I was on the trail that, after ten minutes, pooped out. But that was to my advantage. The terrain was easy, there was little offensive vegetation, and the direction I was heading was unmistakable. Beautiful country, and the superb peaks up ahead would make Southern Colorado's mountain gods cringe with shame. Think of the ironies: minutes below, opulent California tourism ran amok; here, not even a trail, nary a tourist hiker, venturing into the sacred high country.

Come late morning I regretted not having brought along my climbing guide to the High Sierras: Matterhorn's summit seemed impregnable. I had to third-class it to the pass below the summit's east side where, throbbingly unprotected, I ventured up to gain an impressive ridge. Then, after traversing south below the vertical fortress, my route ended because a steep snowfield, not yet in the sun, could not be penetrated by kick-steps. With no other choice, I reversed my path then proceeded up the steep west side, weaving around two snowfields and scampering up easy rock. All was airy and majestic. But there was no scamper route to the summit. Understand this: I'm a middle-aged climber; the beauty of it all compensated for not having reached the summit. So, turning around, I retraced my path back to civilization. Well, almost. For the last hour I ended up brush crashing to finally emerge into the huge commercial campground. And now I was Yosemite-bound.

For three days I was able to pick up partners via the message board at the Tuolumne Meadows campground. We climbed early to get off the baking rock before 11 a.m. For my first roping up of the season I welcomed the superb rock and excellent protection. Hooray! For at least one more year the goddess of aging had not yet deprived me of my confidence and face-climbing ability. We climbed routes on Daff and Stately Pleasure Domes (right above Lake Tenaya), but the most memorable was a 5.8 route up the impressive Mendicoff Dome: dreamy Yosemite face climbing with security-blanket bolts every fifteen feet.

When I ran out of partners in the high country, I descended 6,000 feet in 50 minutes to arrive by car at the Valley. I knew how to spend the first night undetected by the rangers, then got in line early the next morning to pay for my maximum seven legal nights in Camp IV. But who would believe it? Among all the trekkers and the handful of climbers, nobody was seeking a partner like me. I counted a half-dozen European rope teams, even a few from Mexico! But one demographic was sorely underrepresented: young American males (well, a second one too: the bears.) Where was the young generation of wall scalers if not in Yosemite? You tell me.

It's impossible not to have a great time in the Valley. But how many of my friends over 40 confront the same quandary as I: the great routes in their majority are rated a difficult 5.9 and above, and I can only trust myself leading 5.7—and an occasional 5.8. So I satisfied myself with doing a few routes on the nearby Manure Pile Buttress, where I was humiliated having to prussic up a 5.8 mantel on Nutcracker—good thing I was following! (You can be assured that pull-ups are now emphasized on my daily and weekly workouts!) On two other days I accompanied new friends on long hikes. Another day I realized with surprise that in no previous trips here had I made the drive to Glacier Point. There, for the first time ever, I was able to stand exactly where Ansel Adams had snapped several of his familiar, unforgettable photos.

Proceeding. A few days visiting my son near Santa Rosa, and then an unremarkable day to the summit of Mt. Shasta (14,000+ feet). That peak looks beautiful from a distance, but what a pile of shit! With every step up I slid a third of a step down. But it has a nice summit, reminiscent of Rainier—and a bit like Popo.

Look on the map and trace the shortest highway route from Shasta to the Tetons. Beware if you take it: in one stretch I drove 200 miles without passing a gas station! I've warned you.

In the Teton's American Alpine Climbing Camp I finally found what I had been looking for all month: a cadre of young eager climbers. I have to qualify the last word: sport gymnasts don't go to the Tetons; only mountaineers willing and able to suffer long approaches and exhausting days. Within hours I made the acquaintance of John Young—I could not have dreamed into existence a more perfect partner: a real nice guy possessing a touch higher technical ability than my own, and in great shape. Two other things about John turned out to be essential: he could get off the Grand with a flashlight, having summited recently by three different routes; and he possessed a thin 60-meter rope for that long rappel down the Owen-Spaulding. On our first shakedown climb to the summit of Nez Percé he demonstrated that he could go light and long and was comfortable climbing unroped on 4th and easy 5th class. On a new route up the West Buttress of Ayer's Crag 5 (at the end of Glacier Canyon), he was adept at simul-climbing and took positively my insistence on a maximum 30 seconds of turnaround time on each belay.

Now we were ready, and the weather collaborated marvelously, for our ascent of a route that I had dreamed of doing for decades: Grand Teton's East Ridge (III, 5.7). This is the mighty rib that predominates in every photo taken of the peak from Jenny Lake to Jackson Hole. It took five hours to get to the bivy site on the top of the Teton Glacier moraine. Early the next morning we were in tennies; I wore shorts and a long-sleeved white shirt, and carried wind pants and a windbreaker. We carried no ice axes, against the advice of all route descriptions, because we were hesitatingly confident that the above-normal heat had left bare rock exposed on the right side of the upper snowfield. I carried half the rope in my pack, and we only belayed for short stretches some five (or perhaps ten) times. The towering gendarmes make that route one of the most majestic that I have ever climbed. All went smoothly and, except for the 45 minutes we spent on the south side of the Molar Tooth, we had comfortable sun on our backs the whole way up. Climbing can't get any better that this. We summited in early afternoon, descended the tedious Owen-Spalding Route, hiked down and out of Garnet Canyon, and just before dusk we again reached the bivy site and our sleeping bags. Hungry but exuberant, the next morning we hiked out and then refurbished calories at the Mexican restaurant in Jackson Hole. What more can I say? A fabulous route that we did in superb style. A dream come true. Will the Mountain Gods grant me another summer junket as good as the one just past? Tell me, capricious gods, how many summers do I have left? Friends, rest assured: for each and every summer still remaining I will try as hard as I can to get on the rock, to get up some routes, to enjoy yet another glorious summit. *Berg Heil*!

# Chapter 13

# A Plucky Old Climbing Warrior Revisits Tahquitz Rock

One thing that Royal Robbins and I have in common is that we both cut our climbing teeth at Tahquitz Rock, in Southern California—he, beginning in 1952, and me in 1964. (Let it be understood: I have never spoken with the man, whose physical abilities and climbing exploits have far exceeded my own.) On a certain day in May 2016—more than 50 years later—I felt like RR when I led all but the first of the six-pitch Sahara Terror, and even felt confident on the 5.9 finger-jam alternative near its top. On that route I was a stronger and better climber than I was last time there. Over that time span much has changed in how climbers typically get to the top of one such route. This is the topic of my recorded thoughts here.

To begin with, Tahquitz—with its majestic alpine environment up to the summit at 7,973 feet—has hardly changed. The hard, smooth granite at its base becomes rougher and weathered (and better for face climbing) near the top. Occasional pine or mountain mahogany stub-trees still provide solid anchors. An abundance of smaller cracks makes for easy placement of pro: back then, primarily small pitons up to three-quarters of an inch; and now, small- to middle-sized cams.

What else has changed? I have to begin with me. A half-century ago, what a great vertical playground to initiate my training as a climber! Indelibly imprinted on grey-matter memory cells are memories of one of the most terrifying experiences I have ever had, furiously tugging the rope up a zig-zag lead on the 5.5 Ski Tracks (new guide: Left Ski Track, 5.6).[1] Or trembling—eighteen months later—to dare the 5.7 Jam Crack (new guide: 5.8). Those experiences constituted, so to speak, my rites of passage from novice to mature climber. Imagine: all that to attain the 5.7 level, when younger climbers today get up protected 5.9 pitches on their first weekend out!

There must also be mythological significance to my return 50 years later. It is pure coincidence that my 2016 visit brought together three of us (read below about Mr. Jitters and Mr. Bo-Jangles), all suffering the "plucky old warrior" syndrome, knowing that our best climbing years already belong to the past, and all of us embracing an attitude of resistance and fight-to-the-end. Could we regain a degree of former rock mastery and leader confidence? For this, two of us dared a new visit to the massive pinnacle inhabited by the rock-devil known locally as *Tahquitch*—on what would be, hopefully, a rite of renewal and not blood sacrifice.

Little did we imagine back then that we were going up (what we now recognize as) historical routes put up only a decade or so before by now historic climbers such as Robbins, Chouinard, Frost, and T.M. Herbert. Back then, Yosemite was still six years into my future. I must have suspected what Chouinard later wrote—in words quoted by Bob Gaines in the introduction to the newest guide—that Tahquitz "has been a teaching ground for nearly every prominent Valley Climber." Gaines adds, "Arguably, the first climbs in America to be rated 5.8, 5.9, 5.10, 5.11, and 5.12 were done here. Tahquitz Rock is also the birthplace of the Yosemite Decimal system … the rating system still used throughout the United States."[2]

Back then Tahquitz meant pure multi-pitch piton-protected (or sling-around-a-bush) climbing. What hasn't changed is Tahquitz's concentration of "trad" climbs (short for "traditional"—that is, protected by the hardware which leaders themselves put into the cracks and the rope that is secured by their belayers below). We had no need to call it "trad" climbing, because the highly protective "sport" climbing (whether by bolts or top ropes) was not yet practiced. Also, the total elimination of crack-maiming pitons from the typical leader rack was still a decade into the future. As to be expected, the new climbing guide recommends a typical trad rack of only "clean" stuff: nuts and cams.

Climbing difficulty? Chuck Wilts, in the 1962 climbing guide, includes only a few routes with a 5.10 difficulty—this rating system, he wrote, was only beginning to be applied.[3] Contrast that to 50–60 percent of the newer routes, ones that are rated at 5.10 and above—as Bob Gaines includes in the 2013 guide. Also, it is understandable that several of the hardest routes listed in the old guide, which were climbable only using aid (Wilts used a now-discontinued scale of 6.0 to 6.8 to indicate nailing difficulty), are now free-climbed by gifted athletes at the 5.10 a, b, or c levels. Due to my modest technical abilities, none of these newer, or now totally "free," routes interest me in the slightest. But, thank goodness, the new Tahquitz guide still provides accurate descriptions, and an occasional topo, of the dozen or so routes at the 5.2 to 5.8 levels—all classic lines—many of which I had climbed decades before and now lusted to venture upon again.

**The third Cathedral Spire, in Custer State Park (only 20 miles from Mt. Rushmore) offers a very pleasant, 2½-pitch climb up to an exhilarating summit. Here Karen is beginning the second of three rappels to get back down.**

Hmm. Jump to 2016. Climate change must account—at least in part—for our unseasonably warm day, that required us to wear only long-sleeved shirts, with windbreakers untouched in the climbing pack. I have no firm data, but I do suppose that here, as almost everywhere else, the climbing season now begins earlier and extends later than before. And perhaps the increased heat of summer discourages climbing on the rock's sunny south side for a larger number of summer days. But I was there in mid-spring. Snow at Tahquitz's summit was visible from the town below. In our north-gully descent we plunged into previously untrodden snow for almost half the distance down to the climbers' trail. (Is it possible that we were the first party to descend there that season?) What a magnificent setting. For me, the general coolness of the air constituted a welcome change from the glaring desert environment of Joshua Tree National Park—some two hours away.

Could I be mistaken? My impression is that these days there might be even fewer climbers attacking Tahquitz routes than a half-century before. During that warm weekend, I saw only one other climbing party. A year later when I passed through again (but did not climb for lack of a partner): ditto—and that one party was on the easiest route, the Trough (5.0). Additional anecdotal evidence: over the past few years I have talked with climber after climber at Red Rocks (just outside of Las Vegas) and Joshua Tree who have not even heard of Tahquitz!

I have the impression that this is not simply a case of Tahquitz ignorance, but rather of declining interest in trad climbing in general. More anecdotal evidence: instances are multiplying of me unable to recruit a ready-and-able partner due to a scarce climbing demographic at demanding trad sites: Yosemite Valley (August 2014), Rushmore and Custer State Park (August 2014 and 2015), and the Tetons (August 2015). Luckily, in 2016 I was able to snag a partner, unlike a year before or after: I hit gold by responding to a note posted on a bulletin board at the climbing store in Idylwild, the small community at the base of Tahquitz. But that was after a whole month of futile messages sent to the email site, Mountain Project. How to account for this (perceived) scarcity of climbers? I'll venture some hypotheses.

First, the small number of climbers at Tahquitz contrasts grotesquely with the flood of climbers—young and old—at Joshua Tree and Red Rocks. In these two other close-by sites, climbing has become a popular sport. Sport climbing, that is. Hot weather climbing. There, you'll find at least two groups. First, a growing number of physically gifted youths, lusting for verticality-induced adrenaline and reading *Climbing* magazine in their spare time. And second, a greying population haunted by memories of past physical prowess, who now seek safe routes without the threat of unpredictable alpine weather or fatigued legs and arms at the end of a long, long day. All this explains why so many of today's climbers prefer to spend a weekend at Red Rocks and (the belay-from-your-bumper setting of) J. Tree.

And yet, there are other reasons for this preference—reasons which have affected a whole generation of younger enthusiasts whose climbing practices are the (sometimes unconscious) result of instruction or information propagated by risk-aversive climbing schools, liability-scared Boy Scouts, or the "grandmother" mentality of the Seattle Mountaineers or the American Safe Climbing Association. Gaines, in his introduction to the currently available guide, is only partially correct when he implicitly associates a "daring, go-for-it style" in the climbers of old, for whom "boldness was a virtue." This, in implicit contrast to "safe" climbers of today with textbook practices and an overabundance of certified equipment.

That's it! The above paragraph explains the unsavory reactions I unintentionally provoked from two different individuals during that 2016 climbing trip. These were instances of perceived safety. First, it was a (haughty) young female, a recent graduate of a three-day climbing-safety class, who—I'm not making this up—went bananas over me protecting her friend with my trusty ol' "Eight" instead of an ATC or grigri. The second instance was when a Joshua Tree belayer, struggling with an advanced case of the jitters, caustically condemned me for placing only two pieces of pro in a sixty-foot 5.2 gully with bomb-proof holds every five feet. I assure the reader: my lead was hardly an example of an irresponsible, "daring, go-for-it style."

My experience on the Tahquitz climb adds further evidence to what I perceive as a chasm separating old from new climbing mentalities. There I was at 8 a.m. rendezvousing with the partner whom I had the good fortune to snag via cell phone the afternoon before. Imagine my surprise when he pulled from his car trunk a Pancho Villa–type chest-crossing-belt contraption with surely fifty pieces hanging! That sight would spellbound any tourist. A vision of my 15-pin standard rack—back then—slithered into mind.

Then, he pulled out a humongous 5-inch cam. "I think I'll take it: I remember a nasty move near the top that was hard to protect, and this big cam is made to order." *Gads, I thought. How much does it weigh? It must have cost $200! How—where—will he carry it? Boy, this piece sure would have been nice on the Steck-Salathé or the Durrance at Devil's Tower. But here? Come on, partner. Leave it!!! Hmm. Well, it's true that, back then, I had never dared to do any of the 5.8 routes here (after the sewing-machine leg shake experienced on Jam Crack's first pitch), and had never even contemplated attempting a line up Tahquitz's north side: the perceived verticality, as seen from the road below, had been simply too intimidating. And he does know the route, which I don't. On this issue it's politically expedient to defer to him.* Which I did.

Then he took out three grigris, hanging one on his rig, handing me the second, and packing the third in his pack: "Just in case. The grigri is safer than your 'eight.'" *Hmm. Really?* I asked myself. *Admittedly, with regard to new equipment, I have been out to lunch for the past few decades.*

*Using it would be a learning experience. But each one must weigh three or four pounds. Ouch! And an extra one in the pack? Back then we had followed three iron-clad rules: "No emergency equipment"; "Eliminate duplication" (one device for both rapping and belaying); and: "When in doubt, leave it." But then … a grigri? I had used one before, and my first reaction was: like the "miraculous" cams compared to pitons, it must be better than anything else we had used for belaying back then.* "It's pretty heavy. I'm not sure I even know how to use it." *Discretion, Katra! "When in Tahquitz do as the Tahquillians do."* I decided not to put my Eight away. We might have to rap off something. He gave a brief demonstration on how to load and unload the grigri and how to best pull the rope through it, while I silently worked through a mild case of culture shock.

Through all this, and via his words, he continued to project the confidence of a time-proven, competent, 5.9 climber that (I have no doubt) he *had* been.

"No need to carry the guidebook." He was confident he would recognize the route's start. Wrong! After the half-hour approach, all the cracks and trees resembled each other. He hadn't told me *how many years* had passed since his last climb here. *I was able to ask myself only hours later, "How much had new fears altered his mind's eye about the route's features?"* But, let it be admitted: weeks later—with the benefit of having both the 1962 and 2013 guides open before me in my study—I was relatively convinced that we had indeed climbed the route we had intended: Sahara Terror. But his uncertainty about this, added to latent fears, made for his very hesitant lead up the first roped pitch. At the belay he willingly—and eagerly—yielded the lead to me for the rest of the climb. Hurray. I was feeling my oats. Brer Rabbit was finally back in the ol' Briar Patch!

Chalk one up for the 1962 guide, whose descriptions for route starts on Tahquitz's north and northeast areas are consistently good and helpful. (With a copy of the Wilts guide, we would have had no doubt about where we ended up climbing!) And give a "D" rating for Mr. Bob Gaines, whose two-color pictures of those routes—with their squiggly white lines—help very little when you have to cock your head awkwardly upward to get a view of the rock's imposing majesty.

Now, beginning with the second pitch, I was in glorious lead. The Mountain Gods had responded favorably to my supplications: surprise of surprises, I felt strong and confident. The choice of route certainly helped: I can now describe it as an ultra-safe 5.2–5.4 crack except for perhaps a dozen short 5.6–5.8 moves every fifty feet or so. A sling around an occasional shrub meant that pro was almost not needed, except for a prudent placement before each mini-crux. At the end of almost every pitch I encountered bomb-proof sit-down belay stances alongside trusty trees or shrubs. For my leads I carried only ten cams, and none bigger than 1.5 inches. I left the rest of the pro with Mr. Bo-Jangles: imagine, him decked out in bomber jacket, with that superfluous 5-inch cam banging against the backside of his pack the whole way up.

About belay anchors: it took me less than a minute to loop the climbing rope around a tree, haul up the slack, and then yell my "On Belay." Or—if needed—I would place a bomb-proof cam and lean back into the crack with perfect foot support. Inevitably, my buddy criticized me for an inadequate number of anchors. I agreed with him in part, promising that at the beginning of every lead I would whip in a second piece of pro in order that on difficult or exposed sections we would always have a minimum of two pieces placed. (This was our standard procedure back then.) And, inevitably, I heard his textbook response, that if it really became difficult he would only feel safe with three bombproof anchors at all belay stations. My answer to him was that I considered that to be "safety overkill," that it would take far too much time, and that on long trad routes our speed up the route guaranteed safety much more than a redundant placement of anchors.

The climb gave me the opportunity to evaluate the relative merits of the grigri—and newer belaying techniques. (Here, I do not dispute the grigri's superior status for belaying at the bottom of a Boy Scout tower or gym wall.) But it proved to be very awkward to use, when I was anchored above in order to belay my buddy climbing on up. This is because the grigri restricted me from pulling in more than a half-arm length of rope at any one time, far too slow when he was barreling up an easy pitch. By the third belay I had disconnected the grigri in favor of my "Eight": a bit better, a bit faster. But by the second-to-last belay I had reverted to the method we had used back in the day. I am now convinced of its superiority to any of the other methods: with me facing inward, the belay rope ran directly to a biner attached to my anchor: one rope ran down to my climbing buddy and with the other I performed a waist belay. This was fast and efficient, and in the event of my buddy's slip, the major force of the fall would be absorbed by the biner and not my waist.

I would recommend the same method for a belayer securing the leader, but with a few remarks: the main anchor—and belayer—must be positioned for a downward jerk until the leader announces that he or she, upon beginning the ascent from the belay, has clipped into a new piece of pro. After that, both anchor and belayer must be positioned for an upward pull.

None of this rules out the tried-and-true waist belay from a bomb-proof sitting position—and without any pro at all. But this last belay, for either follower or leader, should be used only in the case of very easy terrain and the near absence of risk.

In performing my six-or-so rope leads, I placed a total of ten cams—in addition to about five slings around stout bushes. *Hmm. In most future trad climbs, and especially in a return trip to this Heavenly Place, should I contemplate leaving behind all the hexes, stoppers, and wire nuts?* The cams go in and come out so easily. (Who designed this four-wheel *maravilla*? Hail to American ingenuity.) I ended up placing—in total—only ten pieces of pro. *While seated in the summit sunshine to belay my buddy on up, my unleashed imagination concocted a surreal image of the pro, dangling from his super harness, swelling up to grotesque proportions.* Then, weeks later, I finally had the chance to open up the 1962 guide to read that Chuck Wilts, back then, had recommended the placement of only seven pins for the entire route! Right on, Chuck. I'm with you, RR! Twenty-first century: do I belong here?

One more thing to say. While I was sitting there on belay and basking in the summit sunshine, the thought entered my head that Heaven could be no better than this. Except for one factor: I was feeling significant fatigue in my hands, arms, and shoulders. Was my physical condition that deficient? Well, perhaps this was a contributing cause. Were the years catching up with me? An emphatic *no*: about this I'm committed to an attitude of permanent denial. A better explanation: the weight of the rope. Back then they measured 150 feet, whereas today they are either 200 feet (60 meters) or 230 feet (70 meters). Or—to translate lengths into equivalent weights—back then our ropes (12mm or the equivalent) weighed some seven pounds, whereas today they are nine or even ten pounds. Add to that the inevitable friction from my rope passing around gentle rock corners or through slightly zigzagging pro. Think about it: with me on lead, each time I belayed my buddy meant that my arms and shoulders were pulling up every single foot of the rope's length. And while climbing, my leg muscles also had to do the bulk of the work: each upward step was pulling an ever-increasing drag. Indeed, I distinctly remember having registered a significant rope drag while negotiating the delicate 5.9 finger-tip layback slab near the top. Flashing amber light: rope weight heightens fatigue, which lessens safety. This is one clear example of how sport climbing—its equipment and procedures—has contributed to undermining the safety of trad climbing.

With good reason I was tired by the end of the climb! I was mildly ticked off when my buddy, upon reaching the summit sun, began chirping that we two should venture onto an even more demanding route on the morrow. He, who had been able to scurry up every one of my leads, he who did not have to bear the burden of his own rope. "Sorry," I told him, even before initiating the descent, because I was feeling the need to spend at least one full day of R&R in order to recharge the corporal battery.

What are the rope lessons to be learned? One, on these easier classic routes here at Tahquitz (and elsewhere) perhaps a 150-foot rope is sufficient, and perhaps one with a thinner diameter (for example, a 10mm rope). Or, I could take shorter leads so that my buddy could share the upper-torso burden of pulling up the rest upon arriving at the belay station.

I like the idea of climbing with a vastly thinner rope. I'm a risk-taker. Why not take along a thin, 7–8 mm "twin rope," of 165 feet, that weighs under four pounds? It would have a test strength more than adequate for even a long leader fall. Although this thin rope would not be appropriate for hard technical stuff, it might be ideal for those long pack-ins: Snake Dike, Robson, Assiniboine, the North Palisade, any of the easier Teton summit routes. Or for Rainier glaciers. Or for easier trad routes with long spates of fourth class: Royal Arches, the East Ridge of the Grand. Think about it.

It was easy going: the first descent of the season down the soft snow of Tahquitz's North Gully. Emerging from the woods and breaking out onto the paved roadway near the parked cars, we met up with a dozen young Sierra Clubbers carrying overnight packs. Evidently, they had spent an enthusiastic night camping near the summit of San Jacinto. One young Asian girl from that group, seeing Mr. Bo, draped with technical gear, innocently inquired whether he was "the professional"—implying that I, in my simple clothing and transporting the rope, had the appearance of either a white-skinned sherpa or a paying client. I replied ambiguously that both of us were highly skilled amateurs. She was so cute.

## Chapter 14

# Trying to Climb in Argentina

In 1970 I had followed the mule trail to the summit of Aconcagua in the northern part of Argentina, near the Chilean border (the highest peak in the world outside of the Himalayas), and had successfully summited several of the crags around Bariloche. All that is another story. In 2014 I had explored the climbing areas of Patagonia, but without doing any roped or high-altitude peak bagging (see Chapter 11). Then, in December 2016, I completed a trip to perhaps the country's most prestigious rock-climbing area that is located in the Province of Cordoba. This is my topic here.

First of all, the issue of the language. I would recommend a visit to these areas only to those who are bold, since English is not spoken by very many people. And given that the existing sources of information are faulty and sometimes misleading, it is handy to have verbal skills to get yourself out of a fix and onto the right bus or trail. That being said, bus travel to and from the provincial capital, Cordoba, and then to the small vacation city of Carlos Paz, offers no problem. This is not the case, however, with the local buses that would carry you to the climbing areas. A tourist center at the bus terminal of this last city proved somewhat helpful, but they also did provide some misinformation.

It was early summer—only two days after Christmas—and one would expect the climbers to be out in force. I was bound for Los Gigantes, billed as Argentina's best for sport and trad climbing. Anticipating good times and a crowd of climbers, I stuffed five days of food into my pack that was already heavy with rope, rack, shoes, and a bivy tent. I also carried into the bus two gallons of water plus iodine purification pills, being unsure whether water would be available. Finally, after arriving at the start of the trail I cheerfully left behind the plastic jugs when I learned, much to my relief, about the abundance of clean water almost everywhere. I packed no stove, fully expecting to use my charm to gain cooking favors at one of the three climbers' huts some three sweaty hours away.

Shucks. I arrived at the bus terminal in the city of Cordoba at 9:00 a.m. and promptly learned that the only daily bus traveling the 2.5 hours to the trailhead leading to Los Gigantes had left an hour earlier. But there were other ways to get there. I got on a different bus that, in an hour, left me at the terminal of the small touristy city of Carlos Paz. There, I found yet a second bus which, after 15 minutes, left me at the turn-off for the 30-kilometer dirt road. There, I sat down in the last shade I would experience over the next two days and bared my thumb to the air. In less than an hour I was riding with a young orthodontist from Venezuela who was making plans to relocate to the area. He would accompany me the rest of the day, driving into the confusing entrance to Los Gigantes and then hiking with me up near the summit—he without a pack and me loaded down and sweating. Two hours before dark we were a half-kilometer west of the Cerro de la Cruz, where the region's best routes, sometimes reaching two pitches in length, are located. From that distance we watched a man and woman team completing the second of two raps down its vertical face. These were the only people I would see actually climbing over the whole next week. One individual gave me an unfathomable explanation for the lack of climbers: "Climbers here don't climb during vacation time." That's what he said. I kid you not.

There exists a printed guide to the climbing routes for Los Gigantes (it must be a pamphlet), but I have not had the opportunity to examine it. As a very poor substitute, the tourist office in Carlos Paz had provided me with a dual-sided color page with three small 3 × 3-inch photos. The first, a small road map, had not helped me to avoid problems involved in getting from Carlos Paz to the correct trailhead. The second photo was a miniature trail map. It, also, was less than useless for finding the three alpine huts (refugios) that were up, up, and far away (and me with that heavy pack!). The third small photo was of the actual Cerro de la Cruz; it showed about 40 different routes, with climbing difficulty varying from "4+" to "7a." I later learned that these notations might be the equivalent of our 5.5 and 5.12c.

After my Venezuelan friend left me, I kept wandering along an inadequately marked trail and finally stumbled upon the first of the three climbing huts. It was deserted, the doors were firmly bolted shut, and I saw no signs of use over the previous few years. There and then, I decided that my poor bod was going to suffer no further that day. So, on a level rock in front of that hut, I passed my first night. There was a bit of dew in the morning, but I have nothing else to report.

Early the next morning I realized that with no partner I would do no climbing in the area, so it would be foolish for me to stay. But I had a whole day ahead of me before the 5:30 p.m. departure of the bus that would take me back to Cordoba City. I left my equipment at the hut and went scampering upward. Surprise of surprises, within a half hour I found another rock-walled hut, again totally locked down, but with five friendly young men dressed in military garb who had camped around its perimeter. They explained to me their curious hobby of going on "military-like" hikes to wilderness spots, where they would fire plastic pellets from replicas of historical revolvers—I think that is what they said. They offered me a ride back to Cordoba if I were to get back to the trailhead by three o'clock.

None of them was so energetic as to desire accompanying me in my scampering, so I set off alone. Another surprise: I found yet a third stone hut, but this time occupied by two young men (self-proclaimed "sometime climbers") from the Club Andino of Carlos Paz. They gave me an email address of the club—that later proved dysfunctional. Their recommendation was that I should call or email a week ahead of time and someone from the club would be eager to go off climbing with me on a future occasion. Great. Perhaps I can find an alternative email address via the web.

I unloaded on them almost all my food and began walking down a better but unfortunately longer trail with my now lightened pack. I missed my rendezvous with the *pistoleros* and, as a result, had to walk an additional five kilometers to arrive at the pick-up point for the once-a-day bus back to Cordoba and the youth hostel (inexpensive and convenient).

It took me two days to rehydrate and recover, before I returned to Carlos Paz to visit a second climbing area called La Ola ("The Wave"). Advantageously, it is located right on a highway, meaning I had to accomplish no exhausting hike in. Furthermore, I would have no problem flagging down a bus to return after some inviting climbs. But the unanticipated half-day delay in my bus's departure meant that I arrived at La Ola with only an hour left of cloudy daylight. I sauntered down to a very scenic, but wet, camping grotto. In the threatening wind I found a single pitched tent, with a young climbing couple from Poland closed up inside. But no Argentine climbers were to be found. Given the thunder clouds (the pair also reported a heavy hail the previous night) and the damage done to their tent by the local dog, they now had plans to hitch back to Cordoba the next day. The positive side to all this was their willingness to share a few bottles of wine with me while we viewed for two uninterrupted hours an incredible lightning show on the horizon. Thank goodness, the heavy rain held off till daybreak, when I was able to cram my body comfortably against the wall of a semi-cave in order to pass the time reading my book. By late morning the rain had stopped. Then I scampered around to check out the many inviting routes. Finally, when my Polish friends rolled out of their tent, I wished them luck as I headed for the road to flag down a bus and return to Cordoba. This is a place to return to, in better weather and with my own climbing partner.

Back in Cordoba, I stumbled into the best climbing-related experience I enjoyed during the entire week. It occurred in a clean hostel—the Rupestre—located just six blocks from the bus terminal. It even had a climbing gym! The personnel, super friendly, were all dedicated climbers. Imagine my luck: I spent a balmy New Year's Eve on its third-floor terrace, surrounded by climbers and enticed by superb food and beverages! Even though I got absolutely no climbing in during my whole week in Cordoba, that night made it all worthwhile.

## Chapter 15

# "A Gory Way to Die": Song Lyrics Modified by Bill Katra

The following is an improved version of the traditional Army cadence "Blood Upon the Risers."

1. "Can you get around the chockstone?" cried the belayer looking up
Our hero feebly answered "yes" and slowly inched on up
He was trying to drive a piton in a hellish awkward stance
When his feet began an airy dance.

*Chorus*
Gory, gory, what a helluva way to die (3×)
And he ain't a gonna climb no more.

2. He tumbled down the chimney and he quickly gathered speed
He shot past his belayer who'd forgot the climber's creed
An anchor to a piton would have satisfied his need
And they ain't a gonna climb no more.

3. The belayer felt the rope grow taut, he tried to let it run
It jerked him from position and he knew his time had come
He left the ledge he sat on and it shot up toward the sun
And he ain't a gonna climb no more.

4. They shot on down the chimney and across the southern col
They slithered 'cross the friction pitch and sped on down the wall
Such a grand exposure that they had a lovely fall
And they ain't a gonna climb no more.

5. The days they lived and laughed and loved went rushing through their minds
They thought about the girls back home, the ones they'd left behind
They thought about the ranger and they wondered what he'd find
And they ain't a gonna climb no more.

6. A reporter in the valley watched it through a telescope
The scoop was his, his pulse sped up, a guilty sense of hope

**On a typical outing day near Mt. Rushmore, the best climber leads, clipping into the bolts positioned about every ten feet. After leaving the rope threaded through the bolted anchors at the top, the belayer lowers the leader. Then, anyone else in the party can climb the same route safely with an upper belay. When everyone's finished, we pull one end, and the whole rope falls at our feet.**

The headlines and the morning news would feature his own lines
A sensation in these boring times.

7. They hit the ground, the sound was "*splat*," the blood it squirted high
Their comrades all were heard to say, "What a colorful way to die"
They lay there on the talus in the welter of their gore
And they ain't a gonna climb no more.

8. One had a sling wrapped round his neck, a piton thru his spleen
The ice axe in his rucksack fell and split the other's bean
Two bloody stripes marked their descent into the valley green
And they ain't a gonna climb no more.

9. There were brains upon the rucksacks, there was blood upon the ropes
Intestines lay there all strewn out across the rocky slopes
The stillness of the moment witnessed just a marmot's peep
As from stone to stone it ran and leaped.

10. A rescue team camped in the park they tittered full of glee
To move their butts, six hours of time, would earn them quite a fee

No need to work the whole next month and endless beer to boot
The whole thing was quite a hoot.

11. Crude jokes occupied their thoughts while hiking up the slope
They scraped all into baskets after salvaging the ropes
Not a serious word to say about the unlucky blokes
Who ain't a gonna climb no more.

## Chapter 16

# "Climbing Majesty": Song Lyrics by Bill Katra

Sung to the tune of Willie Nelson's "To All the Girls I've Loved Before."

Our muscles glow, our spirits soar
When we're tied into that nylon cord
We embrace the ephemeral goal
Of climbing skyward hold by hold
On up the mountain wall.

*Chorus*
Partners in this strange delight
Where ritual pre-empts normal life
We contract with the Mountain Gods on high
To share in the glory of earth and sky.

Select the route and sort the gear
Place small cams and hexes near
Add stoppers, biners too
Pack water, slings, and food
We leave at dawn.

With queasy gut we find the crack
Ready rope and shoes, now light the pack
Cat move onto the rock
Climb out, no idle talk
No turning back.

I glance up and ask if it will go
You reach out and place a piece of pro
The rope goes through
Relieved us two
You continue on.

You reach the ledge, shout down to me
I undo my anchor from the tree
I hurry on up

At Devil's Lake, guidebook author Olle Swartling—in spite of his 80-some years—is still one of the best climbers in the Midwest. For a better grip, he'll thrust a hand into the small bag to cover his fingertips with chalk.

Remove the stuff
Your belay secure.

Switching leads, we move along
A sustained climb it's like a song
Our strength and cheer
Rule fatigue and fear
The summit's nigh.

We reach the top I shake your hand
Our eagle gaze above the land
In misty breeze
A short reprieve
Before starting down.

Set rappel and off we go
Danger fuels the adrenaline flow
At the next safe stand
Pull hand by hand
The rope falls free.

As daylight fades we reach the scree
Then along the trail 'n' thru the trees
We're headed down
To camp we're bound
The climb's complete.

As the years pass by, remembrance pales
Of heavy packs and rainy trails,
What shines bright
In memory's light
Are those fine friends who've climbed with me.

# Glossary

**aid climbing** See **6th class**

**anchor** Noun or verb. Before belaying, a climber either places a piece of **pro** or uses a sling to tie around a tree, then clips in with a **biner**, to make himself secure from either falling or being pulled off his perch in case he has to catch the fall of his partner.

**belay** Noun or verb. One partner, who is stationary and anchored to the rock, keeps the climbing rope taut between himself and his buddy, who is climbing. Therefore, the belayer minimizes the distance of the latter's possible fall. If the belayer is positioned below the partner who is climbing, the latter's fall can still result in an injury—even after the belayer "catches the fall."

**bergschrund** The **crevasse** at the top of a glacier, where the latter separates from the (normally) vertical rock face.

**beta** Since the 1980s climbers use this term in reference to pertinent data (type of **pro** needed; specific obstacles) about a particular climb or climbing area.

**biner** See **carabiner**

**bivouac** Also: "bivy." Noun or adjective. A forced or planned night out with a minimum of equipment. For climbs in the Bugaboos or in Alaska, Fredrickson and I always carried an impermeable "bivy sack" that both of us would climb into, use the drawstring to close the top opening, and—body to body—shiver the night away.

**bolt** Noun and verb. Where no **piton**, **nut**, or **cam** is possible, the climber holds a protected drill bit in one hand and a hammer in the other, in order to make a hole and insert an expansion bolt and hanger. This can be a strenuous and time-consuming labor. Later, climbers use this bolt as an anchor, as protection while free climbing, or as a clip-in point for an aid ascent. Over the past few decades, interested individuals, climbing clubs, and park services have funded campaigns to increase climbing safety by installing at each **belay** station on popular routes a pair of bomb-proof bolts.

**cagoule** A roomy rain garment that reaches down to the knees.

**cam** Also: "Friend." An ingeniously-designed four-wheeled protection device that—like **pitons** and **nuts**—can be inserted into a crack to offer protection to a lead climber. Since their appearance in the 1980s, climbers now almost universally prefer to use cams (if placement is possible) due to their versatility and ease of placement and removal.

**carabiner** Also "biner." A four- to five-inch oval-shaped, (usually) aluminum, device, with a spring (and sometimes locking) gate, that climbers use, among other applications, to fasten slings or ropes to protective devices.

**chimney** Between two walls facing each other, climbers must use arms, feet, butt, and back to wiggle up.

**chockstone** A rock of any size that is jammed into a crack or gully.

**clip in** Climbing slang for fastening a **carabiner** into the eye of a **piton** or the sling of a different protective device.

**col** The low point between a pair of summits or **gendarmes**.

**couloir** French. A "gully" or "valley" between two ridges on a mountain. Couloirs, often with year-round snow or ice, sometimes offer the least difficult route to a summit.

**crampons** Metal "spikes" that one fastens to the bottom of the boot to facilitate ice climbing.

**crevasse** A deep slit or wide crack in glacier ice. In spring and early summer, if covered by snow, they can offer extreme danger to an unsuspecting climber who must cross the glacier in order to reach the beginning of a rock climb.

**cut steps** On hard snow or ice, climbers sometimes use the adze of their ice axes to—literally—cut steps into the hard snow or ice in order to facilitate their ascent or maximize their safety at a belay site.

**5th class** Also: "free" climbing. Noun or verb (e.g., "I'll have to 5th class it the next 40 feet"). In the United States, climbers universally use the Yosemite Decimal System to rate (by general consensus) the technical difficulty of different climbs. Fifth class means that the climber uses **protection** for safety, but not for physical assistance. 5.0 might be the equivalent of ascending a ladder; 5.3, a ladder missing two out of three steps; 5.7 will require gymnastics moves; 5.8 strong and practiced arm moves; a 5.10 route (with more difficult routes rated 5.10a or b or c) can be ascended only by physically gifted individuals. In recent years some routes have been rated up to 5.14b.

**flared crack** A crack that widens or is rounded at its opening, making it extremely strenuous for a climber to obtain secure hand holds and therefore to maintain position.

**4th class** On a steep but not overly dangerous slope, the strong climber, dragging a rope, ascends without being belayed and without putting in **protection**. He then places himself on **belay** to protect the ascent of the weaker climber who follows.

**friction** Noun, adjective, verb. The climbing shoe does not slip if the rock has a sufficiently rough surface (i.e., it has enough friction).

**front-point** Noun and verb. Many climbers, with ice tools in their hands, prefer to thrust their boots straight forward in order that the two forward-pointing "spokes" of each crampon enter an adequate distance into the hard snow or ice to provide sufficient support for upward climbing.

**gaiter** A nylon sock-sleeve that keeps snow or gravel from entering into the top of a hiker's or climber's boot.

**gendarme** Small towers or summits on a mountain ridge.

**grigri** See **jumar**. Used after about 2010.

**ice tools** Climbers fasten **crampons** to their boots and hold in either hand an ice hammer or (four decades ago) an ice axe modified for climbing.

**jumar** Also: ascender, gri-gri. Noun or verb. A metal device, measuring about 6 inches in length, that clips onto the (normally 7⁄16-inch-diameter) climbing rope. With "teeth" pointing downward, it easily slides up the climbing rope but brakes with a downward pull. Normally, on big-wall climbs, the second climber, after **belaying** from below his partner (who is on lead) will then "jumar" on up. That is, he will clip both jumars (plus stirrups) onto the rope that the leader has tied off, and slip a toe into the lower step of each stirrup. By sliding up one jumar, and then the other, he will literally "walk up" the vertical rope. This was the accepted practice for big-wall climbing between about 1965 and 2010.

**In the late 1960s only a climber such as Marek was able to escape from USSR-dominated Poland. Here, after descending from a mixed climb in the Sierra Nevadas (California), it's snack time on the rocks bordering Glacier Lake.**

**kybo** A primitive toilet.

**layback** A strenuous climbing move: given an appropriate crack, climbers find decent handholds at the side, place feet high and lean back using arm strength to move feet and hands progressively higher.

**lead** Noun, adjective, verb. In **trad** climbing, one partner leads, or goes first. Because he is belayed from below, he confronts most of the risks associated with climbing. He provides partial protection against long falls by placing and clipping into **pro**.

**mixed climb** The path to the summit involves ascending regular rock (using a rope and **pro**) as well as moving over up near-vertical ice or snow-covered rock using **crampons** and **ice tools**.

**nail** See **6th class**. Verb ("He had to *nail* the crack running up from the bolt.")

**nut** Also: "chock" or chockstone. An aluminum protection device with an attached sling, with sizes varying from ⅛ to 2 inches. The lead climber wedges an appropriately-sized nut into a crack that will "catch" him (hopefully) if he falls. Nuts became popular in the 1970s. Although not as secure as **pitons**, they offer the advantage of not leaving permanent "scars" (the holes left after numerous piton placements and removals) on rock. Types of nuts: stoppers, hexes, offsets, etc.

**pitch** A rope length, i.e., from 140 to 170 feet. Normally, in multi-pitch **trad** climbing, partner A **belays** from below while partner B **leads** the first pitch, ties into an **anchor**, and then belays his partner on up. Switching leads, partner A then takes the **rack** and leads the second pitch while partner B, still anchored to the wall, is on belay.

**piton** Also: "pins." A type of **protection** device used by climbers up through the 1960s. Most common were soft-steel European pitons or American hard-steel (chromium molybdenum or "chromoly") devices with widths varying from knife-blades up to about 2½ inches. Typically, the lead climber uses his hammer to drive the appropriate piton into a rock crack, clips a **carabiner** into the piton's eye, then clips the free-running climbing rope into the carabiner. When the second climber follows, he "cleans" the route, that is, he recovers a driven piton by pounding its head in the direction of the crack until the piton works its way out. Types of pitons: knife-blades, angles, aluminum bongs (4+ inches wide), rurps ("realized ultimate reality pitons"—the smallest piton imaginable—which are driven into hair-line cracks for aid climbing).

**protection** Also: "pro." Those devices are either hammered or inserted into rock cracks in order to "catch" the lead climber in case of a fall or to anchor the belayer to the wall. Examples: **pitons**, **nuts** or **chocks**, **cams** or Friends, a sling (usually a closed loop of ½-inch webbing) around a tree.

**prussic** Verb or adjective. A climber uses this knot to fasten a sling around the thicker climbing rope. Tied properly, it will function like a **jumar**.

**rack** Verb or noun. The lead climber carries, arranged on a sling, the yet-to-be-used **chocks**, **cams**, and **biners**.

**rappel** Verb or noun. Also "rap." A procedure for safely descending a vertical wall. After the climber threads the rope through an **anchor** at the top, he fastens his rappelling device (most common: an ATC or an "8") to the double rope and descends to the ground. He then recovers the rope by pulling one end until it passes through the anchor and (ideally) falls neatly at his feet.

**REI** Recreational Equipment Incorporated, an outdoor equipment retailer. Its many outlets sell good climbing and outdoor gear.

**scamper** My personal definition: "free-solo" climbing, meaning that a slip might result in serious injury. To attain an easy summit, I'd pack a minimum of clothing and food for a very long day. I'd carry neither technical equipment nor specialized rock-climbing shoes, even though I'd be climbing (and descending) easy 5th class moves.

**scramble** An arduous hike over rough terrain for which most climbers would forgo the use of technical equipment, because a slip would not result in a serious bodily injury.

**simul-climbing** On 5th class routes, a pair of climbers with more or less equivalent technical ability will rope up and ascend simultaneously, while placing a minimum of **protection**.

**6th class** Also: "aid" or "direct aid." Noun or verb (as in: "I'm going to aid, or sixth class, the next five feet"). When lead climbers use devices not merely for protection, but also for physically assisting the ascent. Most typically—in the 1970s—climbers, when confronting an extremely difficult vertical crack, would pound in a **piton**, use a **carabiner** to clip the climbing rope into the piton's eye, then clip in another "biner" supporting their *étriers* (or stirrups), and then climb up as high as possible in order to pound in the next piton—and repeat the process. According to the Yosemite Decimal System, aid moves or pitches are rated A1 (easy) to A5 (extremely difficult placement). In the 1970s the Salathé Wall on El Cap—to give one example—was rated 5.9 A3.

**skins** Tough, thin, coverings that one fastens to the bottom of skis. Originally, they were made of short-haired animal skin. But—beginning in the 1940s—synthetic "skins" became commercially available. Skis outfitted with skins allow the mountaineer to glide up a moderate snow slope without slipping back down.

**sport** Adjective. A type of climbing. Climbers, **belayed** from below, clip into already positioned **bolts** in order to protect themselves from long falls. Or: climbers at indoor gyms or some outdoor areas can thread the rope through an anchor at the top in order to belay from below. Sport areas became popular beginning in the 1970s.

**stirrup** Also: *étrier.* A 5–6 foot "ladder" made of webbing that the climber stands in when performing **aid climbing**.

**swami belt** Climbing harnesses became commercially available in the 1980s or '90s. Before harnesses, we looped and tied webbing around our waists, e.g., a swami belt.

**top-roping** The rope passes through an **anchor** at the top of the climbing wall. At the bottom the climber ties into one end, and his partner uses the other to fix a **belay**.

**topo** A stick-diagram that shows for each **pitch** the essential information of a route: existing **bolts**, technical difficulty, size of **cams** needed, etc.

**traditional** Also: "trad" climbing. A lead climber is **belayed** from below by his buddy. By inserting "pro" into rock cracks, then clipping in with the climbing rope, he (ideally) minimizes injury in the case of a long fall.

**From my home in La Crosse, Wisconsin, it is only a "short" eleven-hour drive to South Dakota's vertical granite at Mt. Rushmore and the nearby Cathedral Spires. While I and my buddies climb the easy stuff, we glance over to see Spiderman scaling a much more difficult line.**

**wands** Small-diameter, one-meter long, bamboo sticks that climbers use to mark their path through crevasses or up a snow-covered summit.

**webbing** A very strong woven nylon strip, usually one-half to one inch in width, that—among other uses—connects the climbing rope to **pro** or an **anchor**.

# Chapter Notes

## *Introduction*

1. Svetlana Alexievich writes of "war" in *The Unwomanly Face of War: An Oral History of Women in World War II*, Trans. Richard Pevear and Larissa Volokhonsky (New York: Random House, 2017), xxi.

2. I provide information about these first ascents in the following chapters: 3. "North to Alaska," 6. "Huascarán," and 7. "Crossing the Line in the Tetons."

3. Quoted by Steve Roper, Camp 4: *Recollection of a Yosemite Rockclimber* (Seattle: The Mountaineers, 1994), 42.

4. Alex Honnold with David Roberts, *Alone on the Wall* (New York: W.W. Norton, 2016), 46.

5. Lynn Hill with Greg Child, *Climbing Free: My Life in the Vertical World*, prol. John Long (New York: W.W. Norton, 2002), 42.

6. A friend of Alex Honnold is quoted as having remarked: "It's like he doesn't feel fear or any of the normal emotions that anybody else feels. He has this ability to just shut his brain off and do the sickest climbs that have ever been done." Honnold, Alone on the Wall, 42.

7. Roper, Camp 4, 111.

8. Roper, Camp 4, 93, 106, 147, 150, 156, 165, 175 (the quoted words are of Royal Robbins).

9. Borges also has some unhelpful ideas. First, I cannot agree that "to remember" is a "ghostly verb" ("Funes the Memorious"). Heavens, I swear that I have not left in my wake the carcass of any former rope partner. And second, if my memories produced only "vague shadows insinuat[ing] a vague history" ("The Golem"), then I never would have been motivated to tap into the vaults of memory in order to write this book.

I feel compelled to mention, but not explore further, Borges' perplexing idea that the act of remembering subsumes "a single identity" for a person existing in two distinct moments in time. We can legitimately inquire whether is it the same Bill Katra—performing the act of remembering in the year 2018—as the Bill Katra of 1973, when "he" ascended the North Face of Mt. Temple.

In contrast to the dilemma of personal identity—as mentioned in the previous paragraph—the gap in time better affirms the speculation of Heraclitus: the raging torrent in which I almost lost my life at Confluencia (on Mount Aconcagua) late in the afternoon of a hot day in January 1971 was clearly not "the same stream" as the gentle glacier run-off some twelve hours later—even though both flows were in exactly the same geographical location.

10. A note for only the most erudite of readers: "memory" resembles "the oral tradition" (as defined by Ramón Menéndez Pidal), in that a given detail of the narration treating an actual historical event will "survive" (and perhaps in embellished form) in a fresh retelling only if it is "remarkable" or "enticing" or enthralling.

11. Eternal gratitude to the following people who have helped with the preparation of this book: Diane Bone, Peter Craig, William (Bill) Dietrich (Chicago Mountaineering Club—CMC), Sister Maria Friedman FSPA, Jean Hammons, Lynn Jarvinen, and Tom Pignet.

## *Chapter 1*

1. Big Rock is located in Riverside County of Southern California, on the shore of Lake Perris.

2. In addition to Chouinard pitons—with angles up to two inches in width—we also carried a few "Lost Arrows," but were never convinced of the utility of "Leepers."

3. See the Glossary: "5th class."

4. See the Glossary: "6th class."

5. By 1980, when the "clean-climbing" movement became dominant (that is to say, piton use was discouraged, in favor of nuts—and later cams—that didn't do harm to the rock), new editors appraised the difficulty of the Salathé Route differently: it was henceforth rated VI 5.12 A3. See George Meyers' [with Merrill Ann Wilson] Yosemite Climbs: A Rock Climbing Guide to Yosemite Valley (Denver: Chockstone Press, 1982).

6. Steve Roper, *Climber's Guide to Yosemite Valley* (Sierra Club, 1971).

7. See the Glossary for information about these devices.

8. Only beginning with Meyers, Yosemite Climbs (1982), were more specific indications available in written "topo" form (that is, as stick or line diagrams) for individual pitches. Meyers indicates for pitch 14's crack leading up to the Hollow Flake Ledge: "5.9 ow"—meaning "off width." My translation: extremely difficult.

9. This statement is based on my reading of Roper's Camp 4.

10. I refer to the well-known text by Alan Steck and Steve Roper, *Fifty Classic Climbs of North America.*

11. Roper, Camp 4, 156, quoting Mike Borghoff.

12. On the Stevens Pass Highway, 60 miles east of Seattle.

13. Sven Olof Swartling and Peter Mayer, photos by Erie Andre, intro. by George J. Pokorny, *Climber's Guide to Devil's Lake*, 3rd edition (Madison: University of Wisconsin Press, 2008).

14. The famed English poet A.E. Housman, in "To an Athlete Dying Young," mistakenly projected that "glory" was a prime motivation for committed athletes.

15. Paraphrased from "The Tell-Tale Heart."

16. Information here about the difficulty of Lost Arrow Chimney is taken from Roper's 1971 Climbing Guide. The fact that Roper had literally copied the data for this climb from his 1964 first edition is an indication that few (wiser and more informed) climbers ever chose to attempt the route and therefore update the relevant beta. Meyers, Yosemite Climbs (1982), 114, rates fully half of the ten pitches at 5.9 or above.

17. Hard not to disagree with Greg Barnes, Chris McNamara, Steve Roper, and Todd Snyder in *Yosemite Valley Free Climbs*: Supertopos (Mill Valley, CA: Supertopo, 2003), that "the first visit to Yosemite is overwhelming—there's so much rock on an incomparable scale" (11). Half Dome: "too massive to be of this world" (11), "the most beautiful and sublime of all the wonderful Yosemite rocks" (146, in the words of John Muir). Snake Dike Route: "one of the most glorious moderate climbers on the planet" (147).

18. I've found information about the Palisade Glacier in Hervey H. Voge, ed., *A Climber's Guide to the High Sierra* (San Francisco: Sierra Club, 1965), 149–50: About the Palisade Group, none others in California's Sierra Nevada are "bolder or [of] more rugged relief, or more beautifully alpine in character." They rise "nearly two vertical miles above the desert environs of the little town of Big Pine to the east" on Highway 395—that which runs in a north-south direction along the whole eastern escarpment of the range. Glacier Lodge, offering appropriate parking, is located some 14 miles east of Big Pine.

19. Chris McNamara, *High Sierra Climbing: California's Best High Country Climbs* (Mill Valley, CA: Supertopo, 2004), 73.

20. For over forty years I have admired the research (and writings) of Dr. Kenneth Cooper who, through his decade-long research with U.S. Air Force recruits, has bequeathed to us both the concepts and vocabulary related to "aerobic fitness" and "conditioning."

## *Chapter 2*

1. Jim Hodgson, *How to Mount Aconcagua: A Mostly Serious Guide to Climbing the Tallest Mountain Outside the Himalayas* (Middletown, DE: n.p., 2017), 20, 24.

2. Ibid., 31.

3. Much of this is treated by R.J. Secor, Aconcagua: A Climbing Guide, 2nd ed. (Seattle: The Mountaineers, 1999).

4. Hodgson, *How to Mount Aconcagua.*

5. Perusing indexes, I see that the first serious treatment of this issue by the edi-

tors of the *American Alpine Journal* is as late as 1972: Charles S. Houston, M.D., "High-Altitude Pulmonary and Cerebral Edema," AAJ 18, 1 (1972): 83–90.

## Chapter 3

1. As listed in *The Freedom of the Hills*, a mountaineering classic both then and now.

2. In the early 1970s the common name was "Alas-Can" highway. According to a more recent information source, it has also been known by the name "Alcan." "The Alaska Highway was the engineering marvel of World War II and was once described as the largest and most difficult construction project since the Panama Canal … stretching 2,224 Km/1,382 miles (originally 1,422 miles) from Dawson Creek, British Columbia to Delta Junction, Alaska." This was an "emergency" project, constructed with continual curves in order to minimize damage from possible aerial bombing. Most of the part passing through Alaska was paved in the 1960s, but in Canada that same improvement did not occur until the late 1970s or early 1980s.

3. David S. Roberts and Richard G.C. Millikan, "Kichatna Spire," *American Alpine Journal* (1966). I have in my hands a digital printout of the original article that doesn't give me the original page numbers. For writing this chapter I have not been able to obtain a copy of the same authors' article in *Summit* magazine which—I assume—contains virtually the same information.

4. Alvin DeMaria, "Middle Triple Peak, Kichatna Mountains, Attempt," *American Alpine Journal* (1973), 409.

5. Royal S. Robbins, "Californians in Alaska," *American Alpine Journal* (1970): 58–62.

6. The now legendary Yvon Chouinard—then in his youth—personally schooled a whole generation of young American climbers in techniques he had learned from the Brits and the French. Furthermore, he founded his own enterprise—predecessor to both the Patagonia and Black Diamond companies—to design, manufacture, and then sell newly designed ice and rock-climbing equipment.

7. I suspect that the Robbins party was influenced by—in addition to the articles written by Roberts—the photographs of legendary mountain photographer Ed Cooper. Two of the latter's aerial photos of Triple Peaks grace pages of the *AAJ*'s 1970 edition.

8. William Katra, "Gurney Peak and P 8520, Kichatna Mountains," *American Alpine Journal* (1973), 408–9.

9. The final lines of Joseph Conrad's short story, "Youth."

10. According to Bill Dietrich, this peak is now known as Citadel.

11. Sean Dougherty, *Selected Alpine Climbs in the Canadian Rockies* (Surrey, B.C.: Rocky Mountain Books, 1991), 310.

12. According to Bill Dietrich, "the ability to get back to the U.S. on battery power without trouble would be hard now. Then the cars used a mechanical fuel pump, and the only required drain was the ignition system. Now fuel pumps run down the battery as they are electric."

## Chapter 4

1. Full names Peter Brashaw and Andy Parkin. I would appreciate news about these two individuals from any reader knowing of their current whereabouts or of their subsequent mountaineering accomplishments.

2. Gaston Rébuffat, in *The Mont Blanc Massif: The 100 Finest Routes*, trans. Jane and Colin Taylor (New York: Oxford University Press, 1975), 122–23, states that the first ascent was in 1906, and that its difficulty was "D sup" (several pitches of IV and IV sup): "mainly crack climbing … a fairly strenuous climb."

3. This was the common nickname for the very hard chromolybdenum steel pitons first made and used by Yosemite climbers.

4. I ignore the date of the téléférique construction—probably in the late 1960s or early 1970s. It is most impressive. Combining its two trams, it rises some 3,777 meters above the valley floor to near the summit of the Aiguille de Midi.

5. Rébuffat calls it the "Fissure Brown, which is vertical with smooth edges and back (VI, very strenuous free climbing; A1 using aid with wedges or very large pitons)" (174). Yes, they would have to be extremely large pitons.

## Chapter 5

1. Parts of this chapter were first published as "Canadian Rockies Déjà vu" in *The*

*Chicago Mountaineer* 40, 1 (March 2015): 39–46.

2. Sean Dougherty, *Selected Alpine Climbs in the Canadian Rockies* (Surrey, B.C.: Rocky Mountain Books, 2008), 282.

3. Ibid., 25.

## Chapter 6

1. David M. Sharman, *Climbs of the Cordillera Blanca of Peru* (Lima: Dolphin Creative, 1995), 122. John F. Ricker, *Yuraq Janka: Guide to the Peruvian Andes.* Part I: Cordilleras Blanca and Rosko (Banff: The Alpine Club of Canada; New York: The American Alpine Club, 1977, 1981), 82, gives the height of 6,654 meters.

2. Gerald Holdsworth and John Ricker, "A Map of the Northern Cordillera Blanca," *The American Alpine Journal* (1971), 263–5 [plus fold-out map].

3. There is hardly any agreement as to this route's name. Geoff Wayatt ("Huascarán's East Face: Camino del Enfermo," *AAJ* 1972: 30–4; this information might also be included in a 1972 article of the *NZAJ—New Zealand Alpine Journal*), a member of the first-ascent team, calls it the "ANZUS Route," a name derived from the three nationalities of members of the first-ascent team: Australia, New Zealand, and the U.S. Ricker, *Yuraq Janka*, 84, refers to this route ambiguously as the "1971 traverse, route B." Wayatt, however, explains clearly that two different members from his larger party actually made a "traverse" with their first ascent of Huascarán's southeast ridge, followed by their descent down the northeast ridge. Simultaneously, Wayatt and three others of the same group accomplished the first ascent of the east-face route that we—Katra, Milne, and Andrews—two years later, would climb for the route's second ascent. Sharman, *Climbs*, 59, provides a fair description of the route, but for unknown reasons calls it the "ANZAC Route." During my 2016 visit to Huaraz, I talked with a half-dozen guides and came to the conclusion that none of them possessed specific knowledge, nor maps, nor photos, of any routes up Huascarán Sur's East Face.

4. Ricker, *Yuraq Janka*, on the map of the northern part of the Cordillera Blanca that accompanies his book, marks this "Ln [laguna, or lake] Sajuna."

5. The 1971 *AAJ* map gives no altitude for this smaller peak, which is marked only by a small circle (indicating "minor peak"). Apparently, neither Ricker nor the climbing community have accepted the quichua name that our party suggested, "Mishac Shipash"—the "youngest virgin" (see William Katra [with James Milne], "Northern Cordillera Blanca," *The American Alpine Journal* [New York: The American Alpine Club, 1975], 94–100, with two accompanying photographs on unnumbered pages). Ricker, *Yuraq Janka*, 68, provides the name for the peak which is used in the body of this essay. Sharman, *Climbs*, 29, gives its altitude as 5,700 meters.

6. I have "pirated" much of this paragraph—as I will with several others here—from (my own) Katra, "Northern Cordillera Blanca."

7. William Katra [with James Milne], "Northern Cordillera Blanca," *The American Alpine Journal* (New York: The American Alpine Club, 1975), 94–100, with two accompanying photographs on unnumbered pages.

8. Wayatt, "Huascarán's East Face," includes a few photos taken during the first ascent of this route. Plate 25 captures particularly well the right-bearing sleeve of snow/ice that constitutes the upper third of the route (before attaining the loose-rock summit ridge). It also shows (in the photo it has the shape and size of a fingernail clipping)—as seen from 2,000 to 3,000 meters below—what might be the crevasse-bergschrund that served both the Wayatt party and our own as the bivouac site before summit day.

9. Although Brad Johnson, *Classic Climbs of the Cordillera Blanca, Peru* (China: n. p., 2003), 130, states that the view of the east side of Huascarán "is nothing short of spectacular" from Punta Olímpica, he includes no such photo in his fine book.

10. Both identical printings of the Ricker guide—respectively dated 1977 and 1981—come with four excellent 30 × 90 cm. fold-out maps (two two-sided sheets).

11. Here is what I copied from that map: "Mapa de Cordillera Blanca / Herausgegeben im Rahmen … vorn Oestereichischer Alpenverein / 2000 / Kartagraphische Bearbeiting."

12. An early climbing account by C.G. Egeler [in co-operation with T. de Booy, trans. (from Dutch) W.E. James], *The Untrodden*

*Andes: Climbing Adventures in the Cordillera Blanca, Peru* (London: Faber and Faber, n.d.), narrates his 1952 (?) expedition, accompanied by famous French alpinist Lionel Terray, that put up new routes on the Pongos Massif and Nevado Huantsán. He mentions their use of a "particularly fine topographical map ... scaled 1:100,000" (16), and adds that their party made a new "geological map of terrain covering roughly 1,000 square kilometers ... most of it above the 13,000-ft. level" (199).

13. Yet a third "climbing guide" (but in many respects more a "coffee table book" on account of its excellent color photos) is Johnson, *Classic Climbs*, that describes scores of "popular" climbs "that are not ... too dangerous" (23), and therefore includes no East Face routes for Huascarán Sur.

14. Friends brought to my attention the website "andesmadness.com" that has two marvelous photos of the East Face. Studying these (most probably recent) photos, I judge that much of the ice/snow existing nearly a half-century earlier has disappeared. Snow/ice still covers the upper third of the ANZUS Route—the right-tending "sleeve"—as well as two-thirds of an imaginary vertical line stretching downward from the start of that "sleeve" (where the—still visible—bergschrund-crevasse of bivouac fame is situated) to the glacier at the East Face's base. I would imagine that danger from rock falling from the summit ridge has increased considerably, and that hard ice (rather than the ideal-consistency hard snow we found) predominates during much of the climbing season.

15. Karla Bardales Farroñay, "Casi la mitad del hielo en los glaciares ha desaparecido," *El Comercio* (Lima: 25 de marzo de 2012), 20.

16. [Rex Broekman], "Interview: Lonnie G. Thompson: 'The Pastoruri Glacier will probably disappear within ten years,'" *The Huaraz Telegraph* (Huaraz: August 2016), 4–6. For the past five years Mr. Broekman (from the Netherlands) has almost single-handedly written and published this fine English-language monthly newspaper. See the website thehuaraztelegraph.com.

## Chapter 7

1. Peter Craig and I were perhaps the first serious climbers from Pomona College. Dabblers in the sport were Kurt Wagner, Bob Michaels, and Pete Van Kuren. Andrew Embick, a few years later, also gained a reputation as a serious climber (in the 1971 *AAJ*, 375, he suggests that he and Dave Goeddel were members of the Claremont Outing Club).

2. The III signifies "Grade 3," meaning that the route could be done comfortably in a day by skilled climbers. Grade IV: a day and a half; Grade V: two days; Grade VI: multiple days.

3. On the back cover of my copy of Leigh Ortenburger, Illus. Eldon N. Dye, *A Climber's Guide to the Teton Range* (San Francisco: Sierra Club, 1965). On the inside back cover of my personal copy I diligently made note (probably at a later date) the climbs I had personally completed in the range: "Durrance Ridge" of Symmetry Spire, "South Face" (?) of Owens, "Dike Route" (only to top of pinnacle) of the Middle [Teton]."

4. Through Google, I have learned that the old climbers' camp at Jenny Lake was closed in 1966 (it had been in use since the 1950s), and the actual camp, administered by the American Alpine Club (via a special use permit issued by the national park), was opened in 1970.

5. Leigh N. Ortenburger and Reynold G. Jackson, *A Climber's Guide to the Teton Range*, 3rd edition (Seattle: The Mountaineers, 1996), 259–60.

6. Aaron Gams, *Teton Rock Climbs: A Select Guide to the Classic and Not-So-Classic Routes* (Jackson, WY: Ground Up Press, 2012), 214.

7. Ibid., 216.

## Chapter 8

1. Parts of this chapter were first published as "Glacier National Park," in *The Chicago Mountaineer* 39, 1 (March 2013): 34–8.

2. Cribbed from General Douglas MacArthur, a soldier and not a climber.

## Chapter 9

1. I don't mention in the text that for every Mexican climb we made sure, one way

or another, that our parked car would always be protected.

2. I wonder what the latest research has to say about aging and acclimatization. A few years after Popo, I went on a climbing trip to Bolivia. There, my body failed to adjust, even after (what I had assumed to be) the obligatory 15 days of preparatory high-altitude jaunts.

3. El Iztaccíhuatl (in Náhuatl: Iztac, "blanco"; cihuatl, "mujer"—"mujer blanca") is the third highest mountain in Mexico (5,286 meters), after Orizaba (5,610 meters) and Popocatépetl (5,500 meters). It's located on the border between the states of Mexico and Puebla.

4. More specifically: the town of San Agustín Amatlípac, in the Municipio (county) of Tlayacapan, State of Morelos.

5. It's appropriate to explain that, after turning about 50, my own body has demonstrated a diminished capacity to acclimatize. I remember two instances when, accompanied by my son, Dan (Long's Peak, Iztaccíhuatl), with my strength dwindling when approaching the respective summits, I chose to not continue on up. Then, in about 2008 in Bolivia, even after spending the obligatory 15 days at higher altitudes, my body never felt comfortable enough to attempt proceeding beyond the climbers' base camps on three separate peaks.

## Chapter 10

1. After reading all this, if there are still any readers nourishing the dream of climbing in Uruguay, Pablo's telephone numbers are 5982-708-0342 and/or 9923-3989.

## Chapter 11

1. Parts of this chapter were first published as "Patagonia," in *The Chicago Mountaineer* 39, 1 (March 2013): 86–96.

## Chapter 12

1. Stewart M. Green, *Rock Climbing in Colorado* (Helena, MT: Falcon Guides, 1995).

## Chapter 13

1. Bob Gaines, *Best Climbs: Tahquitz and Suicide Rocks* (Guilford, CT: Falcon Guides, 2013), 127.

2. Ibid., 14.

3. Chuck Wilts, *Climber's Guide to Tahquitz Rock* (Glendale, CA: La Siesta Press, 1962).

# Bibliography


Alexievich, Svetlana. *The Unwomanly Face of War: An Oral History of Women in World War II*. Trans. Richard Pevear and Larissa Volokhonsky. New York: Random House, 2017.

Barnes, Greg, Chris McNamara, Steve Roper, and Todd Snyder. *Yosemite Valley Free Climbs: Supertopos*. Mill Valley, CA: Supertopo, 2003.

Broekman, Rex. "Interview: Lonnie G. Thompson: 'The Pastoruri Glacier will probably disappear within ten years.'" *The Huaraz Telegraph* (August 2016): 4–6.

DeMaria, Alvin. "Middle Triple Peak, Kichatna Mountains, Attempt." *American Alpine Journal* (1973).

Dougherty, Sean. *Selected Alpine Climbs in the Canadian Rockies*. Surrey, B.C.: Rocky Mountain Books, 1991.

Egeler, C.G., (in co-operation with T. de Booy). *The Untrodden Andes: Climbing Adventures in the Cordillera Blanca, Peru*. Trans. W.E. James. London: Faber and Faber, n.d.

Farroñay, Karla Bardales. "Casi la mitad del hielo en los glaciares ha desaparecido." *El Comercio*. Lima: 25 de marzo de 2012.

Gaines, Bob. *Best Climbs: Tahquitz and Suicide Rocks*. Guilford, CT: Falcon Guides, 2013.

Gams, Aaron. *Teton Rock Climbs: A Select Guide to the Classic and Not-So-Classic Climbing Routes of the Teton Range*. Jackson, WY: Ground Up Press, 2012.

Green, Stewart M. *Rock Climbing in Colorado*. Helena, MT: Falcon Guides, 1995.

Hill, Lynn, with Greg Child. *Climbing Free: My Life in the Vertical World*. New York: W.W. Norton, 2002.

Hodgson, Jim. *How to Mount Aconcagua: A Mostly Serious Guide to Climbing the Tallest Mountain Outside the Himalayas*. Middletown, DE: n.p., 2017.

Holdsworth, Gerald, and John Ricker. "A Map of the Northern Cordillera Blanca." *American Alpine Journal* (1971): 263–5.

Honnold, Alex, with David Roberts. *Alone on the Wall*. New York: W.W. Norton, 2016.

Houston, Charles S. "High-Altitude Pulmonary and Cerebral Edema." *American Alpine Journal* 18, 1 (1972): 83–90.

Johnson, Brad. *Classic Climbs of the Cordillera Blanca, Peru*. China: n. p., 2003.

Katra, William. "Gurney Peak and P 8520, Kichatna Mountains." *American Alpine Journal* (1973).

Katra, William, [with James Milne]. "Northern Cordillera Blanca." *American Alpine Journal* (New York: The American Alpine Club, 1975): 94–100.

McNamara, Chris. *High Sierra Climbing: California's Best High Country Climbs*. Mill Valley, CA: Supertopo, 2004.

Meyers, George, [with Merrill Ann Wilson]. *Yosemite Climbs: A Rock Climbing Guide to Yosemite Valley*. Denver: Chockstone Press, 1982.

Ortenburger, Leigh, illus. Eldon N. Dye. *A Climber's Guide to the Teton Range*. San Francisco: Sierra Club, 1965.
Ortenburger, Leigh N., and Reynold G. Jackson. *A Climber's Guide to the Teton Range*, 3rd edition. Seattle: The Mountaineers, 1996.
Rébuffat, Gaston. *The Mont Blanc Massif: The 100 Finest Routes*. Trans. Jane and Colin Taylor. New York: Oxford University Press, 1975.
Ricker, John F. *Yuraq Janka: Guide to the Peruvian Andes. Part I: Cordilleras Blanca and Rosko*. Banff: The Alpine Club of Canada; New York: The American Alpine Club, 1977, 1981.
Robbins, Royal S. "Californians in Alaska." *American Alpine Journal* (1970): 58–62.
Roberts, David S., and Richard G.C. Millikan. "Kichatna Spire." *American Alpine Journal* (1966).
Roper, Steve. *Camp 4: Recollection of a Yosemite Rockclimber*. Seattle: The Mountaineers, 1994.
Roper, Steve. *Climber's Guide to Yosemite Valley*. Sierra Club, 1971.
Secor, R.J. *Aconcagua: A Climbing Guide*, 2nd edition. Seattle: The Mountaineers, 1999.
Sharman, David M. *Climbs of the Cordillera Blanca of Peru*. Lima: Dolphin Creative, 1995.
Swartling, Sven Olof, and Peter Mayer, photos by Erie Andre. *Climber's Guide to Devil's Lake*, 3rd edition. Madison: University of Wisconsin Press, 2008.
Voge, Hervey H., ed. *A Climber's Guide to the High Sierra*. San Francisco: Sierra Club, 1965.
Wayatt, Geoff. "Huascarán's East Face: Camino del Enfermo." *America Alpine Journal* (1972): 30–4.
Wilts, Chuck. *Climber's Guide to Tahquitz Rock*. Glendale, CA: La Siesta Press, 1962.

# Index

Numbers in ***bold italics*** indicate pages with illustrations